Introduction to Social Administration

Introduction to Social Administration

R.B.S. Verma

SHIPRA

ISBN: 978-81-7541-741-0

First Published in India in 2014

Introduction to Social Administration

Published by:
SHIPRA PUBLICATIONS
H.O.: LG 18-19, Pankaj Central Market, Patparganj,
I.P. Ext., Delhi-110092, Tel: 91-11-2223 5152, 2223 6152
Br.Off.: 4617/18, Ansari Road, Darya Ganj,
New Delhi-110002, Tel: 9650028065, 9810522367
E-mail: info@shiprapublications.com
www.shiprapublications.com

Preface

Human Society, from its very beginning, has been engaged in making varied kinds of efforts for helping its every member for leading a healthy and satisfying life and living. However, in every society, there exists persons who are not alike to lead a life having minimum standards due to various kinds of handicaps may be social, cultural, economic, structural, political etc. These persons are given help through institutional framework of society which may be of state intervention or voluntary effort. These interventions or efforts are organized, directed, coordinated and managed by the process of administration, generally known as social administration which connotes the administration of social and community services such as health, housing, education and recreation meant for people in general and needy people in particular.

The present book is a humble effort in introducing different dimensions of social administration for the purpose of equipping social service personnel with the required scientific knowledge, technical skills and philosophical base for tackling the problems of marginalization and social exclusion in this era of globalization. Thus, the role of social administration (both as method and process) becomes vital since it (a) makes various services (community services, social services, social security services, and social welfare services) available to needy people without any discrimination, makes analysis of services in view of their historical development, moral values implicit in these services, roles and functions of these services as well as meeting the needs of social process, (c) improves in the condition of life of individuals in family and group by providing services, removing prevailing disabilities as well as creating opportunities for their well being, and (d) establishes machinery of administration for organising and dispensing of social assistance for the purpose of improving overall lives and relations and meeting the needs of community members to whom services are being made available.

The present book has been presented into twelve chapters giving detailed analysis of social welfare, administration, social administration, social policy, planning and decision making, organizing, staffing, directing, budgeting, controlling and project formulation, administration in government and voluntary agencies as well as administration of important organizations. I am sanguine that the book would be able to meet the objectives of teaching, research and practice of administration specially in meeting the contemporary challenges of good governance, inclusive development and establishment of civil and sane social order.

I am extremely thankful to the library of Udaipur School of Social Work, Udaipur (Rajasthan) for providing original texts related to this subject.

Udaipur
April, 2014

Pref. R.B.S. Verma
Principal
Udaipur School of Social Work,
Udaipur (Rajasthan)

Contents

1

Social Welfare: An Introduction

SOCIAL WELFARE: CONCEPTUAL ANALYSIS

In this era of globalisation, people in the developing societies, particularly in India are facing several challenges as an individual, member of groups, communities, institutions and larger society. These problems are poverty, discrimination, exploitation, ill-health, ignorance, bad housing and living conditions, lack of proper educational, recreational and development facilities, mushroom growth of slums, family change, family breakdown, widowhood or orphanhood, old age, isolation, juvenile delinquency, crime, youth intolerance and unrest, psychological strains and stresses, psychological breakdown, lower status of women and unprivileged groups, minorities, refugees, terrorist and separatist activities, physical, mental and social disabilities, offences against weaker sections including women, corruption, scams, etc. These existing as well as emerging challenges used to be met by strong commitment as well as joint action on the part of politicians, administrators, framers as well as executors of policies and programmes in a welfare state having the mandate of assuring minimum standard of living to every citizen, removing economic disparities and social distances, providing help and support to weaker sections as a matter of right, giving access to resources (like health, education, housing, recreation, food security, development opportunities, etc.) to each and every citizen, enhancing citizen's participation in governance and establishing democratic norms and values.

The above mentioned state of affairs demand the enhancement and restoration of capacities of individuals for smooth social functioning and establishing such societal conditions which are favourable towards the fulfilment of goals of individuals, especially of the weaker sections of society, since socio-economic status of population determines the progress and prosperity of a nation. After independence, the Indian Constitution strived to establish a social order based on Equality, Liberty and Fraternity through the provisions of Fundamental Rights and Directive Principles of State Policy.

MEANING AND DEFINITIONS OF SOCIAL WELFARE

The term social welfare contains two words, i.e. social and welfare. The term social is being used in several senses. According to V.M. Kulkarni (1972: 4-5) this term is mostly used in three senses:

(1) Social means, the ultimate, the total, the societal.
(2) As an adjective 'social' is used by economists for a provision or a service or a programme which is not thrown up by a free play of market forces. Such a provision has a hidden element of subsidy or help.
(3) In sociological sense, the term 'social' refers to relationships between man and man, man and a group and between groups of men and all that is associated with these.

Thus, 'social' is mainly concerned with relationships among people and what is relational is social.

CONCEPTION OF WELFARE

In India, the earlier conception of welfare was labelled as Dana, which refers sharing and dharma or dhamma having different meanings ranging from duty or obligation to charity or equity. In Muslim period dana or charity was known as khairat.

In West, right from the earlier period of industrial revolution upto about second decade of nineteenth century, the terms charity or philanthropy were used and after the middle of nineteenth century Charity Organisation Movement was in operation in England where the term 'scientific charity' was in use.

In contemporary parlance, welfare is taken as a condition of physical health, emotional comfort and economic security and the efforts of a society to help its citizens achieve that condition.

APPROACHES TO THE STUDY OF WELFARE

Misra (1977) has discussed five approaches to the study of welfare.

(A) Welfare as Social Reform

This approach is represented by the work of scholar reformers like Titmuss, Townsend and Dannison whose work is influenced by the writings of Booth, Rountree Webbs, Beveridege and others. Main features of this approach are as follows:

(1) Here, welfare is studied from interventionist idea having a course of action.

(2) Welfare is taken as having the context of specificity in its concerns.
(3) The central theme in social reform is poverty.
(4) The state based on democratic traditions is supposed to assume the responsibility of institutionalised character of welfare.
(5) In this approach, liberal capitalism is recognised and structural constraints are not taken into account.
(6) Here, information regarding relevant maladies is sought and policy options within the given resource constraints are discussed and debated for effectively dealing with them.
(7) Development in the field of welfare takes place on two counts i.e. (a) economic development of society; and (b) realisation and acceptance of moral responsibility on the part of state regarding maintenance of minimum standards of welfare.

(B) Welfare as Citizenship

Marshall (1963) advocated that there exists a close bonding between development of social services with the development of citizenship rights in the democratic states. Marshall propounded that citizenship rights consist of three different elements having following details:

Elements of Citizenship Rights

(1)	Civil	Body referring to individual liberty and equality before the law.	This led to the establishment of legal institutions.
(2)	Political	Referring political enfranchisement. The right to vote and seek political office.	This led to the establishment of political institutions.
(3)	Social	Economic welfare and security and the right to share to the full in the social heritage and have a civilised existence as per the standards prevailing in the society.	Institutionalisation of welfare.

However, the welfare concept in this approach refers only to the statutory welfare and ignores voluntary and charitable welfare.

(C) Convergence Theory

The main features of this theory are as follows:

(1) Emphasis is laid down on the role of industrialisation in shaping the welfare institutions.

(2) This theory puts forth that in industrial societies, the nature and development of the social institutions can be explained in terms of the 'pull' (requirements or functional necessities) and the 'push' (consequences) of an industrial technology and economy.
For example:

(I) Industrialisation transforms	Self-employed labour force such as farmers, craftsman etc. into 'employed workers on regular wages'. This leads to the demand of uninterrupted income which can be interrupted by unemployment, sickness, work injury, old age, etc.	This results into the establishment of protective welfare measures against the contingencies of unemployment, sickness, work injury etc.
(II) Industrialisation and Urbanisation creates	Problems of public health, housing, control of urban environment	This demands educated and skilled manpower leading to occupational mobility which weakens traditional family and local community affiliation. For this, alternative arrangements in forms of custodial care of children etc. are needed.

(3) According to Kerr (1973), each industrialising elite influences the welfare institutions in its own way. For example:

(I)	Middle Class is	For maximisation of state intervention	Development of a residual system of welfare
(II)	Dynastic and Traditional groups	Behave as paternalistic	Institutional pattern of welfare

(*Contd.*)

(III)	Communists	Role of State enhances	Lowly role of family, market, individual in the provision of welfare provisions.

(4) Finally, above all this theory argues that there is progressive narrowing of differences as industrialisation increases.

(D) Functionalist View of Welfare

The functionalist view (a) sees society as a system – a set of inter-related patterns constituting the parts of an integrated whole; and (b) analysis of these patterns – social institutions in terms of the contributions made by them towards working of whole i.e. 'function'. Thus, functionalists remain concerned with:

(1) For the survival of society, specification of function to be performed, (2) looking and seeing the functional division of labour among the society's institutions; and (3) Examination of inter-relationship between various institutional patterns for the purpose of knowing of 'good fit' or harmony (Mishra, 1977).

Views of Classical Functionalists

The analysis of society on the basis of part-whole analogy as well as the functional notion i.e. 'system analysis' is quite old in sociological thought. But, the writings of Durkheim (1964) have made their influence on founders of functionalism. Though, their theoretical presentations are not directly related to the analysis of welfare, but some interpretations may be made in this regard: (a) there has been increase in scale and complexity in modern social structure requiring coordination and regulation on a large scale; (b) consequently, state emerges as central organ of society having multitude of functions; (c) as per Durkheim, there exists social regulation in constraining the individual in the interests of his own and the common good; and (d) addressing of the problem of social justice is must for attaining solidarity in modern societies.

Views of Modern Functionalists

The leading proponents of modern functionalists have been Parson, Merton and Smelser.

According to Parson, survival of any system (or society) depends upon four functional requirements which he labelled as basic elements (sub-systems) of society.

(a) adaption referring to economic tasks.
(b) goal attainment is for political tasks.
(c) integration is concerned with maintenance of harmony and solidarity.
(d) pattern maintenance is related to the continuation of basic value patterns.

As per the view of functionalists, welfare is primarily belonging to the third, i.e. integration which is labelled as process making a social system more cohesive and harmonious. Thus, integration is of two types:

(a) System integration referring to integration of institutions, mainly concerned with the 'instrumental' aspects of collectivity i.e. efficiency.
(b) Social integration is concerned with the integration of social groups involving reduction if conflict between social groups (workers and management, minority or majority groups etc.). It enhances morale, commitment and loyalty towards a collectivity on its members. Thus, it is concerned with expressive aspects i.e. with morale and cohesiveness.

In this way, functionalists suggest the following:

(a) Maintaining order is a good deal of welfare activity.
(b) Society or other collectivity, in which members have a sense of belonging to it (community feeling), has a sense of solidarity meaning thereby that existence of institutions and practices having an expression of altruism (a concern for member) is normal affair.
(c) This suggests that social welfare institutions are both cause as well as consequence of community.
(d) This communal character of welfare is seen due to the principle known as individuals have a claim on the resources of community not because of their earning but due to demands of solidarity. Their wants be recognised and met (Siddique, H.Y.: 1990: 9).

(E) The Marxian View

According to Marx:

(1) Structure and processes of society are decisively influenced by mode of production;
(2) Means of production are controlled/owned by small majority whilst vast majority lack resources and live at subsistence level;
(3) This leads to the existence of small class of rich and privileged and vast mass of more or less poor people;
(4) In this, mode of production i.e. capitalist, wealth and poverty are generated and reproduced through: (a) private ownership of the means of production; (b) production for profit; (c) private property and inheritance; and (d) the allocation of incomes and resources through the mechanism of market.

In this way, Marx argued that above mentioned core institutions of capitalism and underlying values constitute the very anti-thesis of welfare society. For the institutionalisation of welfare as central value, Marx suggested that:

(a) production must be governed by social criteria; and (b) distribution must be done as per needs of human beings; and (c) for this dominance of market, private ownership of productive resources and production for profit should be curbed.

Regarding state in a capitalist society, Marx pointed out that though the state represents the larger community yet it generally serves the interest of dominant class and maintain the integrity of system. For this, he cited the failure of social legislation which state in a capitalist society passes this legislation but fails to exert effective influence in the implementation of this legislation.

According to George and Wilding (1976) theoretical approached to welfare broadly could be divided into two major groups:

(A) Order and Pluralist Theories

The basic features of these theories are as follows:

(1) Residual Approach to Social Welfare

In this theoretical framework, this approach envisaged the following:

(a) Conceptualisation of human need in terms of basic amenities needed for the survival of individual and social order.
(b) The welfare programmes are required when normal structure of society fails to cope with the needs of common people.
(c) The state is entrusted the responsibility of initiating ameliorative action to fulfil the minimum standards for maintaining the social order.
(d) The thrust of welfare programmes has been to ensure a basic standard of decency in relation to the physical and mental well-being of citizenry (U.S. Encyclopaedia of Social Work: 1972)

(2) Institutional Approach to Social Welfare

The basic features of this approach in this theoretical framework are as follows:

(a) Acceptance of need of establishing welfare institutions considering it as one of the functional elements in the structure of society.
(b) This approach takes non-fulfilment of needs of individual as an aberration of system.
(c) Institutions are establishing for preventing these aberrations of system converting in social problem and threatening the very structure of society.
(d) Here, certain measures are initiated to as corrective device or mechanism for correcting the structure.

(B) Conflict Theories

The main features of these theories related to social welfare are as follows:

(1) Poverty and unemployment exist due to inherent contradictions of the societies based on capitalist mode of production.
(2) Here, structural approach to welfare is recognised where strategy of welfare relies on the total ban on private property with a view to redistribute societal wealth equally and justly among the needy people.
(3) Moderate segment of conflict theories have been of the view that existence of conflict between different classes is inevitable and state should function as a neutral arbitrator between warring factions or classes.
(4) In this way, this approach envisaged that the state is given major responsibility of devising measures to provide services for meeting the needs of people on an equitable basis rather than on a minimum needs scale.

H.Y. Siddique (1990) has presented the following typology of welfare models:

	Subjects	*Models*		
		Residual	*Institutional*	*Structural*
(1)	(2)	(3)	(4)	(5)
1.	Entitlement of individual vis-à-vis. The society (concept of need)	Basic minimum	Minimum opportunity for development	Equal with others
2.	Collective responsibility	Minimum	Accepted in principle	Obligatory
3.	Mechanism for delivery of services	Largely voluntary	State with voluntary efforts	State through local authority
4.	Range of programmes	Primarily curative	Curative with emphasis on prevention	Preventive and curative
5.	Coverage	Only handicapped	A large section of general population	All
6.	Level of benefits	Low	Medium	Low

(*Contd.*)

(1)	(2)	(3)	(4)	(5)
7.	Percentage of national expenditure on welfare	Less than 5 percent	Between 10 to 20 per cent	Difficult to measure generally considered high around 20-30 percent
8.	Status of clients	Low	Low with efforts to non-stigmatise	Equal with others
9.	Role of voluntary agencies	Primary	Supportive	Marginal

MODELS OF WELFARE

There are different conceptions of welfare. These are as follows:

Wilensky and Lebaux (1965):

(a) **Residual** : Welfare institutions should come forward when the established structure of supply (the family, the masket etc.) fails to deliver their responsibilities or services.

(b) **Institutional** : Modern industrial society has first time functions of providing welfare services or the people.

Richard Titmuss has given three models of welfare which are given as follows:

(a) *The Residual Welfare Model*: Social welfare institutions come into play when two natural (or socially given) channels (family/market) fail to satisfy the needs of individual.

(b) *The Industrial Achievement Performance Model*: This model envisages a vital and important role of social welfare institutions as adjuncts of economy. It sets standards that on the basis of merit, work performance and productivity, social needs should be met.

(c) *The Institution Redistributive Model*: This model envisages social welfare as important integrated institution of society. This institution makes services available to individuals (a) outside the market; (b) on the principle of need; (c) based on the thinking of multiple effects of social change as well as of economic system; and (d) partly on the principle of social equality.

THE TERM SOCIAL WELFARE

Combined together the terms social welfare has two meanings: (a) Traditionally, social welfare means some nursing depend on methods to teach the person to protect his surroundings effectively; and (b) As modern concept, social welfare is a planning by which men will mitigate his problems under any social organisation.

The term social welfare is related to the concept of welfare state and in this context Encyclopaedia Britannica refers social welfare as "a system of laws and institutions through which a government attempts to protect and promote the economic and social welfare of its citizens usually based on various forms of social insurance against unemployment, accident, illness and old age". In the same parlance, Encyclopaedia of Social Sciences refers welfare state by explaining that the 'welfare state' is the institutional outcome of the assumption by a society of legal and therefore formal and explicit responsibility for the basic well-being of its members.

DEFINITIONS OF SOCIAL WELFARE

The term social welfare expresses an ambiguous and changing concept. It has both a negative and a positive connotations (Romanshyn: 1971:3). It expresses a changing views of a changing institution (Compton: 1980: 25). The definitions of the terms are being presented as follows:

(1) *Social Security Administration (1950)*: "... Social welfare has been encompassing the development and administration of (1) social insurance, (2) social assistance and (3) other social services designed to strengthen family life and to provide care and protection for social groups such as children, the aged and mentally, socially or physically handicapped persons".

(2) *Friedlander, W.A. (1955)*: Social welfare is the organised system of social services and institutions, designed to aid individuals, and groups to attain satisfying standards of life and health, and personal and social relationships which permit them to develop their full capacities and to promote their well-being in harmony with the needs of their families and community.

(3) *Wilensky, H.L. and C.N. Lebeaux (1958)*: "Social welfare as those formally organised and socially sponsored institutions, agencies and programmes which function to maintain or improve the economic conditions, health of interpersonal competence of some parts of all of a population".

(4) *Wilensky, H.L. and Lebeaux, C.N. (1965)*: "Two conceptions of social welfare seem to be dominant in the United States today: the residual and institutional. The first holds that social welfare institutions should come into play only when the normal structures of supply, the family and the market, break down. The second, in contrast, sees the welfare services as normal "first line" functions of modern industrial society".

(5) *Wickenden, Elizabeth (1965)*: Social welfare as "... including those laws, programmes, benefits and services which assure or strengthen provisions for meeting social needs recognised as basic to the well-being of the population and the better functioning of social order".

(6) *U.S. Department of Health, Education and Welfare (1966)*: "In the current views of social welfare, two concepts predominate: The residual and developmental. The first holds that social welfare activities should come interplay only when the normal structures of society breakdown. This places social welfare activities in a residual role, ameliorating the breakdown and filling gaps. The second, and for more promising view of social welfare defines welfare activities as a frontline function of modern industrial society, in a positive, collaborative role with other major social institutions working toward a better society".

(7) *Philip Klein (1968)*: Social welfare as "the administration of certain services to individuals and families who find it difficult or impossible to maintain themselves and their dependents in material solvency and in health by their own efforts".

(8) *Crompton and Keiser (1970)*: Social welfare as "a system that embodies a multi-faceted approach to social and economic problems, reflecting social values and using the expertise of interrelated disciplines for the collective good".

(9) *Smith and Zeitz (1970)*: While defining social welfare, the statement has been given as "the social services institutionalise as public policy, the philanthropic impulse".

(10) *Romanyshyn, John. M. (1971)*: "Social welfare as including all those forms of social intervention that have a primary and direct concern with promoting both the well-being of individual and of the society as a whole".

(11) *Encyclopaedia of Social Work (1971: 1146)*: "Social welfare, generally denotes the full range of organised activities of voluntary and governmental agencies that seek to prevent, alleviate or contribute to the solution of recognised social problems or to improve the well-being of individuals, groups or communities. Such activities use a variety of professional personnel such as physicians, nurses, lawyers, educators, engineers, ministers, social workers and para professional counterparts of each".

(12) *Romanyshyn, John. M. (1974)*: Social welfare is "a field of activities and policies directing efforts to deal with social problems".

(13) *Martin Woolins (1976)*: "Social welfare is a device for maintaining or strengthen of the existing social structure of an industrial society".

(14) *Turner (1974)*: Social welfare as including "(1) the wide range of services designed to attain ways of life acceptable to individuals and the community, sometimes thought of collectively as the "social aspects of development and including services designed to strengthen the individual confronted with economic, physical, mental or social disabilities, together with (2) those aimed at including the remedy of conditions leading to dependency".

(15) *Federico (1976)*: The concept of social welfare as an institution of society which has its purpose "improving social functioning and minimising

suffering through a system of socially approved financial and social services at all levels in the social structure". "... focus of the social welfare system may be on solving existing problems (curative) preventing the future occurrence of problems (preventive) or rehabilitating those with problems to prevent future problems (rehabilitative)".

(16) *Encyclopaedia of Social Work (1977: 1503)*: "Social welfare is an organised effort to ensure a basic standard of decency in relation to the physical and mental well-being of the citizenry ... (it) includes considerably more than assuring the necessities to support life ... is characterised by a large complex of interlocking preventive and protective laws and organisations designed to provide, at the least, universal access to the mainstream of society.... (involves). The ever present, active assistance to individuals and groups to facilitate their attaining and maintaining a respectable life style.

(17) *Compton, B.R. (1980)*: "Social welfare is a social institution charged with the necessary function of helping both individuals and the other social institutions to move together more productivity for the sake of individual and family welfare.

(18) *Dologoff R. and D. Feldstein (1980)*: "In its narrowest sense, social welfare includes these non-profit functions of society, public or voluntary, which are clearly aimed at alleviating distress and poverty or at ameliorating the conditions of casualties of society".

(19) *Dologoff R., D. Feldstein and L. Stolnik (1997)*: "All social interventions intended to enhance or maintain the social functioning of human being".

BASIC FEATURES OF THE TERM SOCIAL WELFARE

According to Wilensky and Lebeaux (1958), there are five features of social welfare:

(1) *Organisation*—delivered through government and non-government organisations.
(2) *Social sponsorship and accountability*—service providers answerable to funding sources (government and donations to provide quality service).
(3) *Non-profit motive*—sometimes charging of fee.
(4) *Functional generalisation*—to meet different aspects of need of society.
(5) *Direct focus on human consumption*—that is housing, medical services etc.

Thus, basic features of social welfare can be summarised (on the basis of definitions given) as follows:

1. Social welfare establishes an organised helping system.
2. This system improves the well-being of individuals, groups, communities or whole society.
3. It provides active assistance and help to persons having difficulty in obtaining access to ways of developing a respectable life style.
4. The help and care are rendered on the principles of non-profit as well as accessibility based on means test.
5. The principle of 'normalisation' is fundamental to social welfare system which refers that regardless of physical, psychological or social handicap, a person should be enabled to live, work and develop in a normal environment.
6. This system was the expertise from different disciplines.
7. The help and care are rendered to persons and groups facing problems and having needs to be met through family of legislative enactments, developing policies, organising programmes and rendering services.
8. This help, care and protection are provided through public or private institutions.
9. The ultimate purpose of this help, care and protection is to promote public welfare to make social system more effective.
10. As an institution, social welfare—
    (a) encompasses policies and laws;
    (b) these policies and laws are operational by organised activities of voluntary (private) and/or governmental (public) agencies;
    (c) these agencies distribute defined minimum of social services, money, and other consumption rights (medical care, education and public housing etc.);
    (d) this is distributed to individuals, families and groups by criteria other than those of the market place or those prevailing in family system; and
    (e) the purposes have been prevention, alleviation or contribution to the solution of recognised social problems for improving the well-being of individuals, groups and communities directly (Compton: 1980: 34).

OBJECTIVES OF SOCIAL WELFARE

These can be presented as follows:

(1) Overall well-being for human being leading to welfare for all.
(2) Helping in filling of human rights.
(3) Helping for poor and vulnerable sections of society leading to improve their social functioning in society.

(4) Developing person-in-environment.
(5) Solving problems of people through organised help and support.
(6) Developing human resource leading to good citizenship.
(7) Bringing social change.
(8) Developing and improving human relationships.
(9) Establishing social control.
(10) Empowering and capacity building of weaker sections of society.
(11) Introducing better socialisation opportunities.
(12) Maintaining balance between distribution of resources and amenities.
(13) Establishing, fixing and facilitating the role people in society.

FUNCTIONS OF SOCIAL WELFARE

Compton (1980: 33-34) has maintained that the social welfare institution must be concerned with three types of activities:

(1) *Maintenance activities:* (a) Acting to protect the individuals by supplying necessary limits, supports and resources for enabling them to cope with life. (b) Acting to ensure the coherence, continuity and stability of the other social institutions of society.
(2) *Developmental activities:* (a) Providing assistance to orderly growth of both individual and all kinds of institutions within the framework of national plans and aspirations. (b) Furnishing a foundation for the optimal development of individuals and families.
(3) *Change activities:* (a) Changing the functioning of individual, family and group as per desire of individual wanting change or when change is vital for the protection of self and others. (b) Changing the significant elements of social structure by seeking pressure within the boundaries of existing laws and working of other institutions when their functioning is harmful to individuals or groups.

Thus, social welfare functions at different levels which may be described as follows:

(1) *Remedial*: Refers to removal of disabling and regaining normal functioning of needy groups, weaker and under-privileged sections of society, providing emergency relief and remedy in cases of hardships and human sufferings, alleviating abnormalities, providing care services to individuals and families, fixing minimum standard of services and giving other residual services.
(2) *Preventive*: Refers to early detection and prevention of abnormal behaviour and conditions, generating new conditions, eliminating causes of problems, screening services, conducting research on effective prevention of causes of problems, preparing systematic plans

and striving for universal services and so on.

(3) *Developmental*: Refers to improvement in situations, developing individual and society, preparing constructive plans, making social investment, generating awareness about social commitments and responsibilities, developing potential and capacities, making mature and responsible citizenship.

(4) *Supportive*: Refers to the achievement of goals and targets of different sectors of society, organisation of mutual support system among different services and clientele, providing education, training as well as community support to individuals and families, framing interrelated and responsive social policies and developing a system having better effectiveness and efficiency and establishing a sustainable economy based on equity and social justice.

CONCEPTS RELATED TO SOCIAL WELFARE

There are concepts related to social welfare. Sometimes, these concepts are confused with term social welfare. A brief description of these concepts is being presented in following paragraphs.

Social Services and Social Welfare

Social welfare is different from social service since social services are meant for the normal population and strives for meeting the basic requirements and needs of life such as education, health, housing, recreation and so on. The concentration of social services is to develop human resources of country.

Social welfare is directed towards upliftment of weaker and vulnerable sections of the society. Welfare services are given to persons who are suffering from some kind of handicap and need support and help.

Difference

Social Services	*Social Welfare*
1. Organised activities for every member of society.	Activities for weaker and vulnerable sections of society.
2. No means test for availing the services.	Means test for availing the facilities/services.
3. Mostly cooperative action.	Individual and cooperative actions.
4. Fulfilling the needs and solving the problems.	Maintenance of minimum desirable standard of living.

Social Work and Social Welfare

In the profession of social work, help is made available to persons having problems by individual (professional social worker) or organisation (agency). The help is rendered on the basis of scientific knowledge, methods and skills after assessing and developing capacities and resources of problematic person so that he may be able to help himself and able to make adjustments with environment. Social work also strives to bring change in the situation for attaining social justice and maintaining human rights and humanitarianism.

Social welfare is a system where services are offered to weaker and vulnerable sections of society on the basis of means test.

Social Work	*Social Welfare*
1. It is a professional activity.	It is normally based on religious/ philanthropic thinking.
2. Remuneration is charged by professional social worker for providing services.	No remuneration is charged.
3. Services provided to every person having problems.	Services provided on the basis of certain eligibility criteria.
4. Help is based on the principle of self-help.	Help is not based on the principle of self-help.
5. Focus on individuals, group and community.	Generally focus on group/ community.
6. Persons approaching for help are known as clients.	Persons getting services are known as beneficiaries.
7. Help is rendered on the basis of scientific knowledge, methods and skills.	No specific knowledge, methods and skills are required.
8. Individual differences are taken into account.	No individual differences are taken into account in case of eligible beneficiaries.
9. Promotes independency among seekers of help.	Promotes dependency among beneficiaries.
10. Emphasis on evolutionary change.	Emphasis on maintenance of system.

Social Justice and Social Welfare

Social justice has been interpreted as distribution and redistribution of resources, provision for equity and equal opportunities, just allocation of advantages by preventing the abuse of power and liberty as well as just decision about disputes and adoption of change.

Social welfare is oriented towards providing facilities and concessions to that sections of society who are lagging behind and not able to cope with the needs and wants of day-to-day living.

Difference

Social Justice	*Social Welfare*
Opportunities and resources as a matter of right of weaker sections of society	Opportunities and resources as matter of duty of community and state.
Providing protection or prevention of exploitation/discrimination mostly through legislation.	Using policies and programmes generally for alleviating the situation.
More emphasis on change.	Emphasis on maintenance of system.

Social Security and Social Welfare

Social security provides protection to people against various contingencies or risks such as accident, unemployment, handicap, old age, retirement, widowhood etc. by providing assistance (social assistance and public assistance) and social insurance mainly chalked out through legislative action.

Social welfare provides services to special section of society both under government and private auspices.

	Social Security	*Social Welfare*
1.	Protection provided against contingencies such as unemployment, accident, old age, etc.	Services rendered to special section of society for maintaining minimum desirable standard of living.
2.	Assistance is provided through assistance and insurance.	Assistance/help provided through well planned programmes and services.
3.	Here, contribution from beneficiary may be taken.	No such contribution from beneficiary is taken.
4.	It is generally provided through legislative action.	Provided both through programmes/schemes and legislative action.
5.	Main purpose is the maintenance and sustenance of life.	Main purpose is to fulfil minimum needs of persons who are not able to cope with their needs.

Social Reform and Social Welfare

Social reform is undertaken against any particular social evil or social problem by an individual or group of individuals as a movement in order to change or restructure the existing system. It is an organised activity launched by a person or group of persons having other persons as followers of reform.

Social welfare is generally carved out to maintain the status quo and persons getting benefits of programmes/services are beneficiaries (not followers) who fulfil certain eligibility criteria.

Social Reform	*Social Welfare*
1. Movement against any social evil/social problem.	It is not movement by a system of giving help and support to weaker sections of society.
2. Casual and temporary activity.	Undertaken for long time.
3. Restructuring or changing the existing system.	Maintaining the existing system.
4. Individual or group of individuals as leaders or reformers and others are simply followers.	Persons getting benefits on certain conditions are known as beneficiaries.
5. No means test only faith in movement.	Existence of means test.

Social Development and Social Welfare

Social development is (a) a process of systematic change purposefully initiated through the instruments of social policy and planning for the enhancement of the levels of living and quality of life of masses, (b) a programme as well as a movement, approach and method of treating any broad based issues, (c) involved in long-term planning based on investing in people, environment and social systems, and as largely concerned to improve the social situation in regard to development, housing, health, nutrition, education, social stability and social welfare (Atul Pratap Singh and Arun Kumar Singh: 2010: 8-9).

Social welfare provides services/programmes for the maintenance of life and living of weaker sections of society having less emphasis on charge.

Social Development	*Social Welfare*
1. Wider in scope.	Narrow in scope.
2. Development of totality of society i.e. its economic, political, social and cultural aspects.	Development of individual or family mostly economically and socially.
3. Macro approach.	Both macro and micro approaches.
4. Long term planning and policy.	Short term as well as long term both.
5. Emphasis on change.	Emphasis on system maintenance.

Empowerment and Social Welfare

Empowerment is a process of enabling or authorising an individual to think, behave, take action and control work and decision making in autonomous ways, refers to a state of mind having a feeling of being worthy and competent or perceiving power or control resulting into self-empowerment to take control of one's own destiny and modifies social structure in order to distribute resources for overcoming the effects of discrimination and oppression. Thus, empowerment is a process of change through active involvement of persons who strive for change.

Social welfare is mainly concerned with improving the conditions of downtrodden through policies, programmes and services as well as providing protection through legislative measures.

Empowerment	*Social Welfare*
1. Develops capacities of people to get their rights.	Provides services to improve the conditions of people.
2. Enhances sense of prestige and worthiness among people.	Develops feeling of inferiority and marginalisation.
3. Enhances independence.	Develops dependence.
4. Change is vital.	Change is in subordinate position.

2
Administration: An Introduction

ADMINISTRATION: CONCEPTUAL ANALYSIS

With the advancement in science and technology, industrial revolution, population increase and unprecedented growth in information technology have created a situation that state should play a positive and responsible role to care and protect the people who are not able and capable to care for themselves. This demands state intervention and the concept of welfare state came into existence in which importance of administration for rendering services to the needy has increased.

MEANING OF ADMINISTRATION

The English word 'administer' is derived from the Latin words 'ad' and 'ministrate'. This means "to minister to", "to serve", or "to manage". The Dictionary meaning of administration is the management of affairs. Thus, the meaning of administer to manage or direct or serve.

There are two views regarding administration.

(a) *Integral view*: All activities (physical, mental, clerical, managerial) for attaining the purpose comprise administration. In this sense, administration means the activities of groups, cooperating to accomplish common goals.

(b) *Managerial view*: According to this view, administration is concerned only with the management, direction, supervision and control of human beings who are cooperating to achieve a purpose.

In this way administration means the following:

(1) Administration is conceived as the necessary activities of individuals in an organisation.

(2) These persons are charged with ordering, forwarding and facilitating the associated efforts of a group of individuals.

(3) These individuals brought together to realise certain defined purposes.
(4) Thus, administration is viewed as 'doing of work' or 'getting the work done' by others.

DEFINITIONS OF ADMINISTRATION

Administration normally conveys that leaders in the top echelon of an organisation facilitate the work of the organisation and staff by involving all members of the organisation working at different levels of organisation. In order to explain the concept of administration, the following definitions are being quoted.

Tead (1939): "Administration is the process of direction, oversight, coordination and stimulation in an agency designed to carry out some agreed purpose with economy and effectiveness in the means employed (material and personnel) and with all possible regard for the claims of the individuals involved".

Leopard Maya (1945): Administration may be defined "as the determination and clarification of function; the formulation of policies and procedures; the delegation of authority; the selection, supervision and training of staff, and the mobilisation and organisation of all available and appropriate resources to the end so that the purposes of the agency may be fulfilled".

Arlien Johnson (1947): Administration as "a process and method by which objectives of programme are transformed into reality through a structure and a mode of operation that make possible the coordinated and unified work of people in the movement towards the defined objectives".

L.D. White (1948): "The art of administration is the direction, coordination and control of many persons to achieve some purpose or objectives".

Beavers (1950): Administration "as the process of means by which the aims of an organisation are determined, plans made for achieving these aims and the plans carried out".

Kidneigh (1950): Administration "as the process of transforming social policy into social services… a two way process (1)… transforming policy into concrete social services and (2) the use of experience in recommending modification of policy".

Spenser (1950): "Administration is the conscious direction of the internal relationships and activities of enterprise towards the achievement of goals". She also outlines that it encompasses "the conscious intervention in the interacting forces operating between the agency and the larger community of which it is a part".

E.A. Nigro (1951): "Administration is the organisation and use of men and materials to accomplish a purpose".

Friedlander (1955): "Administration of social agencies translates the provisions of social legislation and the aims of private philanthropy and religious charities into the dynamics of services and benefits of humanity".

Waldo, D. (1955): "An area of study, administration is a science, and as an area of practice it is an art".

Herbert A. Simon (1960): "In its broadest sense, administration can be defined as the activities of groups cooperative to accomplish common goals".

Pfiffner (1961): "Administration is the organisation and direction of human and material resources to achieve desired ends".

Dunham (1962): "Administration as the process of "supporting or facilitating activities which are necessary and incidental to the giving of direct service by a social agency. Administrative activities range from the determination of function and policies, and executive leadership to routine operations such as keeping records and accounts and carrying on maintenance services".

Stein (1970): Administration "as process of defining and attaining the objectives of an organisation through a system of coordinated and cooperative effort".

Warham (1970): Administration is "a problem solving and enabling process. It involves the making of decisions; and if only because present decision affects future functioning, it is directed towards the future".

Schwartz, Edward E. (1970): "In common parlance, the term administration is used to refer both an area of study and an area of practice".

Trecker (1971): Administration "as process of working with people in ways that release and relate their energies so that they use all available resources to accomplish the purpose of providing needed community services".

Saari (1977): "Administration refers to a systematic, interventive process, consisting of interdependent tasks and functions and associated activities, employed by management personnel to facilitate the achievement of selected organisational goals and objectives. It denotes the purposeful application of knowledge, skills, and values to such tasks of defining objectives and planning programmes, mobilising and maintaining resources, and evaluating outcomes".

A review of these definitions suggests some important elements which are as follows:

(1) Administration is a dynamic process having continuity.
(2) The process formulates and implements policies related to collective endeavours.
(3) The collective endeavour is directed toward accomplishment of common goals.
(4) The process goes on for meeting common purpose or goal.
(5) This process organises and mobilises resources for the purpose of fulfilling the common purpose or goal.
(6) Harnessing of resources of people and material is done through coordination and cooperation.
(7) Organisation is the setting of administration through which administrator/social worker should work.

(8) Planning, organising, leadership, decision making, authority and communication are essential ingredients of administrative process.

Thus, administration is a process through with common goals or purposes met by formulating and implementing social policies having an organisation as setting in which coordinated activities are undertaken.

ADMINISTRATION, MANAGEMENT AND ORGANISATION: THE PROBLEM OF TERMINOLOGY

(A) One School of Thought Regarding the Terminology

(1) Administration is Top Level Function

One school of thought (consisting of William R. Spriegel, J.N. Schulz, Oliver Sheldon, G.E. Millward, Ordway Tead, F.J. Wright, etc.) considers administration as top-level function which:

1. Determines major policies and objectives of organisation (i.e. thinking function).
2. Concerns itself with overall determination of institutional objectives and policies followed in achieving those objectives (determinative function – *W.R. Spriegel.*
3. Lays down the object for which an organisation and its management have to strive and the broad policies under which they are to operate (*J.N. Schulz*).
4. Functions in industry concerned in the determination of corporate policy. The coordination of finance, production and distribution, the settlement of compass of organisation and the ultimate control of executive (*Oliver Sheldon*).
5. Determines the aims for which an organisation and its management are to operate and which gives general oversight to the continuing effectiveness of the total operation in reaching the objectives sought (*Ordway Tead*).
6. Implements the policy and coordinates all factors of production in accordance with the general directions laid down by those responsible for the formulation of the policy (*F.J. Wright*).

(B) Management is the lower level Function which is Concerned with

1. Implementation of the policies and giving direction to operators to attain the objectives laid down by administration (doing function).
2. Carrying out of broad policies laid down by the administration (executive function – *W.R. Spriegel*).
3. Leading, guiding and directing an organisation in the accomplishment of a pre-determined object (*J.N. Schultz*).

4. Execution of policy within the limits set up by the administration and the employment of the organisation for the particular objects set before it (*Oliver Sheldon*).
5. Execution of policy in a planned and supervised manner (*G.E. Millward*).
6. Direction and guidance of the operations of an organisation in the realising of established aims (*Ordway Tead*).
7. Carrying out decisions of administration (*F.J. Wright*).

(C) Concept of Organisation: According to this school of thought, organisation is:

1. The combination of the necessary human beings, materials, tools, equipment, working space and appurtenances, brought together in systematic and effective correlative, to accomplish some desired object (*J.N. Schultz*).
2. The process of so combining the work which individuals or groups have to perform with the facilities necessary for its execution that the duties, so formed, provide the best channels for the efficient, systematic, positive and coordinated application of the available effort (*Oliver Sheldon*).
3. The process of dividing work into convenient tasks or duties of group such duties in the form of posts of delegating authority to each post and of appointing qualified staff to be responsible the work is carried out as planned (*G.E. Millward*).

Thus, according to this School of Thought "Organisation is the formation of an effective machine, management of an effective executive, and administration of an effective direction" (*Oliver Sheldon*).

As per this School of Thought the difference between Administration and Management is as follows:

Difference between Administration and Management

Base of Difference	*Administration*	*Management*
1. Policy formulation	Formulates the policy	Implements the policy
2. Determination of targets and goals	Directly related to the determination of targets and goals	Not directly related to the determination of targets and goals
3. Nature of function	Determinative and legislative functions	Executive and largely governing functions
4. Direction of human resources	Not actively concerned	Mainly concerned with the direction of human efforts in the execution of plan as well as policy

(*Contd.*)

Base of Difference	*Administration*	*Management*
5. Main concern	Planning and organising	Motivating and controlling
6. Level	Top-level	Middle and lower level
7. Nature of relationship	Master organisation	Servant of administration
8. Coordinated activity	Coordination of finance, production and distribution	Use of organisation for achievement of target
9. Administrative/technical nature	Understood as administrative activity	Understood as technical activity having some administrative functions
10. General usage	Done mostly in government auspices	Done mostly in Industrial and business auspices
11. Functional expansion	Takes place at the upper level and decreases in importance at lower levels	Contract function at the upper levels and expand at the lower levels

Difference Between Management and Organisation

Base of Difference	*Management*	*Organisation*
1. Nature of function	Executive function (Getting things done with others)	Organisation (Putting different parts of organisation into an order)
2. Performance of functions	Different functions (planning, organisation, staffing, motivation, coordination and control)	Organisation is one of the functions of management
3. Execution of functions	Functions executed in the organisation	Structure or framework in which management functions
4. Levels	Different levels – top, middle and lower	No such levels
5. Use	Management uses organisation developed by administration	Machine of management

(B) Second School of Thought

According this this school, the terms "Administration" and "Management" are synonyms. This view has mainly been taken by Henri Fayol and William Newman. The arguments in this regard is given that:

Executives, at all levels, perform both functions i.e. administration and management. However, there may be difference in scope and degree. At the top level of hierarchy, more time is spent on administration while at lower level more management activities are performed.

ADMINISTRATION: TYPES

The administration can be divided into two types:

(A) *Public Administration*: Refers to government in action where administration consists of getting the work of government done by (a) fulfilment or enforcement of public policy; (b) coordinating the efforts of people for the purpose of accomplishment of their tasks; and (c) organising collective endeavours for fulfilling common purposes or tasks through executives of government.

(B) *Private Administration*: Prefers to fulfilment of common purposes or goals through private organisations where administration is done for meeting the needs of people or solving their problems through collective endeavours.

Both public and private administration provide services to people for solving the problems or fulfilling their needs either with the purpose of getting profit or with the purpose of non-profit motives.

If administration of services are done with intention to earn profit under both public and private auspices. This type of administration is known as Business Administration, which is of two types:

(a) Business administration under public domain; and
(b) Business administration under private domain.

If services are administered without profit motive or no profit and no loss basis, this type of administration is known as Social Administration having two categories:

(a) Social administration under public domain.
(b) Social administration under private domain.

However, the term Social Welfare Administration includes collective, cooperative, coordinated and controlled efforts and endeavours specially designed for weaker, downtrodden, vulnerable and under-privileged sections of society both under public and private auspices having non-profit motive or no profit and no loss basis.

EVOLUTION OF ADMINISTRATION IN SOCIAL WORK

The profession of social work has always been involved in administering social welfare organisations both public and private auspices. But, the profession of social work has been slow in recognising the importance of administration in its professional practice. However, this recognition came slowly and now-a-days administration enjoys an important place in the constellation of social work methods. So, this evolution of administration in social work has passed away through different phases.

First Phase: Earlier Beginning

Earlier in 1874, National Conference of Charities and Corrections resolved that people, their social problems and delivery of social services should be the concern of leaders leading to emphasis on administrative problems and issues.

The observation made by Anna L. Dawes of Pittsfield, Massachusetts in 1893 at the International Congress of Charities, Corrections and Philanthropy that schools should organise to train workers to help to provide effective social services to those in need is an important landmark in this direction.

In 1897, Mary E. Richmond, then General Secretary of Charity Organisation Society of Baltimore, Maryland made same observations at National Conference of Charities and Corrections in United States. These recommendations were made mainly due to the non-availability of competent personnel to take the place of generation than passing off the scene (Bruno: 1944).

In the beginning of the 20th century, the theme of social administration was introduced into a few British Universities. For example, in 1901 The London School of Sociology and Economics was established.

Later on in 1912, this school became the Social Science Department of London School of Economics and Political Science. During the first decade of 20th century training courses for social workers in administration were established leading to their development around the world.

Second Phase: Beginning of Recognition of Administration

From 1900 to 1930s, the social work has been identified and recognised as an occupation in which social case work has been recognised as dominant method of this emerging profession. As an effort in the direction of intensive professionalization:

(a) Social work was introduced in hospitals, schools, judicial organisations, psychiatric settings.

(b) Schools of social work were established, and

(c) Professional organisations were formed for monitoring and setting standards of social work education.

By 1920s, social case work has advanced and become a well formulated field of practice in social work mainly due to the (a) recognition of social case work as core technology for professional practice of social work in different settings, (b) systematic efforts in developing principles of practice by Mary Richmond in Social Diagnosis (1917) and What is Social Case Work? (1922) giving theoretical base later on extended and developed in Freudian Psychology; and (c) schools of social work have developed their curricula mostly around social case work.

But, critics like Edith Abbott along with her colleagues at the Chicago School of Civics and Philanthropy and Sophonisba Breckinridge have impressed upon the profession to adopt a much broader approach to social work education and practice. James Hagerty (1931) on the basis of studies conducted on social work education during 1920s also opined that "most important task they (schools) should be engaged in was the education of leaders, the organisers and the administrators – in short, the executives in social work administration" with these opinions and persuasions, some beginning of the recognition to administration was taken place which is evident from the following:

1. Many schools of social work introduced courses in administration applied to specific agency settings (e.g. child welfare).
2. After 1914, a number of programmes also offered courses in general social welfare administration.
3. 1932, American Association Professional Schools of Social Work adopted its minimum curriculum for the first year of graduate programme in which administration was made the part of group of electives which students, might or might not take in their course of study.
4. Mulford Conference held in 1929 proposed a curriculum for professional training schools that would encompass the 'fundamental techniques of social work including social case work, group work, community organisation, research and administration'.

Thus, in this period, knowledge and competence in social case work was taken as the foundation of all forms of professional practice and administration was not ordinarily distinguished from direct practice, nor thought of as a separate function (Arthur Dunham: 1939).

Third Phase: Intensification of Recognition

Recognition of administration in social work was intensified due to the involvement of Government in providing economic assistance to millions unemployed and economically dislocated people. For this a public welfare system was established by creating federal emergency Relief Administration in 1934 followed by passing of Social Security Act in 1935 which has created a federal state system of public assistance. This situation has made following effects in furtherance of knowledge and skills in the field of administration in social work.

1. Inclusion of courses on administration in course curricula of schools of social work for preparation of personnel to work in public relief agencies.
2. Examination of case work and group work skills for purpose of adapting to administrative and supervisory responsibilities in public welfare and to incorporate contents on public social policy.
3. Social workers started looking into the emerging field of public administration for a theoretical framework.
4. The scholars like Follett, Gulick, Urwick, Dimock and White provided an orderly way of thinking about leadership, administrative processes and principles of structuring of organisation.
5. Many of these concepts such as division of labour, span of control, line-staff responsibilities, coordination, personnel management and managerial functions were adapted to the courses on social agency administration.
6. After world war second, developments in theoretical and conceptual frameworks of administration were directed to evolve a method of practice closely related to the core knowledge, values and skills of social work leading to acculturate administration for the purpose of evolving social work administration.

The need for evolving social work administration as distinct from general administration has been mainly due to the meeting the problems of: (a) expenditure on "overhead" and delay in taking and implementing decisions because of "red tape", (b) adequacy of benefits and services, (c) client insensitivities, (d) professional incompetencies, (e) ineffectiveness of the programme and inefficiency in operation, (f) unilaterism in exercise of authority, (g) undemocratic and non-participatory nature of administration, and (h) uncalled for division of persons into "deciders", "doers" and "receivers".

Thus, during the period of 1930 to 1960 administration has emerged a legitimate method of social work practice but still it was treated as minor method in some quarter. However, it got same institutional acceptance which need further development in order to be accepted as equal partner in realm of social work methods.

Fourth Phase: The Development Phase

In early 1960s, efforts were directed to develop theory and practice of social work administration which is evident from the following:

1. Establishment of Institute in 1960 for conducting research in social work administration and community organisation by the National Association of Social Workers.
2. Establishment of the Council on Social Work Administration in or NASW in 1963.
3. In 1960, the National Conference on Social Welfare also gave attention to administration and a number of papers were presented on this theme.
4. In 1962 and 1969 the Council of Social Work Education permitted individual schools to experiment with new approaches to education for practice making room for specialised courses on social work administration.

Fifth Phase: Meeting Challenges

In 1960s, there was massive growth in social welfare programmes resulting into unparalleled growth in social welfare expenditure. There were problems to manage this expenditure and massive enterprise of social welfare programmes mainly due to a gradual shrinking of the physical dividend because of the combined effect of several tax cuts, the Vietnam war, increased social welfare expenditure, inflation and reduced rate of economic growth leading to policies of scarcity.

This politics of scarcity affected badly the management of social welfare organisations since they have been asked to give information about what was being done at what cost and with what results. This resulted into the shift from programme maintenance and expansion to programme description, control and evaluation. For this, new management techniques such as cost-benefit analysis, programme evaluation and review technique (PERT) etc. were needed which demanded specialised professionals giving new challenges to social work administration.

Besides this, the position of social work professionals involved in managing social welfare organisations become vulnerable due to the wave of political reaction in the country regarding escalating expenditure on social welfare programmes.

The profession of social work responded these challenges by rapid expansion of curricula in schools of social work which increased scholarly attention to this method of practice in forms of

(a) organisation of professional conferences sponsored by CSWE, NASW and National Conference on Social Welfare;
(b) appearance of a number of journal articles on management and related subjects in social work abstracts; and
(c) publication of the Journal 'Administration in Social Work';
(d) by 1979, thirty six schools of social work offered a major in administration, and

(e) with advancement in area of social work administration, the course curriculum of several schools was restructured and included the following:
   (i) personnel – recruiting, selecting, developing, utilising, leading, mediating and evaluating;
   (ii) fiscal resources – acquiring, allocating and controlling;
   (iii) information systems – measuring, analysing, designing and operating;
   (iv) social and organisational policies and programmes – planning, instituting, monitoring, evaluating and changing;
   (v) organisational decision making and sanctioning systems – creating, using, restructuring and modifying; and
   (vi) environmental influences – building, challenging, coping and coordinating (Kazmerski and Macrov: 1976)

In this way, administration in social work becomes more visible. Consequently, the following propositions of curriculum study are noteworthy:

1. The Master's level social work curriculum (or approximate equivalent) should provide to all social workers the essential basic preparation requisite to their proper performance of their roles as (a) employees; (b) professional service workers; (c) supervision; and (d) staff colleagues.
2. The social work curriculum should provide for all students such knowledge and experience in the area of administration as well as support subsequent on the job learning and the application of professional knowledge in positions involving executive and sub-executive level responsibilities.
3. Thus, social work administration became a social work function.

APPROACHES TO ADMINISTRATION

(1) Scientific Method Approach

Use of scientific method in the area of administration has been established by the conceptualisation of scientific management by F.W. Taylor. Coined by Louis, Dr. Brandies in October 1910 at a meeting of engineers, the term: "Scientific Management" gained wide approval and publicity during the year 2012 due to the hearings on Taylor's scientific management by Special Committee of House of Representatives of US Congress.

Conceptualisation of Scientific Management by F.W. Taylor

The basic features of this conceptualisation are as follows:

1. Need for collaboration between management and all workers.

2. Application of scientific methods in the selection of workers, determination of their place on the job and creation of any understanding between workers and management.
3. Understanding between management and workers would lead to industrial efficiency.
4. Reward should be given to worker if his/her output reaches to a level of excellence under the prescribed conditions.
5. There is need for "mental revolution" both on the part of management and workers requiring complete change in the mental framework of management and workers in their day-to-day affairs.

Objectives of Scientific Management

These objectives have been framed by Taylor's society:

1. Help rendered for the development of higher standard of living by increasing income of workers.
2. For getting more income, wastage of human and material resources should be avoided and this increase in income should be shared between management and workers.
3. Provision of happy homes and surroundings to working personnel.
4. Provision of healthy conditions of work to the members of organisation both individually and socially.
5. Provision of maximum opportunities for the development of capacities of individual by scientific method of work assignment, selection, training, transfer, placement and promotion.
6. Imparting training to workers for the development of capacities of worker which make them eligible for promotion.
7. Development of self-confidence and self-respect among workers.
8. Creation of research atmosphere for developing understanding of the aims and objectives of organisation among workers.
9. Avoidance of discrimination in wages for the promotion of social justice.
10. Factors of environment contributing in conflict and development of feeling of neglect should be eliminated.

Principles of Scientific Management Applicable to Administration

(1) Development of True Science of Work. As per this principle:
   - (a) Replacement of rule of thumb in management by the development of science for each task.
   - (b) For this, scientific investigation of working conditions and fixation of amount of work done by each work should be carried out.
   - (c) Performance of work by workers should be properly planned.
   - (d) Workers working as scientific management procedure should get higher remuneration.

(e) Use of carrot and stick theory where worker is penalised in case of his/her failure to achieve required output.

(2) Scientific Selection and Training of Workers. This means:

(a) Scientific selection and training of workers as per their physical and intellectual qualities.

(b) Placement as per suitability of job.

(c) Training and development of workers are the responsibilities of management.

(3) Equal Division of Work Between Workers and Management. This involves:

(a) Acceptance of all suitable tasks by management.

(b) Avoidance of chances of conflict between these two.

(c) Creation of cordial and peaceful environment in the organisation.

(4) Cooperation Between Management and Workers. According to Taylor:

(a) This cooperation would create a good and healthy atmosphere in organisation.

(b) Enhancement and promotion of industrial efficiency and increase in individual productivity.

Mechanisms Envisaged under Scientific Management

These mechanisms have been differentiated from principles by F.W. Taylor who said that mechanisms are related to the performance of work in a planned way based on scientific system leading to efficiency in organisation. These are as follows:

(a) Functional foremanship where eight functional foremen (gang boss, speed boss, inspectors, repair boss, three clerks in planning office and a shop disciplinary) were supposed to guide workers in place of single foremanship.

(b) Use of stop-watch for the application of time study technique.

(c) Separate planning cell or department in every organisation should be established.

(d) Standardisation of tools and techniques of all cadres.

(e) Use of time savings devices (such as slide rules).

(f) Establishment of instruction based system for recording the nature and method of performing particular task.

(g) Adoption of classification of manufactured products and implements of manufacturing process.

(h) Bonus system for efficient performance.

(i) Reward and punishment system should be introduced.

(j) Application and promotion of modern costly system.

2. Bureaucratic Approach

Basic contributions of Max Weber regarding administration were his views on authority and bureaucracy. His views were stemmed from a basic concern with why individuals obey commands, why people do as they are told. For this, Weber made a distinction between power and authority.

Power is the ability to force people to obey, regardless of their resistance. Authority whose orders are voluntarily obeyed by those receiving them.

Types of Authority

In the conceptualisation of Weber, exercise of authority has been a universal phenomenon that characterised social relationships. He classified authority on the basis of legitimacy since the type of obedience, the kind of administrative system and the ways of exercising authority depended on it. He classified authority into three types:

(a) *Traditional Authority*: Here, authority is exercised by leader due to the virtue of his status which is inherited. The extent of authority is fixed by custom. Due to demands of traditions, authority of ruler is obeyed. The ruler may exercise arbitrary authority also.

Under Traditional authority, administrative staff has one of following two patterns:

(i) *Patrimonial form*: Officials are personal servants of the ruler and owe traditional loyalty to supreme head.

(ii) *Feudal form*: Officials have autonomy with their own resources of income but they owe a traditional relationship of loyalty toward leader.

Administrative and Managerial Services under Traditional Authority

1. These are handed down from father to son, so no selectors and appointments are made on the basis of expertise.
2. Administrative staff does not have clearly defined sphere of capabilities and competence.
3. No rational ordering of loyalty.
4. No regular training of promotees.
5. Recruitment and promotions are based on personal contacts, loyalties and kinship.

(b) *Charismatic Authority*: In this type of authority, personal abilities and qualities of person make him/her leader and he/she is treated as super-natural, super-human or bestowed with exceptional powers or qualities. He/she may be a prophet, a messiah or a political leader. This type of authority has followers not subjects and their job is to mediate between leader and masses.

Here, the administrative system does not have separate administrative staff but only group of followers and disciples who are given the position in administration on the basis of his/her charismatic qualities. There exists no legal rules to govern.

Weber suggested routinisation or institutionalisation for the continuance of this kind of authority after the departure of Charismatic leader. The task of routinisation can be done through following devices:

(a) Finding out new charismatic leader having specific qualities.
(b) Oracles or by drawing lots.
(c) Designation of successor by original charismatic leader.
(d) Heredity.
(e) Institutionalisation of plebiscite which can routinize charisma on democratic basis.

(c) *Legal Rational Authority*: This system of authority is called legal since authority is exercised by means of a system of rules and procedures. It is rational because since certain specific ends are achieved through expressly designed means. All final decisions are kept in black and white. Head of the system may enjoy authority either on the basis of tradition or charisma.

The administrative staff in this system is hierarchically organised and termed as 'bureaucracy' which was termed by Weber as most efficient form of organisation.

Nature of Administrative Staff: According to Weber, the existence and functioning of an administrative staff is important for all types of authority but there remained differences in nature of staff and activities as per legitimising of authority.

'Monocratic bureaucracy' has been labelled as most rational form of administrative staff which is located in legal-rational authority system. It is called 'pure' also, it is pure from technical point of view and capable of drawing highest degree of efficiency.

Characteristics of Bureaucracy (Ideal Type Rational Organisation): According to Weber these are as follows:

1. *Division of Labour*: Each person's job is broken down into simple, routine and well-defined tasks.
2. *Well Defined Authority Hierarchy*: Existence of multi-level formal structure with hierarchy of positions or offices ensures that each lower office is under the supervision of higher one.
3. *High Formalisation*: Dependence on formal rules and regulations as well as procedures for ensuring uniformity and regulating the behaviour of job holders.
4. *Impersonal Nature*: Individual members and interests as well as preferences are avoided and uniformly applied.
5. *Employment Decisions Based on Merit*: Qualifications, technical competence and performance are the bases of selection and promotion.

6. *Career Tracks for Employees*: Members of organisation pursue their career in organisation and in turn, organisation gives them tenure which assures for their retention.
7. *Distinct Separation of Members' Organisational and Personal Lives*: The needs, demands and interests of members kept completely separate from the rational impersonal conduct of the activities of organisation.

Thus, this approach of administration strives for a hierarchical system of organisation, competent and efficient staff to run the organisation, working as per rules and procedures for uniformity and avoiding personal discretion etc.

3. Human Relations Approach

This approach has been developed as a result of Hawthorne Experiments (1924-1932). The main features of this approach are as follows:

1. In every society/organisation phenomenon of informal organisation exists and important for establishing network.
2. For increasing the levels of output, the role of informal social groups is important.
3. It was brought out that member of organisation is not an 'economic man' only. He has sentiments, emotions, social relations, etc.
4. The role of superior is important in the equation of morale and productivity.
5. The importance of human relations in personnel administration has been recognised. It has emphasised that administrator should take account of the facts, attitudes and sentiments of workers.
6. According to this approach, the administrator should behave like a guardian or preserver of morale through the function of maintaining a condition of equilibrium which will preserve the social values existing in a cooperative system.
7. Administrator should be equipped with social skills in addition to specialist skills for the purpose of tackling workers through the generation of cooperative feelings and development of informal patterns of behaviour.
8. Administrative elite could help in bringing harmony and increased production.
9. Logical thinking and self-interest appears only when social association fails.
10. Emphasis on the importance of an adequate communication, particularly upwards.

Thus, contributions of this approach has been path breaking and phenomenal. Their impact on administration and management has been tremendous.

4. Technological Approach

All organisations turn inputs into outputs regardless of their nature and style. This approach has been developed on the basis of researches conducted in1960s by John Woodward and Charles Perrow as well as conceptual framework offered by James Thompson. Technology encompasses information, equipment, techniques and processes required to transform inputs into outputs of organisation.

James Woodword's Views

According to Woodword, unit, mass and process are three types of production technologies and these technologies have been treated by her as scale with increasing degrees of technological complexity with unit being the least complex and process the most complex.

Unit	manufactures custom-made products (such as tailor-made suits, turbines for hydro-electric dams, etc.)
Mass	makes large batch or mass produced products (such as refrigerators or Ford automobiles)
Process	produces heavily automated continuous process producers (such as oil and chemical refiners)

Woodword concluded that:

1. There are distinct relationships between these technology classifications and the subsequent structures of firms.
2. The effectiveness of the organisations were related to the fit between technology and structure.
3. The administrative component varied directly with type of technology, that is, as technological complexity increased, so did the proportion of administrative and supportive staff personnel.
4. Thus, these technologies have differentiated features:

Mass Production Technology Firms →
- Highly differentiated
- Relied on extensive formalisation
- Did relatively little to delegate authority

Unit and Process Technologies →
- Structured more loosely
- Flexibility through less vertical differentiation
- Less division of labour
- More widely defined roles and responsibilities
- Decentralised decision making

Charles Perrow's Contributions

Perrow looked at knowledge technology underlying two dimensions:

1. Task Variability	- Few expectations, if job is high in routineness - Large number of expectations if job has great deal of variety. This characterises top management, positions, consulting jobs, etc.
2. Problem analysability which ranges from well defined to ill-defined	- Assessing of search procedures followed to find - out successful methods for responding adequately to task expectations. - At one extreme, search can be defined and described. - An individual can use logical and analytical reasoning in search for a solution. - On other extreme would be ill-defined problems.

Matrix

These two dimensions can be used to construct two-by-two matrix. Four cells in this matrix represent four types of technologies.

Cell-I:	Routine Technologies	Few expectations, Easy to analyse problems
Cell-II:	Engineering Technologies	Large number of expectations can be handled in rational and systematic manner
Cell-III:	Non-routine Technologies	Many expectations and difficult to analyse problems

According to Perrow:

If problems studied systematically with logic and rationality	Cell I or II would be applied
Problems handled only through intuition, guesswork or unanalysed experience	Cell III or IV can be used
If new, unusual or unfamiliar problems appear regularly	Cell II or IV are appropriate
If problems are familiar	Cell I or III can be used

3. As per Perrow, task variability and problem analysability were positively correlated.

Main Conclusions

1. Control and coordination methods should vary with technology.
2. The more routine the technology, the more highly structured the organisation.
3. Non-routine technologies require greater structured flexibility.

Key Aspects of Structure that could be Modified to the Technology

1. The amount of discretion that can be exercised for completing the task.
2. The power of groups to control on the unit's goals and basic strategies.
3. The extent of interdependence between these groups.
4. The extent to which these groups engage in coordination of their work using either feedback or planning of others.

Perrow summarised his predictions as follows:

Cell Technology	*Formalisation*	*Centralisation*	*Span of Control*	*Coordination and Control*
I. Routine	High	High	Wide	Planning and rigid rules
II. Engineering	Low	High	Moderate	Reports and message
III. Craft	Moderate	Low	Moderate-wide	Training and meetings
IV. Non-routine	Low	Low	Moderate-narrow	Group norms and Group meetings

Thompson's Contribution

Thompson classified technologies into three types differentiated by the tasks of organisational units. These are as follows:

1. Long-Link Technology: In this: (a) tasks or operations are sequentially inter-dependent; (b) technology is characterised by fixed sequence of repetitive steps, (c) efficiency and coordination are required by these technologies and for this manager faces major uncertainties on the inputs and outputs sides of organisation; (d) manager responds to these uncertainties by controlling inputs and outputs; and (e) this involves integration vertically – forward, backward or both allowing the organisation to encompass important sources of uncertainty within its boundaries.

Input → (A) → (B) → (C) → (D) → Output

A Long Linked Technology
(This shows sequential interdependence)

2. Mediating Technology: This (a) links clients on both the input and output sides (welfare agencies are one example); (b) mediators perform and interchange function linking independent units; and (c) linking unit standardises the transactions of organisation and establishes conformity in the behaviour of client.

Mediating Technology
(Showing Pooled Interdependence)

3. Intensive Technology: This (a) represents a customised response to a diverse set of contingencies; (b) the exact response depends on the nature of problem and variety of unpredictable problems; (c) achieves coordination through mutual adjustment; (d) the selection, combination and ordering of these resources depend upon feedback from the object itself; and (e) managers respond by ensuring the availability of resources prepare for any contingency.

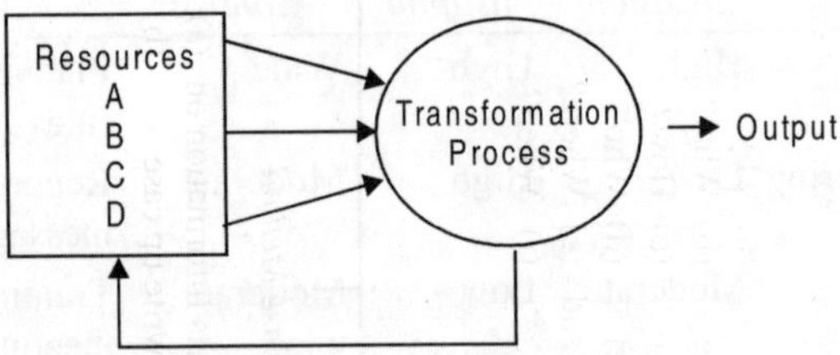

To conclude, it can be maintained that:

1. Routine technology is positively associated with low complexity involving fewer number of occupational groups and the less training possessed by professionals.

   On the other hand, non-routine technology is likely to lead to high complexity involving sophisticated and customised work, narrow span of control and increase in vertical differentiation and greater use of specialists.
2. Routine technology is positively related to formalisation since it permits management/administration to implement rules and other formalised regulations through rules manual and job descriptions.
3. The non-routine technologies heavily rely on specialists and characterised by delegated decision authority while routine technologies are associated with centralised structure.
4. Routine technology is positively correlated with centralisation but only if formalisation is low.

Methods of Approach in Solving Administrative Problems

J.E. Walters has summarised these methods after recognising the limitations of such brief outlines.

J.E. Walters' Methods of Approach in Solving Administrative Problems

1. *Logical Method*

(a) Analyse proposition
(b) Find relations
(c) Syllogic (develop alternatives)
(d) Deduct, in far etc.
(e) Conclude logically

2. *Scientific Engineering or Systematic Method*

(a) Define, recognise, formulate, state problem
(b) Consider alternatives and solutions
(c) Decide principles to apply
(d) Collect facts, experiment etc.
(e) Analyse and classify facts: consider detrnate solutions
(f) Test alternatives and select solution
(g) Base solution on facts and thinking

3. *Administration Elemental Method*

(a) Planning
(b) Organising
(c) Managing (Directing)
(d) Appraisal and control

4. *Industry Engineering Questioning*

(a) why?
(b) What?
(c) How?
(d) Who?
(e) Where?
(f) When?

5. *Organisation, Research, Management Science Method*

(a) Formulate problem
(b) Confer with other scientists
(c) Construct model of system
(d) Device solution from model
(e) Test model and solution
(f) Establish controls
(g) Implement solution

6. *M's of Management*

(a) Methods
(b) Money
(c) Men
(d) Materials, machinery, maintenance
(e) Manufacturing
(f) Marketing
(g) Measuring

7. *Function of Administration*

(a) Finance and accounting
(b) Sales
(c) Personnel
(d) Engineering and Research
(e) Production
(f) Research and development
(g) Purchasing
(h) Legal
(i) Public relations and advertising etc.

8. *Case Method*

(a) Collects information on case: write up case
(b) Discuss case
(c) Determine significant factors
(d) Find alternate soslutions
(e) Select course of action from factors

9. *Democratic Method*

(a) Determine problems
(b) Collect information on problem
(c) Meet or confer with those concerned
(d) Obtain consensus on solutions
(e) Decide upon solution
(f) Reconfer with those concerned
(g) Select best solution (majority)

3

Social Administration: Conceptual Analysis

The term administration has been used in combination of different terms, i.e. social administration, welfare administration, public administration, business administration, social service administration, social security administration, social agency administration, social welfare agency administration, development administration, social welfare administration and social work administration.

Before continuing these concepts and their distinctiveness with social welfare administration, some definitions of terms which are sometimes used interchangeably and sometimes differently are as follows:

DEFINITIONS OF SOCIAL ADMINISTRATION

R.M. Titmuss (1951): "Social administration may broadly be defined as the study of the social services whose object, to adapt Simey's phrase, is the improvement of the conditions of life of individual in the setting of family and group relations. It is concerned with the historical development of these services, both statutory and voluntary, with the moral values implicit in social action, with the roles and functions of the services, with their economic aspects, and with the part they play in meeting certain needs in the social process. On the other hand, then, we are interested in the machinery of administration, which organises and dispenses various forms of social assistance, on the other, in the level, the needs and the mutual relations of those members of the community for whom the services are provided by reason of their belonging to that community".

The Seminar on Social Administration in Developing Countries (1960): "Social administration is the participation of public administration to work with people in the administration of community services like health, education and housing, social security services like insurance, assistance and grants and social welfare services for the destitute, disabled, delinquents, drink and drug addicts, etc."

The Seminar on Social Administration in Developing Countries (1964): "Social administration is that part of administration which provides and operates services leading to the removal of prevailing disabilities and to the creation of opportunities for the well-being of individuals and families in the community".

Slack, K.M. (1966): "The term (social administration) is used in two ways; a fact which is the cause of good deal of the confusion that it generates. First, social administration is used to refer to a subject of study. Second, it is used to refer to a process directed to the solution of social problems, the promotion of social welfare or the implementation of social policy, a process which is furthered by the use of different methods or techniques designed to reach a decision, promote, some action or establish a precedent.

Parker (1966): "Social administration is a study of those aspects of policy and administration which (a) attempt to regulate standards of living and to control the distribution of income within a particular society, and (b) are intended to improve the circumstances or increase the well-being of a particular group or of the whole community".

D.V. Dennison (1968): "Narrowly defined social administration is the study of the development, structure and practices of the social services. Broadly defined, it is an attempt to apply the social sciences including philosophy to the analysis and solution of a changing range of social problems".

Forder (1974): "Social administration is concerned with study of development, structure and practices of social services".

Carrier and Kendall (1977): "Social administration may be understood as the part of administration which provides and operates services leading to removal of prevailing disabilities and to the creation of opportunities for the well-being of individual and families in the community".

CHARACTERISTICS OF SOCIAL ADMINISTRATION

As per proceedings of the Seminar on Social Administration in Developing Countries (1964), social administration consists of the following characteristics:

(a) Social administration is not a distinct discipline but a multi-disciplinary field of study.
(b) Field of study of social administration is essentially statutory welfare provision.
(c) Statutory welfare provision aims at meeting individual needs — There is, thus, a distinction drawn between 'personal' social services and

'public services' that benefit community at large in an indiscriminate manner.

P.D. Kulkarni (1965) enumerated the following special features of social administration:

(1) Promotional in objective.
(2) Directly responsive to the needs, problems and aspirations of the community.
(3) A working partner of citizen's organisations.
(4) Flexible enough to accommodate innovation in the structure of administrative agency, public or private.
(5) Liberal and progressive enough to permit experimentation in the functions, methods and procedures of administration.
(6) Manned with specialists in different branches of social development and welfare who have to acquire full and proper orientation of administration of the jobs (reverse of a generalist administrator who has to acquire specialisation of job).
(7) In closer liaison with research and evaluation so as to be able to formulate and review policies and programmes in the light of changing socio-economic condition and socio-psychological responses of the community.

Thus, social administration is the widest term having following characteristics:

(1) It makes available various services i.e. community services, social services, social security services and social welfare services.
(2) It studies services regarding their historical development, moral values implicit in these services, roles and function of these services and meeting the needs of social process.
(3) It improves in the conditions of life of individuals in family and groups by providing services, removing prevailing disabilities, creating opportunities for their well-being.
(4) Machinery of administration for organising and dispensing of social assistance for the purpose of improving overall lives and relations and meeting the needs of community members to whom services are being made available.

DEFINITIONS OF SOCIAL WELFARE ADMINISTRATION

Friedlander, W.A. (1955): "Social welfare administration (is) the process of organising and directing social agency".

Patti, Rino J. (1983): "The more restrictive definition of social welfare administration conceives it as a method of practice. Viewed in this way, administration refers to a systematic, interventive process consisting of interdependent tasks and functions and associated activities employed by management personnel to facilitate the achievement of selected organisational goals and objectives".

Characteristics

1. Social welfare administration is the part of social administration.
2. It refers as collective and cooperative endeavours specifically designed for weaker sections of society.
3. The services are offered or activities are conducted in both public and private auspices.
4. The basic premise of offering services or performing activities is non-profit motive.
5. The basic element is the improve the life and living conditions of weaker sections which are not able to cope with their needs and wants even at standard manner.
6. It studies and manages both statutory and voluntary services.
7. These services are made available to individuals in setting of family, group and community relations.
8. It prevents, alleviates or contributes to the solution of recognised social problems.
9. It improves the well-being of individuals, groups and communities.

DEFINITIONS OF SOCIAL WORK ADMINISTRATION

Spencer Sue (1959): "Social work administration … involves the making of judgments and the use of professional knowledge and skill which, while not wholly peculiar to social work, nevertheless differ considerably from the knowledge and skill required in business administration, or in the administration of other governmental or voluntary non-profit community services (such as schools, hospitals, churches etc.)".

American Council on Social Work Education (1959): Administration in social work is the process of transforming community resources into a programme of community service, in accordance with goals, policies and standards which have been agreed upon by those involved in the enterprise.

Skidmore (1983): Social work administration is "the action of staff members who utilise social processes to transform in social policies of agencies into the delivery of services. The basic processes, most often, used are planning, organising, staffing, directing and controlling".

Characteristics of Social Work Administration

As a method of social work, social work administration has following characteristics:

(1) It is concerned with administration of professional social workers.
(2) It is related to social organisation or agency for the purpose of achievement of its objectives.
(3) It identifies social objectives, formulates them and try to achieve them through policies and programmes.
(4) It enhances social functioning by (a) restoring it, (b) providing resources both social and individual for effective social functioning; and (c) preventing social dysfunction.
(5) Every agency or organisation has a definite structure in terms of general body, executive committee and highest body for decision-making.
(6) It tries full, efficient and effective utilisation of resources with help and support of participation and involvement of community in which agency and social work are functioning.
(7) Administration of these agencies/organisation is generally based on democratic values based on cooperation, collaboration and collective endeavours.

APPROPRIATENESS OF TERM OF SOCIAL ADMINISTRATION IN USAGE

The above mentioned three terms namely social administration, social welfare administration and social work administration have been used sometimes interchangeably and sometimes differently depending on the context, the background of the user and the purpose in view at a particular time. On the whole, social workers have been more inclined towards using the expressions social work administration and social welfare administration. Without trying to indulge in a hair-splitting exercise, it may be stated that social administration appears to be the most comprehensive of all three, and social work administration the narrowest. Acceptance of the term social administration on a universal basis seems to be the most appropriate course open (Hasan Saiyed Zafar: 1965).

The appropriateness of the term of 'social administration' is also in consonance of the present time, since the emphasis has been shifted from welfare to development to empowerment and presently the focus has been concentrated on right based approach to deal with the problems of needy persons.

Distinction of the Term Social Administration with Other related Terms

Social administration is widest term which includes all other terms which are in use for administering the services to the needy persons. However, these distinctions are as follows:

(A) Difference between Social Administration and Social Welfare Administration

	Social Administration	*Social Welfare Administration*
1.	Management of different services (community services, social security services, social services) available to all persons	Management of those services which are designed for weaker sections
2.	Providing services as per need of people	Maintenance of minimum desirable standard of living
3.	No dependency on the part of people	Generated dependency among people
4.	Administer services without any means test	Administering service through means test
5.	Use of right based approach	No use of right based approach

(B) Difference between Social Administration and Social Work Administration

	Social Administration	*Social Work Administration*
1.	Administration of services provided by persons of different disciplines	Administration of services provided by social workers
2.	Administration of social service organisation	Administration of agency of social workers
3.	As a method, social work administration is a part	As a method of social work
4.	Multi-disciplinary	Uni-disciplinary approach

Difference between Social Administration and Welfare Administration

In simple language, welfare administration means administration of welfare. This envisages:

(1) Administration which administers various plans, programmes and scheme for the welfare of people.

(2) This may not be social only since welfare is a composite concept not including social affairs or social development only but also administration of economic affairs or economic development etc.
(3) The welfare is also limited to the improvement of conditions of weaker and vulnerable sections of society both socially as well as economically.
(4) Thus, the concept of welfare administration includes both social as well as economic services.

	Social Administration	*Welfare Administration*
1.	Administration of social plans, programmes and services	Administration of social and economic plans and programmes
2.	All people	Weaker and vulnerable section of people
3.	Services without means test	Services with means test

Difference between Social Administration and Public Administration

The following explains the meaning of public administration which is:

1. Art of carrying out government policies both in central and local organisations.
2. The activity of the state in exercise of its political power.
3. The process consisting of (a) the actions involved affecting the extent or desire of government, (b) continuously active 'business' part of the government concerned with carrying out the law, as made by legislative bodies (or other authoritative agencies) and interpreted by court, and (c) processes of organisation and management.
4. The action part of administration, this means, by which the purposes and goals of government are realised.

	Social Administration	*Public Administration*
1.	Providing services in both public and private auspices	Only in public (government) auspices, the services are provided
2.	Wide in scope	Narrower in scope
3.	Both statutory and non-statutory services	Generally statutory services
4.	Soft nature of organisation	Hard nature of organisation
5.	Serves large number of people/ clientele	Serves limited number of clientele/people

Difference between Social Administration and Social Service Administration

Social service administration is the administration of social services and their agencies which generally include income maintenance services such as health care, housing, education, manpower and vocational rehabilitation, correctional services, personal social services, social development and change activities

	Social Administration	*Social Service Administration*
1.	Wider in scope	Narrower in scope
2.	Administration of social services, social security services, community services, etc.	Administration of social services and agencies only
3.	Helping to every person	Helping the helpless people

DIFFERENCE BETWEEN SOCIAL ADMINISTRATION AND PUBLIC WELFARE ADMINISTRATION

Public welfare administration is an art and science of those governmental activities directed towards the relief of distress, the care of dependent and neglected children and the treatment of criminals as well as care and treatment of mentally ill.

	Social Administration	*Public Welfare Administration*
1.	Both governmental and voluntary efforts are included	Only governmental efforts are included
2.	Governmental, quasi-governmental and non-governmental organisations are involved	Only governmental organisations are involved
3.	No means test in providing services	Means test in providing services

Difference between Social Administration and Social Security Administration

The term social security administration is used to denote the administration of services provided to the victims of various contingencies which imperil the working capacity of person who finds himself unable to maintain present standard of living.

	Social Administration	*Social Security Administration*
1.	Services to every person	Services given in case of contingencies (old age, unemployment, handicap etc.)
2.	Both statutory and voluntary	Mostly statutory services
3.	No contribution from beneficiaries	Contribution from beneficiary in case of social insurance
4.	No application of means test	Application of means test
5.	Benefits are not as a matter of right	Benefits as a matter of right

Difference between Social Administration and Social Agency Administration or Social Welfare Agency Administration

It is the administration and internal management of social agency either public or voluntary referring collectively, internal audit, internal agency coordination, communication etc. Thus, this administration is related to the structure, functions and management of social agency and social welfare agency.

	Social Administration	*Social Agency Administration and Social Agency Welfare Administration*
1.	Under this social agency/social welfare agency is created	Social agency/social welfare agency is means to provide services to needy
2.	An inclusive concept	One aspect of social administration
3.	End in itself	Means to an end
4.	Macro in nature	Micro in nature

Difference between Social Administration and Social Development Administration

Social development administration is an administration of policies and programmes of social development for bringing out change in the quality of life of people. It includes structure and functioning of organisations which are engaged in chalking out policies, programmes and schemes of development of persons and totality of society.

	Social Administration	*Social Development Administration*
1.	Mostly directed towards maintenance of income	Both maintenance of income as well as social change
2.	Services provided for rendering help in areas of social service	Improvement in the quality life of people
3.	No emphasis on the change of system	Change in the system may be emphasised
4.	Provides benefits of every person	Mostly needy persons are benefitted

DIFFERENCE BETWEEN SOCIAL ADMINISTRATION AND BUSINESS ADMINISTRATION

Business administration is concerned with organisation of services provided with objective of earning profits. It also manages economic and commercial undertakings.

Social Administration	*Business Administration*
1. Services are provided selflessly	Services are offered with the motive of earning profits
2. It is for long term investment	It is treated as short-term investment
3. Human-development oriented	Profit-motive oriented

NATURE OF SOCIAL ADMINISTRATION (SOCIAL WELFARE ADMINISTRATION)

Social Administration is a Science

Social administration is a science since it has a scientific body of knowledge which can be put to use for the effective discharge of social services. Through this knowledge, critical examination of every activity of social administration takes place. It also contains principles which are universally applicable as well as ways of doing things systematically and logically.

Social Administration is an Art

Social administration renders actual services to the needy for which skills and techniques are used. The knowledge is applied systematically for bringing human as well as physical resources together, so that they may be utilised fully for meeting the needs of people or solving their problems. For this, social administrator uses skills, practical knowledge, result oriented creativity and establishes standards for continuous practice for achieving prescribed aims and objectives.

Social Administration is a Discipline

Any discipline has three components known of (a) knowledge, (b) research and (c) consultancy.

Social administration contains knowledge based on scientific method which is tested knowledge and has universal application. This knowledge can be extended through training and imbibed by administrator for doing things.

Through research, the knowledge is updated, corrected, verified as well as expanded. The validity and reliability of knowledge is tested resulting into the incorporation of objectivity in this knowledge.

Consultancy involves application of knowledge through skills and techniques for the well-being of people.

The above mentioned criteria of discipline makes social administration a discipline.

To conclude, it can be maintained that the social administration is a science, an art as well as a discipline.

Social Administration: Scope

Luther Gulick has coined a term entitled as 'POSDCORB' in which words indicate each technique i.e. (P = Planning, O = Organising, S = Staffing, D = Directing, Co = Coordinating and B = Budgeting). Here, technique oriented not subject oriented approach has been used.

As per Henry Fayol, organisation, command, coordination and control are the main categories of administration.

According to P.M. Queen, the administration deals with men, material and methods.

Besides above different views, the following can be included in scope of social administration.

(1) *Legislation*: Here, legislation is concerned with social legislation which means collection of norms created on the initiative of a competent authority. These norms are directed towards fulfilment of social goals for the purpose of revising the social status of individuals who come from socially unprivileged section of society.

(2) *Policy*: The essence of administration is policy formulation. Policy refers to a course of action or intended course of action, conceived as deliberately adopted after review of possible alternatives pursued or intended to be pursued.

Policy formulation involves determination of broad objectives for the fulfilment of social goals.

(3) *Planning*: It is the process of determining objectives of administrative effort for determining most effective means to achieve it. This involves assessment of resources (physical, human and financial), assignment of priorities, selection of short term and long term projects, development of time schedule and bringing coordination among resources and prioritised needs.

(4) *Organising*: Organising is creating a structure designed to achieve certain goals involving creation of positions in organisation; allocation of functions and responsibilities; organisation of efforts and capacities of individual members, and fulfilment of objectives under public and private auspices.

(5) *Staffing*: It involves selection, placement, orientation, training and development, promotion, disciplining, salary and wage administration, organisation of service benefits etc. regarding staff of the organisation.

(6) *Supervision*: It is overseeing of work done by individual. In social administration, supervision means supervising the work of public social organisations but private or voluntary organisations.

(7) *Communication*: It is a shared understanding for shared purpose. In social administration, communication means sharing of information between public and private agencies.

(8) *Coordination*: It is an orderly combination of efforts to provide proper timing for execution of directions for unified action towards objectives. In social administration, coordination is needed among different agencies, between government and voluntary agencies and different programmes.

(9) *Method/Technique*: As a method/technique social administration (social welfare administration) is a way of doing things for fulfilling the needs of people.

(10) *Reporting*: This is concerned with progress of work reported to higher authorities including to administration.

(11) *Budgeting*: It is schedule of activities as well as means of financing these activities with a purpose of bringing out estimate of anticipated revenues and proposed expenditure together.

(12) *Philosophy*: It contains belief in certain values on which foundations are based. In case of social administration, these values are: (a) the worth of the individuals; (b) the inherent dignity of person; (c) individual welfare is the responsibility of society; and (d) the responsibility for contributing towards common good.

(13) *Evaluation*: In the process of evaluation, effectiveness and efficiency of efforts are seen in getting the objectives fulfilled. It also examines failures and analyses their causes and if need be, change of efforts as per requirement.

(14) *Feedback*: Through this process, administration receives the account of successes and failures as well as the causes of failure. This is also the process of putting experiences into practice. If need be, corrective measures are taken and efforts are undertaken afresh.

SKILLS IN ADMINISTRATION IN SOCIAL ADMINISTRATION

According to Curriculum Study of Council on Social Work Education (1959), the following skills are needed:

(1) **Skills related to Organisation:** These are concerned with role, performance and integration of roles:

(a) Ability to take role of agency/organisation employee.
(b) Ability to take role of professional worker and be comfortable with the authority implicit in professional qualification.
(c) Ability to take role of member in the administrative hierarchy.
(d) Ability to take role of colleague (share necessary information, support in feeling, enable in performance).

(2) **Skills related to Policy Process:** These are concerned with ability to contribute appropriately to policy formulation in the agency:

(a) Ability to use professional knowledge to contribute toward the solution of a given social pattern.
(b) Ability to express and to interpret professionally sound positions (within the general objectives of the agency/organisation).
(c) Ability to use one's own area of responsibility in terms of the larger picture.
(d) Ability to act through the established structure of the agency/organisation and in harmony with its purposes.

Ability to be responsive to new policy formulation and to utilise new professional knowledge while maintaining consistency in one's own performance and without loss of coordination with co-workers.

(e) Ability to assess current policy formulation in the light of the day-to-day job.
(f) Ability to sort out and to share necessary information without bias, obscurity and in terms of the agency as a whole.

(3) **Skills related to the Planning Process:** These are related to ability to accept responsibilities as assigned and to contribute one's specific skills towards the achievement of the overall plan.

(a) Ability to the professional knowledge to contribute toward the solution of a given social problem.
   1. Ability to assess current policy formulation in the light of the day-to-day job.
   2. Ability to sort out and to share necessary information without bias, obscurity and in terms of the agency as a whole.
(b) Ability to estimate with reasonable accuracy to resources necessary

to accomplish one's own job every and stated period and within a given plan.

(c) 1. Ability to maintain clarity of function.

2. Ability to maintain stability to performance.

(4) **Skills related to Programming:** These are concerned with ability to take role of member in the administrative hierarchy.

Ability to be responsive to new policy formulations and to utilise new professional knowledge while maintaining consistency in one's own performance and without loss of coordination with co-workers.

1. Skills related to actual allocation of the budget (to a department).
   (a) Ability to make efficient use of designated resources (where "efficiency" is defined by professional standards)
      1. Efficient management of one's own time and energies (where "efficiency" is defined in terms of human values).
2. Skills related to allocation of work.
   (b) Ability to assess one's own capabilities and limitations in terms of specific responsibilities.
3. Skills related to coordination
   (c) 1. Responsibility for learning established procedures and incorporating them.
      2. Responsibility for becoming familiar with the established channels and using them.
         Ability to sort out and to share necessary information without bias, obscurity and in terms of the agency as a whole.
      3. Ability to accomplish one's work as required and in the proper order.
4. Skills related to direction
   (d) Ability to accept supervision and to use it to deepen and to generalise professional skills.

MANAGEMENT TASKS IN SOCIAL ADMINISTRATION (SOCIAL WELFARE ADMINISTRATION)

These tasks are performed to create and sustain an organisation's capability for effective and efficient delivery. These are as follows:

1. Programmes are planned and developed.
2. Financial and other needed resources are required and necessary support from groups and organisations are sought.
3. Organisational structures and processes are designed.
4. Staff capability is developed and maintained.

5. Programmes of agency/organisation are assessed.
6. Necessary changes in agency ogranisation/programmes are brought out.

MANAGEMENT ACTIVITIES IN SOCIAL ADMINISTRATION (SOCIAL WELFARE ADMINISTRATION)

These are as follows:

1. Planning activities such as determining goals, policies, courses of action, strategy setting, work scheduling for entire staff or major units etc.
2. Information processing activities such as reading and writing correspondence, reports, memoranda, dictation, filing out, reviewing, signing forms, etc.
3. Controlling activities consisting of collecting and analysing information as to how the total operation or major segments of it are going by studying records, reports and accounts.
4. Coordinating activities such as exchanging information with other agencies and within agency, organising and attending meeting etc.
5. Evaluating activities such as assessment of proposals and reported or observed performance, appraisal of individual employee performance, programme performance and research related activities directed for evaluation.
6. Negotiating activities such as conferring, bargaining or discussing with a view to reaching agreement with other party, management-union negotiations, handling employee grievances or setting up contractual arrangements, etc.
7. Representing activities such as contacts with individuals, groups or constituencies, speaking before groups, contacts with press, legislative testimony, etc.
8. Staffing activities such as recruiting and interviewing perspective employees, placing, promoting, transferring employees etc.
9. Supervising activities i.e. leading, directing, training and reviewing the work of subordinates.
10. Supplying activities i.e. obtaining space, equipment, supplies, etc.
11. Extra-curricular activities i.e. counselling, treatment or advice to client.
13. Budgeting activities i.e. planning expenditure, allocating resources, monitoring expenditure etc.

COMMON ATTRIBUTES OF SOCIAL ADMINISTRATION (SOCIAL WELFARE ADMINISTRATION)

Thus, these are some common attributes of administration in all the areas may be business, government and professions. These attributes of administration are especially relevant since administration is:

1. Basically a problem solving process involving problem identification, problem study, chalking out action plan for problem solution, implementation of plan and finally evaluating its effectiveness.
2. A system of constellation of interrelated and interacting parts.
3. Involving the use of value judgements in the selection of alternatives.
4. An enabling process making it possible for individuals and groups to function more effectively in individual production and in inter-personal relationships affecting job production.
5. Concerned to a considerable degree with "futures" — The future effects of present functioning and decision-making.
6. Involved in the creative rather than the routinized use of knowledge and skill.
7. Concerned with structuring of programme, services and staff from the point of getting optimum efficiency and production of goods and services.
8. Concerned with greater or lesser extent with the implementation of public will.
9. Involving in maintaining appropriate balance between objectifying management operations in terms of assignment of work, personnel management, standardising of service operations on the one hand and utilisation of human resources in such a way as to take full advantage of capacities and potentialities.
10. Concerned with the importance to the individual staff member of status and recognition as a natural product of his association with the organisation, and also with the necessity for his positive identification with the goals, values and methods of the organisation of which he is a part.
11. Professionally concerned to the communications, interpersonal staff group relations and the appropriate machinery for both vertical and horizontal group participation in agency administration (Curriculum Study: 1959: 21-22).

Besides this, social administration (Social Welfare Administration) has several distinctive characteristics as given by Spencer.

1. Administration within agencies/organisations is established to help them to meet recognised needs within community.

2. The services provided by agencies/orgranisations may be classified as following with three broad categories:
   (a) Restoration of impaired social functioning.
   (b) Provision of resources, social and individual, for more effective social functioning.
   (c) Prevention of social dysfunction.
3. The typical social agency/organisations possesses a governing board that generally represents the community.
4. There are an enormous range and variety in the size, scope, structure and type of programmes of organisation in these agencies/ organisations.
5. The administrator has responsibility for relating the internal operations of the agency/ogranisation in the community.
6. There are constant necessities for making choices about the use of resources.
7. Social agencies/ogranisations used to avoid using a disproportionate amount of their resources for survival. The principal responsibility for producing, maintaining, guarding the agency's optimum functions devolves upon the executive.
8. The service performed by social agencies/ogranisations has an increasingly large professional social work component.
9. All levels of staff participate in the administrative process and affect the agency/organisation project to some extent.

PHILOSOPHY OF SOCIAL ADMINISTRATION/ SOCIAL WELFARE ADMINISTRATION

Webster's New International Dictionary defines philosophy as the science which investigates the most general facts and principle of reality and human nature and conduct specially, and now usually, the science which comprises logic, ethics, aesthetics, metaphysics and the theory of knowledge. Thus, philosophy analyses the body of principles underlying a given branch of learning or major discipline, a religious system, a human activity or the like. It maintains the significance and importance to the values of social life and interprets the ideals and moral behaviours of individuals, society and their relationships.

The principles that constitute the philosophic base are, however, primarily those that are derived from the acceptance of certain values. Social administration believes in certain values on which its foundations are based. These values are derived from values of democratic society. These are:

1. Belief in inherent worth, the integrity and dignity of the individual.
2. Belief in right of individual to self-determination and self-help.

3. The equality of opportunity.
4. Belief in reciprocation of social responsibilities.
5. Acceptance and non-judgmental attitude.
6. Handling the problems scientifically and systematically.

BASIC PRINCIPLES OF SOCIAL ADMINISTRATION/ SOCIAL WELFARE ADMINISTRATION

For effective social work administration, some principles are significant. Trecker has mentioned the following principles:

1. *The Principle of Social Values*: These values should be used as foundations for the development of services to the needy people.
2. *The Principle of Community and People's Needs*: These needs are the bases of existence of agencies and development of programmes.
3. *The Principle of Agency/Ogranisation Purpose*: The social purposes of the agency must be clearly formulated, stated, understood and utilised.
4. *The Principle of Cultural Setting*: The culture of community must be understood in as much as it influences the way needs are expressed and the way services are authorised, supported and utilised by people who need them.
5. *The Principle of Purposeful Relationships*: Effective, purposeful working relationships must be established between administrator, the board, the staff and the constituency.
6. *The Principle of Agency/Ogranisation Totality*: The agency organisation must be understood in its totality and wholeness.
7. *The Principle of Professional Responsibility*: The administrator should provide high quality of services based on the standards of professional practice.
8. *The Principle of Participation*: Appropriate contributions of board, staff and constituency are sought and utilised through the continuous process of dynamic participation.
9. *The Principle of Communication*: Open channels of communication are essential to the complete functioning of people.
10. *The Principle of Leadership*: The administrator must carry the responsibility for leadership of the agency/organisation in terms of goal attainment and the provision for professional services.
11. *The Principle of Planning*: The process of continuous planning is fundamental to the development of meaningful services.
12. *The Principle of Organisation*: The work of many people must be arranged in an organised manner and must be structured so that responsibilities and relationships are clearly defined.

13. *The Principle of Delegation*: The delegation of responsibility and authority to other professional persons is essential.
14. *The Principle of Coordination*: The work delegated to many people must be properly coordinated so that specific contributions are brought to bear upon the major tasks of the agency and all energy is rightly focused upon the mission to be accomplished.
15. *The Principle of Resource Utilisation*: The resources of money, facilities and personnel must be carefully fostered, conserved and utilised in keeping with the trust granted to the agency/organisation by society.
16. *The Principle of Change*: The process of change is continuous, both within the community and within the agency ogranisation.
17. *The Principle of Evaluation*: Continuous evaluation of processes and programmes is essential to the fulfilment of agency's/ogranisation's objectives.
18. *The Principle of Growth*: The growth and development of all participants is furthered by the administrator who provides challenging work assignments, thoughtful supervision and opportunities for individual and group learning.

However, some of basic principles are as under:

1. Adjustment between objectives, policy and programmes of the agency organisation.
2. Coordination between area of work, resources and authority at every level of administration.
3. Leaders and staff members are encouraged and expected to accept one and another accordingly and work with non-judgmental attitude.
4. Staff member should become a part of participatory administration and there should be internal democracy in administrative structure.
5. Establishment of two-way communication in agency/ogranisation.
6. Existence of belief in human dignity, honesty, dignity of individual, self-determination and self-help.
7. Cooperation from the masses.
8. Equality of opportunities.
9. Reciprocity in social obligations.
10. Use of scientific approach and rational thinking.

4

Social Policy

India has been a colonial state of Britishers. So, at the beginning whatever social policies evolved, have been influenced or developed by Britishers. Consequently, the evolution of British Social Policy is being discussed here:

1. The development of industrial society enhances state involvement with the social welfare of its citizens.
2. Political developments also took place side-by-side industrial development where involvement of citizens become more intensive with the activities of state.
3. Thus, role of state was enlarged, character of economy was shaped and nature of political processes took place.

These trends also affected the role of state in social welfare to other industrialised countries like United States, Countries of Western and Northern Europe and Australia.

EVOLUTION BEFORE TWENTIETH CENTURY

With the development of industrialisation and urbanisation, local system of administration came under strain. Development in medicine and education by middle of nineteenth century affected the system of care to sick and diseased persons as well as role of state in imparting education to children. Due to above developments, policies were framed in different fields.

I. Poverty and Protection of Labour

1. Poor Law Amendment Act was passed in1834 and National Poor Law Commission was set up.
2. "Work hours test" and "Doctrine of less eligibility" were evolved.
3. Hours of work in factories were reduced.
4. In 1899, Labour Representation Committee was formed, later on it was converted into Labour Party in 1906.

II. Strengthening Local Government

1. Responsibility was given to local government through Municipal Corporation Act, 1935 for handling local situation.
2. Local Government Acts were passed in 1988 and 1994 and a system of local authorities was set up.

III. Education

1. At the outset, religious societies started giving education to children.
2. By 1833, Government started giving grant to educational institutions and supervision of educational institutions was started at central level.
3. By 1870, Government involved fully in imparting primary education and in 1880, education made compulsory to the children of five and ten through Education Act.
4. By 1890, most of the elementary education was made free.
5. By the end of century School Boards also started in giving their contribution in secondary education.

Thus, in the end of nineteenth century, laissez-faire had given way to collectivism leading to a socialist state which passed factory legislation, intervened in spheres of poverty, health and safety of people.

EVOLUTION AFTER TWENTIETH CENTURY

The perspective of social policy was extended in this century which is evident from the following:

(i) Poverty and Protection of Labour

In 1905, Royal Commission on Poor Laws was set up which submitted its report in 1909, contains a thorough discussion on British Social Policy.

(ii) Strengthening Local Government

Local Government Act was passed in1929 which handed over responsibility for the poor law from the board of guardians to the local authorities.

(iii) Education

1. In 1902, Education Act was enacted which passed the responsibility for state education from the school boards to county and from county to councils.
2. An International Committee on Physical Deterioration was set up and gave its report in 1904. This committee made the provision of school medical services and school meals.

3. In 1944, Education Act was passed.
4. During the period of 1951-64, innovations were taken place in education.
5. To handle issues of education advisory groups were created and they reported on 'early living', 'education between fifteen and eighteen', 'education of less academic children' and 'higher education'.

(iv) Housing

1. Housing Act was passed which made provision for government subsidies to local authorities to build houses for working classes. This Act is known as Adison Act.
2. During 1930s, there was shift in housing policy with government encouraging local authorities to put their emphasis in housing provision upon clearing the slums.
3. In 1947, Town and Country Planning Act was enacted followed by Housing Act in 1949.
4. During 1951-1964, there was boom for house building both private and public.
5. In 1972, Housing Finance Act was enacted.

(v) Health

1. In 1946, National Health Service was created.
2. Mental Health Act was enacted in 1959.
3. In 1976, Royal Commission on National Health Service was introduced.

(vi) Social Security

1. Old Age Pension Act, 1908 and National Insurance Act, 1911 were passed. The adoption of contributing insurance had an important effect on the development of social security policy in Britain.
2. In 1925, contributory pension scheme was started.
3. Beveridge Report was published in 1942 which recommended contributory social security system. This report also argued that other social policies were necessary to underpin his insurance scheme.
4. As social security reforms, National Insurance Act, 1946 and National Assistance Act, 1948 were enacted.
5. Social security changes, introduced in 1965, were learning related supplements to sickness and unemployment benefits.
6. In 1966, 'national assistance' was replaced by 'supplementary benefits'.

In this way, social policies were developed in different areas and ultimately on the recommendation of Seebohm Committee, integrated social services were created.

INDIAN SCENARIO

In independent India, social policies have been evolved mainly from Indian Constitution which declared India as a sovereign, socialist, secular, democratic republic based on social, economic and political justice; liberty of thought, expression, belief in faith and worship, and equality of status and of opportunity. For this, Indian Constitution made provision for Fundamental Rights and Directive Principles of State Policy. Through these provisions, social policies have been evolved for ensuring equity and social justice among different sections of society.

Another sources of social policies have been—

1. Legislature which has framed several laws for protecting the interests of weaker sections of society.
2. The Cabinet is also chief source of social policy, all policies are approved by this.
3. National Development Council also formulates policies regarding development.
4. Public Services. These services implement the policies but during implementation of various kinds of experiences lead to the formulation of policies.
5. Judiciary has played an important role in the direction of framing policies through its far reaching judgments.
6. Professional Associations. Different professional associations engaged in practice of professions all suggest policies.
7. Political Parties. These parties create political will for framing the policies.
8. Planning Commission. It is an advisory body which influences formulation of policies through planned development.

Through these sources, India has evolved several policies for the development and empowerment of citizens. These are as follows:

1. National Population Policy of 1976 and 2000.
2. National Policy for Children of 2001 and 2004.
3. National Policy for Employment of Women, 2001.
4. National Youth Policy, 2003.
5. National Policy for the Older Persons, 1999.
6. National Policy for Persons with Disabilities, 2006.
7. National Water Policy, 2002.

8. National Policy for Education, 1968 and 1986.
9. National Environment Policy, 2006.
10. National Urban Housing and Habitat Policy, 2007.
11. National Policy on Voluntary Sector, 2007.

THE CONCEPT OF SOCIAL POLICY

The concept of social policy can be explained by different perspectives:

(a) General Perspective

Here, social policy has been explained in broader framework of satisfying the needs and problems of society:

Macbeath: "Social policies are concerned with the right ordering of network of relationships between men and women who have together in societies or with principles which would govern the activities of individuals or groups so far as they affect lives and interests of the people".

Pansion: Social policy is a "policy which aims at a continued reform of society in order to eliminate weaknesses and constraints or ameliorate good solutions".

Barber (in Social Work Dictionary): Social policy is "the activities and principles of society that guide the way it intervenes in and regulates relationships between individuals, groups, communities and social institutions".

Lavin: Social policy refers to "the practice of social intervention aimed at securing social change to promote the welfare and well-being of citizens".

Titmuss: "Social policy is concerned with the study of a range of social needs and functioning in conditions of scarcity of human organisation, traditionally called social services or social welfare system to meet these needs".

Myrdal: "Social policy in its broadest sense is simply a convenient way of referring to "the continuous growth in the volume of public, quasi-public and private interventions in social life".

Hagenbuch: "Stated in general terms, the mainspring of social policy may be said to be the desire to ensure every member of the community certain minimum standards and certain opportunities".

(b) Social Policy as Course of Action

As course of action or intended course of action, social policy is concerned with distribution of resources for meeting the needs of fulfilling the stated objectives. Some definitions are as follows:

Kulkarni P.D.: "Social policy is the strategy of action indicating the means and methods to be followed in successive phases to achieve the declared social objectives".

Marshall: Social policy refers to "the policy of governments with regard to action having a direct impact on the welfare of citizens providing them with sources of income".

Donnison: "Social policy deals with the allocation of resources and opportunities between potentially competing groups and as a consequence with relations between groups in society, their status and self-respect, their power and their access to broader social opportunities".

V.N. Institute of Social Development: "Social policy is concerned with redistributive efforts of economic policy protecting people from the vagaries of market and the changing circumstances of the age, enhancing the productive potential of members of society and reconciling the burden of production with that of other social issues as well as sharing of burden of reproduction".

On the basis of above definitions, certain common characteristics of the concept of social policy can be identified. These are as follows:

1. It is statement of a course of action for the purpose of meeting the needs of people or fulfilling the pre-determined objectives.
2. The course of action has knowledge base which is interdisciplinary and multi-disciplinary in nature.
3. It is based on social justice involving distribution of resources.
4. It is a discipline having knowledge, research and consultancy as well as an area of practice involving certain skills.
5. It acts as guideline for ensuring—
   (a) minimum desirable standard of living for every citizen;
   (b) people to develop their full potential and exercise maximum choices in the living;
   (c) protection of every citizen against any kind of exploitation and discrimination;
   (d) human rights and security against various contingencies; and
   (e) reduction of inequalities.

SOCIAL WELFARE ADMINISTRATION AND SOCIO-ECONOMIC DEVELOPMENT

Social administration is the administration of social welfare programmes which are organised mainly for the weaker and vulnerable sections of society. The main objectives of these programmes are as follows:

1. Promotion of social justice by levelling the incomes of rich and poor.
2. Alleviation of poverty and generating employment.

3. Fighting against the discrimination on the basis of gender, race, religion, age or disability.
4. Protection of disadvantaged people and sections.
5. Providing special assistance for social development programmes and working to promote public and private assistance.
6. Integration of poverty reduction and gender equity objective into programmes of structural adjustment.

These social welfare programmes consist of the following programmes for weaker sections:

1. Upliftment and development programmes for raising the levels of living.
2. Housing and accommodation for better living conditions and creating clean surrounding.
3. Health and nutrition programmes for raising the health status.
4. Provision for clean and safe water.
5. Providing education and skill development programmes.
6. Providing opportunities forgetting work and employment as well as creating healthy working conditions.
7. Protecting against any kind of discrimination, mis-happenings, calamities etc. through legislative and non-legislative efforts.

Thus, these programmes are initiated to introduce a process of systematic change and mainly initiated through social policy and social planning so that levels of living and quality of life of masses specially who are weak, vulnerable and disadvantageous may be enhanced. This largely depends on the following:

1. People are motivated to change.
2. People have capacity to change.
3. People have opportunity to change.
4. Services provided and actions performed by social workers.
5. The problem or situation to be addressed by social worker.

The above activities performed by social workers may be effective when there is adequate administrative apparatus for social workers which contains social welfare organisations and administration as well as management of these organisations. For this social welfare administration plays a vital role and through these organisations socio-economic development takes place.

MODELS OF SOCIAL POLICY

R.M. Titmuss has given following models of social policy:

Model A: The Residual Welfare Model of Social Policy

The basic features of this model are as follows:

(1) The basic premise of this model is that there are two channels through which needs of individual can be met.
  (a) Private market.
  (b) Family
(2) When these available channels breakdown, social welfare institutions come into action and then only temporarily.

Model B: The Industrial Achievement Performance Model of Social Policy

Main features are as follows:

(1) Social welfare institutions play an important role as adjuncts of economy.
(2) As per this model, social needs should be met on the basis of merit, performance and productivity.
(3) This is known as 'Handmaiden Model' also.
(4) Economic and psychological theories concerned with incentives, effort and reward and formation of class and group loyalties have contributed to this model.

Model C: The Institutional Redistributive Model of Social Policy
Main features of this model are as follows:

(1) In this model, social welfare is seen as integrated institution of society providing universalistic services outside the market on the principle of need.
(2) This model is partly based on:
  (a) Theories about the multiple efforts of social change and economic system.
  (b) The principle of social equality.
(3) Basically, it incorporates systems of redistribution n command-over-resources-through-time (Titmuss: 1974: 30-31).

OBJECTIVES OF SOCIAL POLICY

According to Tarlok Singh, the central purpose of social policy should be to create conditions in which each area, urban or rural, and each group with distinctive and identifiable problems, is able to lift itself, overcome its limitations, and improve its living conditions and economic opportunities, thus becoming part of the basic social services.

Specifically, the objective of social policy are as follows:

(1) Providing opportunities for the enhancement of standard of living of of society.

(2) Meeting important and vital problems of people.
(3) Establishing social justice.

FUNCTIONS OF SOCIAL POLICY

1. Removal of social disabilities by effectively implementation of various social legislations.
2. Removal of economic disabilities through mass support and institutional services.
3. Rehabilitation of differently abled persons.
4. Removal of problems of victims of deviation, disorganisation and crimes.
5. Making arrangement for corrections by organising correctional services.
6. Organisation of training and educational as well as aware generative activities.
7. Removal of disparities and inequalities.
8. Proving accessibility to resources specially to weaker sections of society regarding their development and empowerment.
9. Organising health and survival activities for people.
10. Development of family welfare and development services.
11. Ensuring protection to downtrodden and under privileged people.
12. Justification of democratic and humanitarian values.
13. Protecting and preserving environment for sustainable development.
14. Ensuring proper distribution of gains of developmental activities.
15. Empowering people specially weaker sections for getting work and resources.
16. Ensuring dignity and importance of every people.

SCOPE OF SOCIAL POLICY

The following are included in the scope of social policy:

(I) Programmes of Social Concern and Related Activities

1. *Social Services*: Health, education, housing, family support and welfare, nutrition, recreation, etc.
2. *Socio-Economic Development and Empowerment Programmes*: These programmes are specially meant for weaker sections of society.
3. *Social Reform Services*: These are related to prevent and educate about the bad effects of prevalent evil practices of society.
4. *Social Security Services*: These are for the protection for victims of different contingency, such as unemployment, old age, handicaps etc.

5. *Social and Economic Change and Development Activities*: These are related to sustainable development and protection and preservation of environment.
6. *Social Policies Related to Different Sections of Society*: These are related to children, youth, older people, women, slum dwellers, landless labourers, organised labour, unorganised labour, employment, providing different rights to people such as right to education, right to work, right to food, etc.
7. *Social Policies for Different Fields*: These are related to agriculture, industry, small and petty businesses, drugs, medicines etc.

PRINCIPLES OF SOCIAL POLICY

These are some principles of social policy:

(1) Promoting the economic and social well-being of people and nation.
(2) Determination of priorities among different needs/wants/problems after analysing the factors (social, economic, political, etc.) important for them.
(3) Collection of facts regarding various needs/wants/problems in order to determine the goals of social policy.
(4) The objectives of social policy are determined through standardisation of resources (locally, nationally and internationally).
(5) Dynamics of population should be the base of social policy.
(6) Social policy should be concerned with the gaps in structures, institutions, attitudes, beliefs, etc.
(7) All services in social policy should be logically interrelated.
(8) There should be a system of measures, evaluation and feedback.
(9) Social policy should have collective concern and effect.
(10) Every social policy should be in consonance with community and society as well as it should have social approval.

SIMILARITIES AND DISSIMILARITIES BETWEEN SOCIAL AND ECONOMIC POLICY

Economic policy is envisaged for the purpose of enhancement of economic development of people with a view to utilise the available resources for that.

Similarities

1. Both social and economic policy have similar goal of making life and living of people good and peaceful.
2. Both are concerned in bringing constructive change in life and living of people.

3. Both have similar content of enhancing standard of living of people.
4. Both are developed, implemented and modified in similar procedure.
5. Both give importance to people's participation.
6. Both are related to bring stability in community.
7. In a welfare state, both are related to public auspices.

Dissimilarities between Social and Economic Policy

Social Policy	*Economic Policy*
1. Based on social concerns related to beliefs, values, attitudes, etc.	Based on purely economic considerations and economic activity.
2. More emphasis on change, reform	More emphasis on increase in Gross National Product (GNP) and per capita income.
3. Wide in scope (education, health, accommodation, recreation etc.)	Narrow in scope (production etc.)

Difference between Social Policy and Social Welfare Policy

Social welfare policy is the stated course of action for organising social welfare services which are specially designed for weaker and vulnerable sections of society. These services may be preventive, alleviative and rehabilitative in nature.

Social Policy	*Economic Policy*
1. Wide in scope since it is related to every person of society.	Narrow in scope since it is related to specialised sections of society.
2. Emphasis on change and development.	Emphasis on protection.
3. Continuous reform of society.	Alleviating weaker sections.

5

Planning and Decision Making

In the contemporary period, there is shortage of resources as compared to needs. For this, it is necessary that resources should be utilised fully. This demands planned utilisation of resources for meeting needs as per their priority. Thus, planning is a rational process characteristic of all human behaviour (Piffner and Sherwood). So, in case of organisation, it is equally important that every organisation should meet their objectives in a planned manner and for every administrator planning is important irrespective of his level in the organisation. For social administrator, planning is required mainly due to the following reasons:

1. Planning is major administrative function.
2. It minimises risk and uncertainty.
3. Its decisions guide future of every organisation.
4. It strives for efficiency in organisation by achieving objectives with a minimum cost and effort.
5. It performs the operations of organisation effectively since without planned operations desired results cannot be achieved.
6. It makes possible to carry out objective research and evaluation of efforts.
7. It facilitates control.
8. It ultimately boasts the morale of organisation by providing an emotional and administrative climate conducive to high morale.

MEANING

Planning involves taking decision in advance, what to do, how to do it, when to do it and who is to it? Thus, planning in 'pre-view'. Some definitions of planning are as under:

Dimock: Planning is "the use of rational design as contrasted with change, the reaching of decision before a line of action is taken instead of improving after the action has started".

Seckler-Hudson:Planning is "the process of devising a basis for a course of future action".

Millet: "Planning is the process of determining the objectives of administrative effort and of devising the means calculated to achieve them".

Urwick: "Planning is fundamentally an intellectual process, a mental predisposition to do things in an orderly way, to think before acting, and to act in the light of facts rather than queries. It is the anti-thesis of gambling, the speculative tendency".

White: "Planning, as the term used in the context of public administration, is not equivalent to make decision on basic policy. Planning in the context of administration begins where general policy stops; it is concerned with the means by which ends can be brought to the fruition".

Farland: Planning as "selecting the best course of action for achieving the pre-determined objectives of a business, after making careful evaluation of the present conditions and future trends regarding the external forces and internal resources".

Review of these definitions suggests the following characteristics of planning.

1. Planning is an orderly process
2. Within this, determination of goal takes place.
3. For the fulfilment of this goal policy is determined.
4. As per determined policy, processes and resources are determined.
5. In order to attain goal, necessary activities are given to different authorities.
6. Evaluation is done by judging the success/failure.

To conclude, it can be maintained that planning is preparation for action and it is the cornerstone around which the foundation of decision making is built.

Planning can be divided on the different bases which are as follows:

Bases	*Types*	
1. Aspects	(a) Planning of Policies	For realisation of objectives of organisation, courses of actions, i.e. policies should be planned.
	(b) Planning of Processes	Processes run the organisation for meeting the needs of people.
	(c) Planning of Techniques	These are ways of handling activities of organisation.

(*Contd.*)

Bases		*Types*
	(d) Planning of Regulations	Regulations, rules, norms and customs run the organisation and every member of organisation is supposed to work as per these regulations.
	(e) Planning of Research	For continuous development of knowledge this type of planning is needed.
	(f) Planning of Budget	Budget is important which are also the part of planning.
2. Use of Planning	(a) Standing Plan or Repeat Use Plan	A standard plan can be developed which can be put to use repeatedly.
	(b) Single Use Plan	This plan is made once and after its use it used to be discontinued.
3. Origin	(a) Planning based on suggestions and applications	The people can suggest or apply for plan for the purpose of meting of their needs.
	(b) Planning from above	This kind of plan is made on the top and implemented at the lower level.
	(c) Planning as per policies dictated from the top	This plan is developed locally but on the basis of policies dictated from the top local level say is absent.
4. Target	(a) Planning after corrections	Situation is first corrected then plan is developed.
	(b) Planning as per implementation	For the implementation of particular idea planning is made on the basis of this idea.
	(c) New Planning	A kind of new plan is chalked out as per will and direction of governance.
5. Process	(a) Short Term	This for some fixed time, i.e. for one month, six months, year or one hundred days etc.
	(b) Long Term	This plan is for long time. Minimum three years or more.

(*Contd.*)

Bases		*Types*
6. Ownership	(a) Govt. Plan	Plan in government enterprises and institutions.
	(i) Administrative Planning	Mainly related to the determination of policy
	(ii) Programme Planning	For the implementation of policies
	(b) Non-Govt. Plan	Planning is related to the plan of a city or country
7. Contents	(a) Physical Planning	The plan is related to the plan of a city or country.
	(b) Administrative and Managerial Planning	Plan related to administrative problems of organisation.
	(c) Economic and Social Planning	This plan is made from the point of fulfilment of social obligations.

PLANNING PROCESS

Planning is rational because it demands a systematic analysis of several possible means and ends, followed by a selection of those means thought best suited to designated end (Pfiffner and Presthus). Planning involves a succession of steps since it is integrative and comprehensive in nature, it is an attempt at coordination, integration and systematisation of efforts for the achievement of self-objectives.

Steps in Planning Process

According to Seckler-Hudson, the steps are:

1. A careful definition and limitation of the problems as far as possible.
2. The exploration of all available information pertaining to the problems.
3. The posing of possible alternative solutions or methods of solving the problems.
4. The experimenting of one or more tentative solutions through actual operations.
5. The evaluation of results in the light of next developments, research and experience.
6. Reconsideration of the problems and the results and re-decision, if justified.

According to Millet, these steps are:

1. The formulation of goals or objectives.
2. An assessment of the means or resources available to realise these goals.
3. The preparation of a work programme designed to achieve the determined objectives.

Schaffer suggests four classic steps in corporate planning:

1. *Research*: To analyse corporate strengths, weaknesses, and other factors, and to determine the opportunities and risks created by external trends.
2. *Formulation of Objectives*: To define what the company should become in the long-term future.
3. *Strategic Planning*: To develop an overall framework outlining how the corporation will move to its ultimate objectives.
4. *Operational Planning*: To create steps that each department and function should take in order to carry out strategic plans.

From management point of view, Carlisle described the following steps:

1. Determine where you stand today.
2. Develop planning premises regarding trends and likely future conditions.
3. Develop and reassess objectives.
4. Establish strategies to achieve the objectives.
5. Programme activities to gain desired results.
6. Determine the support resources required to conduct the activities of step five.
7. Execute the plan.
8. Control the plan.

Thus, the following steps of planning process can be mentioned:

1. Selection of objectives and goals of social welfare/service organisation and fixing of specific targets.
2. Study and appraisal of contemporary conditions and resources and factors involved in meeting the objectives, goals and targets of organisation.
3. Collection of relevant information and analysis of this information intelligently and imaginatively for the development of understanding.
4. Visualising future developments and their impact on organisation.
5. Enumerate the alternative courses of action on the basis of information collected by keeping future trends in view.

6. Weighting of pros and cons of each course of action.
7. Decide best course of action or plan.
8. Chalking out details of the selected course of action by breaking down it into varied aspects of work, establish them in chronological order for taking action. This should be in form of plan of a specific programme of action.
9. Be ready to modify as per situational condition.

Problems Involved in Planning

These are as follows:

1. There remains uncertainty in case of planning since it is evolved on certain assumptions based on some conditions which are changeable.
2. Planning also needs resources which can be spent on actual work instead of wasting them on planning.
3. Planning keeps the activities of an operation into a fixed jacket leading to the absence of discretion.
4. Planning needs intellectual capacity, deep and sustained thinking and some imagination which is very difficult to get in formulation of plan.
5. Problem of developing uniform plan for diverse conditions.
6. Non-determination of priorities among needs, in case of determination of priorities, non-compliance of priorities already chalked.
7. Lack of adequate and reliable information.
8. Differences in views between people's representatives and government officials in formulation and implementation of plan.
9. Use of difficult words and language in the plan.
10. Faulty and unrealistic determination of objectives and goals.
11. Dominance of vested interests, local interests, biases of officers, misutilisation of positions in formulation and implementation of plan.
12. Lack of coordination between government departments, people's representatives and civil society organisations.
13. Non-participation of local people.
14. Lack of commitment on the part of officials involved in planning.
15. More emphasis on economic aspects of planning.
16. Usually planning takes place on the top.
17. Non-cooperation of local people in the implementation of plan since they have no role in its formulation.
18. There are separate institutions for the formulation of plan as well as implementation of plan.
19. Non-availability of financial resources on time.
20. Lack of continuous evaluation of plan.

DECISION MAKING

Decision making is needed at all levels of organisation to execute planning. So, the success and failure of any social work administrators depend to a great extent upon the type of decisions taken by them.

Meaning of Decision Making

Webster's Dictionary explains the meaning of decision making as "the art of determining in one's own mind upon an opinion or cause of action".

Few definitions of decision making are as follows:

Terry: Decision is "the selection of one behaviour alternative from two or more possible alternatives".

Shull and Others: Decision making process is "….a conscious and human process, involving both individual and social phenomena, based upon factual and value premises, which includes a choice of one behavioural activity from among one or more affairs".

Emory and Niland: Decision is, "… the point of selection and commitment… The decision maker chooses the preferred purpose, the most reasonable task statement or the best course of action".

Hodge and Johnson: "Decision making is to solve any obstacle (problem) that stands between decision maker and the accomplishment of the organisation".

Donald J. Chough: "The decision making process involves a problem to be solved, a number of conflicting objectives to be reconciled, a number of possible alternative courses of action from which the 'best' has to be chosen and some way of measuring the value or pay off alternative courses of action".

Ishwar Dayal: "Decision is the commitment of decision maker to act, thereby committing the personnel, material and financial resources of the organisation towards the action objectives".

W. Brooke Groves: "Decision making is the selection from two or more reasonable possibilities of a course that will, at the time and under circumstances provide the most suitable solution of the problem at hand".

Characteristics

On the basis of above definitions, the following characteristics can be listed:

1. Decision is the process.
2. It is process of selecting one best alternative among two or more alternatives.
3. Through this selection, best alternative is found.
4. This best alternative solves the problem or meets the needs of people.

5. Decision making involves facts as well as value.
6. It involves commitment of decision maker.

To conclude, it can be said that decision making is the selection from among alternatives of a course of action, it is core of planning. Decision involves a commitment of resources, direction or reputation. In social work administration, decision making is significant because it affects the morale of the staff and eventual delivery of social services.

Types of Decisions

Decisions have been classified by different writers differently. These classifications are being given as follows:

Writer	*Types*	*Details*
1. Simon	(a) Programmed	These are repetitive and routine since a definite procedure has been worked out to handle them.
	(b) Non-programmed	These are novel, unstructured, and consequential. These decisions need custom-tailored handling.
2. Drucker	(a) Generic	These are programmed decisions as mentioned above.
	(b) Unique	These are non-programmed decisions.
3. Delberg	(a) Routine	These decisions are taken for day-to-day running of activities. They are done under fixed procedure.
	(b) Creative	These are taken for meeting or handling special situation in effective and efficient manner.
	(c) Negotiated	These represent the mutual will of persons involved in handling situation which demands some decisions based on mutual consent.
4. William J. Gore	(a) Routine	Decisions to carry out activities which meet immediate goals.
	(b) Adaptive	For the adoption of routinized activities, these decisions are taken.

(*Contd.*)

Writer	*Types*	*Details*
	(c) Innovative	These are taken to meet the changing goals.
5. Carlisle	(a) Intuitive	These are taken as per feelings of decision maker rather than rationality.
	(b) Judgmental	These are based on knowledge and experience.
	(c) Problem Solving	These are taken after proper study, analysis and reflection. These involve such situations where decisions have to be taken on the basis of adequate information and its analysis.

Decisions also classified as:

(a) Policy decisions are taken by top level of organisation which influences the functioning of the organisation.

(b) Operating decisions are taken by middle level officers for implementing the policy decisions.

On the basis of number of persons involved, decisions are classified as:

(a) Individual decisions taken by one person by taking his/her own initiative.

(b) Group decisions are taken by the participation of representatives of defined interest groups.

To conclude, from the point of view of social administrators, decision may be classified as:

1. Routine	Taken for smooth running of organisation performing day-to-day activities
2. Situational	Taken as per situation arises in order to meet the special circumstances created by situation.
3. Innovative/Creative	Taken for boasting the activities of organisations as well as efficiency and morale of members of organisation.
4. Experimental	Taken for experimenting any course of action

Process of Decision Making

Decision making process in social work administration is important since it affects the lives and livings of individual, groups, families and communities.

Steps Involved in Decision Making

1.	Saturation	To have familiarity with the problem.
2.	Deliberation	Understanding of alternative solutions and arranging them in order.
3.	Incubation	Working on the problem sub-consciously.
4.	Illumination	Striving for new ideas for making decision more creative.
5.	Accommodation	To implement new ideas for getting practical solutions of problems.

Regarding creativity in decision making, Hicks has given the following:

1.	Creativity of thinking new ideas	Innovative
2.	Creativity of absorption, combination and using of ideas from different sources for the purpose to bring out new ideas	Synthesis
3.	Creativity to use old or new ideas	Extension
4.	Creativity to use others' successful ideas	Duplication

However, the following steps are involved in the process of decision making:

1. *Identification and Definition of Situation or Problem*: This implies that in order to understand people and their behaviour, it is imperative to understand the varying problematical situations in which they find themselves as well as their interrelations and feelings about them. This basically involves recognising the problem(s) existence.

Henderson and Suojanen have identified following steps in the identification of problem, however, it is not necessary to use all the steps:

(i) Determination of expectation as per present standards of performance.
(ii) Recording of actual performance through observation and measurement.
(iii) Observing differences between expected performance and actual performance.
(iv) Identification of problem as to who, what, how and why of the observed differences.

Thus, this step envisages the understanding of total situation or problem and its setting and role of psychological, sociological and cultural factors and forces as well as feelings of people about the situation or problem.

2. *Collection and Study of Facts as well as Analysis of Problem*: For proper analysis of problem, pertinent information should be collected from the people asking for decision, their associates and family members, records

and reports etc. This information should be studied and scrutinised objectively and carefully. Henderson and Suojanen have mentioned the following steps:

(a) Classify the problem – separate symptoms from problems; describe the causes and nature of problem, if it is too large – sub-divide it.
(b) Search for and gather data – combine additional information with what is known and determine relationships.
(c) Analyse data – determine of the data is useful in isolating and describing the problem.
(d) Evaluate data – relate data to symptoms and causes for initial development of solutions.

3. *Determination of Possible Alternatives or Formulation of Choices*: The available alternatives is the solution of the problem may be listed and understood because whenever one has to judge, one must have alternatives among which one can choose (Drucker).

4. *Evaluation of Impact of Alternatives or Choices*: The likely outcomes of each alternative should be considered in the light of: (a) available resources, (b) combination of resources, (c) suitability, feasibility and acceptability of resources, and (d) benefits, cost, time and risk associated with it.

5. *Consideration of Feelings of Decision Maker*: Besides rational view, careful consideration of facts, alternatives and anticipated outcomes, the feelings possessed by administrators such as fear, hate, uncertainty, anger and trust need to be scrutinised and understood for the sake of effective and sound decisions.

6. *Choosing Sound Alternative or Choice*: Among different alternatives or choices, one alternative/choice has to be chosen by applying some criteria such as:

(a) weightage of each alternative regarding its risks and expected gains; (b) economy; (c) timing; and (d) availability of resources.

7. *Follow-Through*: After taking decision, it should be fully supported for the purpose of its implementation. The decision should be properly communicated to concerned persons.

8. *Flexibility*: The decision should be firm for the sake of firmness but it is necessary to have open mind, if situation demands or any error in decision is located, it should have room for necessary modifications.

Evaluation of Decisions

Janis and Mann have suggested that decision maker as for his/her ability and capacities of information processing should do the following:

1. Thoroughly canvass wide range of alternative courses of action.

2. Survey the full range of objectives to be fulfilled and the values implicated by the choice.
3. Carefully weighs whatever he knows about the costs and risks of negative consequences as well as the positive consequences, that could flow from each alternative.
4. Intensively searches for new information relevant to further evaluation of the alternatives.
5. Correctly assimilates and takes account of any new information or expert judgment to which he is exposed, even when the information or judgment does not support the course of action he initially prefers.
6. Re-examines the positive and negative consequences of all known alternatives, including those originally regarded as unacceptable, before making a final choice.
7. Make detailed provisions for implementing or executing the chosen course of action, with special attention to contingency plans that might be required of various known risks were to materialise.

Approaches to Decision Making

There are three approaches:

1. *Rationalist Approach:* This approach assume that (a) a number of choices are available based on logical analysis, and (b) the source of knowledge is precise criteria and certain values.
2. *Humanist Approach:* According to this approach decision is taken within the framework of social and environmental conditions – past and present. Here, perceptions and past experiences influence greatly the decision making.
3. *The Integrative Approach:* This is the integration of rational and humanistic approaches which envisages that decisions are made by those who are involved in work rather than those occupying executive offices.

Problems of Decision Making

Carlisle suggested some restrictions of problem solving:

1. People have limited rationality and knowledge.
2. Lack of time often presents intensive synthesis.
3. Goals sought are generally not maximal.
4. Pressures brought by others are often more significant than the "facts" collected to support each alternative.

Skidmore has listed following pitfalls in decision making:

1. *Procrastination*: Tendency to let matters slide with the hope that problems will resolve themselves or go away. So, better not to take decision or postpone it.
2. *Oversimplification*: This tendency exists to follow simple steps is problem solving and/or decision making and figure that such action will take care of everything.
3. *Irrational Behaviour:* There is always the possibility that decisions will not be made on an objective and fair basis. Complexities and feelings, as well as differences in people, cause many detours from sound decisions.
4. *Mistakes Bring Discouragement:* Administrators and staff members need to be accepting one another when mistakes occur. They should be rectified as soon as possible but errors should not be punished.

Thus, the problems of decision making are as follows:

1. Routine decision making takes too much time and efforts.
2. Problem in fixing priority among needs due to vested interests.
3. Lack of adequate data base.
4. Delay in decisions due to lengthy procedures.
5. Lack of requisite capacities on the part of decision makers.
6. Lack of knowledge of surroundings and environment in which decision has to be taken.
7. Dominance of biases in decision making. These biases are two types:
   (a) Prejudice – an unfavourable opinion or falling formed before taking decision.
   (b) Predilection – mental preference of a favourable predisposition towards a particular issue or matter or person.
8. Problems of unethical considerations i.e. favouritism, corruption, nepotism, etc.
9. Non-familiarity with aspirations and conditions persons affected by decision.
10. Lack of proper system of follow through or follow-up.

6

Organising

The contemporary age is the age of organisations which involves cooperative efforts by a number of people to achieve certain common objectives. It is social unit which structures individuals and functions into productive relationship. Organising is the subject of larger activity of managing and it is a process by which the structure of an organisation is created and maintained.

IMPORTANCE OF ORGANISATION

Organisation is important since it:

1. Pervades all the vital aspects of life of man.
2. Satisfies different kinds of needs of people.
3. Helps administration in giving knowledge for completing work effectively.
4. Serves as a laboratory for behavioural scientists.
5. Makes possible for people to work cooperatively.
6. Resembles cooperativeness.

MEANING OF ORGANISATION

Dictionary definition of organisation is "the work of connecting inter-dependent parts so that each has a special function, act, office or relation to the whole". The following are some definitions of organisation.

L.D. White: "Organisation is the arrangement of personnel for facilitating the accomplishment of some agreed purpose through allocation of functions and responsibilities".

Pfiffner: "Organisation consists of the relationship of individual to individual and of group to groups which are so related as to using about an orderly division of labour".

Luther Gullick: "Organisation is the formal structure of authority through which work sub-divisions are arranged, defined and coordinated for defined purpose".

M. Mark: "Organisation refers to the structure developed for carrying out the tasks entrusted to the chief executive and his administrative subordinates in government".

William Schulze: "An organisation is a combination of the necessary human beings, materials, tools, equipments, working space and appurtenances brought together in systematic and effective coordination to accomplish some desired objectives".

Simon: "By organisation we mean a planned system of cooperative effort in which each participant has a recognised role to play and duties and tasks to perform".

Gladden: "Organisation is concerned with the pattern of relationship between persons in an enterprise, so constructed as to fulfil the enterprise's function".

Urwick: Organisation is "determining what activities are necessary to any purpose and arranging them in groups which may be assigned to individuals".

J.D. Mooney: "Organisation is the form of every human association for the attainment of a common purpose".

Amitai Etzioni: "The term organisation refers to planned unit, deliberately structured for the purpose of attaining specific goals".

APPROACHES EXPLAINING THE MEANING OF ORGANISATION

The traditional approach explains the meaning of organisation as a 'structural' arrangement by which work is divided, arranged, defined and coordinated for defined purpose. It is a systematic bringing together of independent parts to form a unified whole.

The structural approach emphasised on tasks to be performed and entry of individual in organisation is for performing specific tasks. This approach did not take into consideration the role of individual in organisation.

The contemporary approach explains that organisation is a combination of human beings with defined duties and responsibilities for the accomplishment of desired objectives and in this cooperative endeavour, a complex pattern of relationship in the organisation is developed by these individuals.

ELEMENTS OF ORGANISATION

Review of above description brings out the following elements of organisation:

1. Two or more persons constitute the organisation.

2. Constituted for the fulfilment of objectives.
3. Cooperation among members of organisation.
4. Organisation arranges sufficient resources, material and goods for the fulfilment of desired objectives.
5. There exists unity and mutual coordination among these resources.
6. Functions of every organisation are specifically described and classified.
7. Every organisation has one or more than one power centres.
8. Members of organisation are continuously placed.
9. Every organisation contains formal and informal communication system.
10. Reward and punishment systems exist in every organisation.
11. Division of work with coordination in every organisation is an important aspect of organisation.
12. Relationships among lessons and groups of organisation are vital.

BASES OF ORGANISATION

There are four bases:

1. *Function or Purpose*: Performance of function or achievement of purpose becomes the basis of organising. For example, departments of Governments such as Health Department, Education Department, Defence Department, etc.
2. *Process*: It is a technique or primary skill of a specialised activity such as engineering, accounting etc.
3. *Clientele*: This means the body of persons to be served such as Department of SC/ST, Department of Youth Affairs, etc.
4. *Area or Place*: When area or place becomes the basis of organising such as Ministry of External Affairs, Indian Mission Abroad, etc.

However, there is no single basis for establishment of an organisation. Establishment of organisation has multiple bases.

BENEFITS OF ORGANISING

Carlisle suggests the following benefits:

1. Determine the flow of work and hence influences organisational efficiency.
2. Provides guidelines for individual performance.
3. Aids in planning and control through creating a framework for these efforts.
4. Establishes channels for communication and decision making.

5. Avoids duplication of work and conflict over jurisdictions.
6. Saves effort by relating all activity to desired goals.
7. Institutes a promotional ladder and basis for evaluating and paying workers.
8. Provides a mentor for each employee and identifies where support services can be obtained.

THEORIES OF ORGANISATION

Organisation theory is the study of structure, functioning, appraisal, problems, performance and behaviour of members of organisation in the form of individuals and groups.

Before industrial revolution, organisations were small and work under the direct control of one person or one family because of the prevalence of handicraft and domestic system of production. But due to industrial revolution and later on developments taken place, organisations become large and complex. These factors pave the way of scientific thinking in this field. Broadly, theories of organisation may be grouped as follows:

I. The Classical Organisation Theory
   (a) Scientific Management Theory
   (b) Bureaucratic Theory
   (c) Fayol and Classical Theory

II. The Neo-Classical Approach

III. Modern Organisation Theory
   (a) Behavioural Theory
   (b) The Systems Approach
   (c) The Contingency Approach

I. The Classical Organisation Theory

(a) Scientific Management Theory

The term "Scientific Management" was first coined by Louis D. Brandies at a meeting held in October 1910. Later on this term got publicity during the year 1912 when a special committee of the House of Representatives of the U.S. Congress held hearings on Taylor's Scientific Management. Main features of this theory are as follows:

1. Scientific management concerned itself with micro aspects such as physical activities of work through time and motion study and examination of man-machine relationship.
2. It laid emphasis on activities at shop floor or work unit level.
3. Taylor's major emphasis in his conceptualisation was on the

collaboration between the management and workers through the application of scientific methods.

4. The management should perform functions of planning, organising, controlling and determining method of work.

Objectives of Scientific Management: These objectives have been elaborated by Taylor's Society.

1. Developing high standard of living by increasing the income of workers.
2. Avoiding wastage of human and material resources and sharing of income accrued from avoidance of this wastage.
3. Assurance by management a happier surrounding to worker by removing disagreeable factors.
4. Providing healthy conditions of work to members of organisation individually and socially.
5. Providing opportunities for higher development of capacity of individual through scientific method of work assignment and selection, training, transfer and promotion.
6. Training should be imparted to workers for the development of more capacities which make them eligible for promotion.
7. Self-confidence and self-respect among workers should be developed.
8. Creating an atmosphere of research for the development of capacity of workers to express and understand aims and objectives of organisation.
9. Discrimination in wages should be avoided so that justice can be promoted.
10. Elimination of factors causing conflict and a feeling of intolerance.

Principles of Management: Taylor outlined the following principles of scientific management.

1. Developing a science for each aspect of work of man which replaces the old rule-of-thumb method.
2. Selecting, training, teaching and developing workman scientifically.
3. A true feeling of cooperation between management and worker should be developed so that work can be done scientifically.
4. There should be almost equal division of the work and responsibility between the management and workman. The management should take all the task in its hand for which it was suitably prepared.
5. Financial incentives to be used to motivate workmen.

Taylor's Main Contributions: These are as follows:

(a) *Mechanical.* For improvement of output. Taylor proposed mechanical devices:
   (i) Time study.
   (ii) Functional foremanship or divided foremanship.
   (iii) Standardisation of all tools and implements and also of the acts or movements of workmen for each class of work.
   (iv) Use of slide rules and similar time saving implements.
   (v) Instruction cards for workman.
   (vi) Routing system.
   (vii) Modern cost system.

(b) *Organisational.* Taylor proposed that:
   (i) There should be a separate planning department.
   (ii) The work of planning should be divorced from the work of doing.
   (iii) Right man should be selected for the right job.
   (iv) Tasks should be clearly defined for the subordinates by management.
   (v) Rewards should be based on differential piece role – large bonus for the successful performance of given task.
   (vi) Management by exception principle.

(c) *Philosophical*
   (i) Provision of reward to worker if he achieves excellence in work, if he fails to complete work, the worker should be punished.
   (ii) There should be mental revolution both on the part of management and the worker.

Acknowledged as 'Father of Scientific Management', F.W. Taylor's views of scientific management have developed into a movement and dominated the scene of industrial management/organisation for several decades. Later on, his followers refined and enlarged his concepts and principles, noted among them are H.L. Gantt and Frank and Lillian Gilberth.

Gantt's Contributions

1. Recognised the importance of human element in productivity and propounded the concept of motivation.
2. Introduced two new features in Taylor's incentive scheme:
   First, every worker finishing the whole assigned work of the day was to win 50 cent bonus for that day.
   Second, the foreman too was to get a bonus for each worker finishing the work assigned for the day plus an extra bonus if all the workers reached the daily standards.
3. He originated a charting system for production control known as 'Gantt Chart'.

Frank and Lillian Gilberth's Contribution

They contributed the following:

1. Conducted motion and fatigue study.
2. Classified all movements employed in industrial work into 17 basic types known as 'Therbligs'.
3. Provided a shorthand symbol for each so that the analyst could easily and quickly jot down each motion as he observed the worker in action.

Contributions of Scientific Management

1. Time and motion studies have brought efficiency and rationality in tools and physical movements involved into fulfilling a task.
2. Emphasis on scientific selection of workers having adequate ability and training.
3. Importance given to work design encouraged managers to seek the 'one best way' of doing job.
4. Provides guidelines to management to develop an effective organisation.
5. Stress on the concept of research and use of standards in management as well as planning and control in management.
6. Introduction of guidelines between workers and management.

Limitations.

1. Emphasis on economic incentives as motivators for increased production is not correct since man is not only an economic man but he is a social man having security, egoistic as well as social needs.
2. Taylor's emphasis on 'mental revolution' on the part of management but he did not emphasise much on relations between worker and management.
3. Scientific management concerned itself wholly with production and was unconcerned with the problem of monotony of workers (Robert Hoxie).
4. Time and motion studies have not been accepted as entirely scientific since two persons are not expected to work in the same way, at the same rhythm, with same attention and same learning speed.

However, besides these limitations, most of the developments in the field industrial engineering, human resource management and organisation vow to concepts developed by scientific management. There are time and motion study, specialisation, standardisation, planning, slide rules, and other work saving implements, work standards and guidelines, piece rate, wage systems, routing system and modern cost system. In this way, it can be unequivocally maintained that scientific management is more relevant to mechanisation and automation which are technical aspects of efficiency than to the broader aspect of human behaviour in organisation.

(b) Bureaucratic Theory

Strict adherence to administrative structures, rules and procedures creates a situation known as bureaucracy. Coined by Vincent de Gournay, a French economist, bureaucracy refers a large, complex administrative system working with impersonal detachment from people. Max Weber (1864-1920) developed this theory and according to him, bureaucratic organisation structure has the following characteristics:

1. *Specialisation and Division of Labour*: This refers the following:

(a) The organisational structure is characterised by a specific sphere of competence.
(b) This is marked off as part of a systematic division of labour.
(c) The whole work is divided into some broad groupings and these groupings further sub-divided into small groupings.
(d) The process of this division of work remains continued till the job of incumbent becomes specific leading to specialisation.
(e) The incumbent primarily occupies each office upto his/her tenure but he/she cannot own personally the office or means of production and administration.
(f) This specialisation and division of labour improves the efficiency incumbent.

2. *Hierarchy*: This means the following:

(a) The structure is characterised by separation between super and subordinate offices i.e. each lower office is under the supervision and control of a higher office.
(b) Every member in the structure remains under control.
(c) Orders are sent by superior to his subordinates and subordinates report results or actions on the orders of superior.
(d) Every subordinate reports to only one boss and every superior controls the behaviour of subordinate(s).

3. *A System of Abstract Rules*: This model contains the following:

(a) This model operates as per rules and procedures.
(b) The bureaucratic structure requires a continuous organisation of official functions bound by rules and regulations.
(c) Works are planned and executed with rational approach requiring a set of formal rules for ensuring uniformity and coordination of efforts.
(d) The rules provide administrative structure stable, continuous and predictable.

(e) The role of rules has been stressed so that personal favours, arbitrarieness, grace or gratitude may not hinder the working of an administrative structure.

4. *Impersonal Relationships*: Here, in this model:

(a) The organisational structure remains formal and the structure of relationship corresponds to the authorised network of communication channel.
(b) Interpersonal dealings remain formal and impersonal and avoid sentiments and emotions.
(c) Emotional attachment to subordinates and customers must be avoided.
(d) Due to these relationships, bureaucrats can take rational and objective decisions.

5. *Employment Based on Qualification*: Here, the following things take place regarding employment:

(a) Employment and job placement are based on technical qualifications.
(b) Special training is organised to individual for improvements in his performance.
(c) Bureaucrats are protected against arbitrary dismissal.
(d) Promotions are made as per seniority or achievements.

Besides these characteristics, this approach also contains the following:

1. Coordination of decisions is the chief purpose of this structure.
2. The head of structure is responsible for and authority to fulfil all work.
3. Authority and responsibility are commensurate at the head and at each lower hierarchical levels.
4. Delegation of authority, responsibilities and resources to sub-heads is done by the head of structure.
5. Sub-heads can also further delegate for effective work and such delegations are administrative in character and do not relieve the responsibility holder of his ultimate accountability.

Functional Aspects of Bureaucracy: For the administration of any big task bureaucratic form of organisation is needed for the purpose of maintaining some degree of efficiency in accomplishing their goods since most of the large organisations usually depend upon specialisation, hierarchy, rules, important and technical training. The following are considered as functional aspects of 'ideal' bureaucracy.

1. *Specialisation.* Every organisation may be a government organisation, industry or social service organisation is a bureaucratic organisation.

Member of organisation functions in a chain and performs his functions in a pre-determined manner. He is assigned a routine work with fixed duties and responsibilities with pre-determined jurisdiction. These things lead to specialisation of task.

2. *Structure*. Structure of organisation fixes the duties and responsibilities as well as control and reporting relationships in a hierarchical system. Structure develops the framework of organisational processes.
3. *Stability*. Organisation becomes stable since certainty and stability are ensured through rules, regulations, training and specialisation.
4. *Rationality*. The organisational problems are solved and functions performed in a prescribed routine manner leading to consistency and objectivity.
5. *Democracy*. In bureaucratic organisation, emphasis is laid down on qualifications and technical competence for recruiting the staff and performance of duties and roles as per laid down rules, regulations, and practices. There is very less scope of autocracy. These things ensure democratic functioning of the organisation.

Dysfunctional Aspects: The following are some dysfunctional aspects of bureaucracy:

1. There is rigidity in bureaucracy since rules and regulations sometime become rigid and lack flexibility.
2. It is argued that bureaucracy resist change and believes in status quoism.
3. Bureaucratic structure performs the work mechanically emphasising on rules and regulations rather than the needs and emotions of people. This structure does not give importance to human relations.
4. Due to emphasis on hierarchy as downward orientation, individual initiative and participation are often blocked and upward communication is impeded.
5. Rules strive for the achievement of organisational goals at each level becomes an end in themselves independent of organisational goals.
6. Watertight division of jobs and steel framing of structure in which person even capable of performing job other than assigned cannot perform the tasks.
7. In bureaucracy, people take their office which they hold and privileges they get as personal ownership and fulfil their self-interests or the interests of sub-unit they represent. This is known as empire building.
8. The procedures laid down in bureaucracy sometimes become lengthy, need much paper work leading to delay in decision making. This is called red tape.
9. This structure believes only in formal network of relationships while

in the continuous interactions, people develop informal network of relationships.

Conclusion. Besides these deficiencies, bureaucracy still is an important aspect of organisation structure. The need of the hour is that contemporary realities should be realised. The following things can be done:

1. The primary goals of organisation should not be neglected at any cost.
2. Individual needs should not overpass the organisational goals.
3. Realisation of human aspect of organisation as well as the role of informal organisation and network in the organisation.
4. Bureaucracy should have both downward and upward orientations. Upward orientation should not be neglected.
5. Communication and innovative ideas should not be distorted.
6. Introduction of adequate means for resolving differences and conflicts between ranks and between functional groups.
7. Assimilation of new ideas, technology and scientific temper in organisations.

(c) Fayol and Classical Theory or Mechanical Theory

This theory believes in formalism, law, structure and rules. The main proponents of this theory are Henri Fayol, Luther Gullick, L. Urwick, J.D. Mooney, A.C. Railley and Mary Parker Follett.

Characteristics and Assumptions of Theory

1. In this theory, emphasis is given on structure of organisation and it is assumed that all problems of organisation generate from its structure so, structure of organisation should have scientific base.
2. This theory assumes that organisation has certain definite principles, so contributors of this theory have taken more interest in developing principles of organisation.
3. Here administration is taken as technical problem, all concentration is on efficiency of the organisation.
4. In this theory, it is said that there is no difference between public and private administration since administration is an activity common to all. The main problem of organisations is to obtain efficiency.
5. Working personnel and their responsibilities in organisation are separately assessed.
6. It is assumed that law, regulation, process, structure and control system exercise decisive role in administration.
7. It is important in this theory to establish maximum coordination between organisation and its different units.

8. It is specially assumed that every organisation has formal structure which operates according to pre-determined regulations, principles, laws, work processes and administrative structure and other components can be explained with the help of chart and rule book.
9. This theory assumes that there is no effect of environment and human behaviour at internal level on the working, structure and principles of organisation.

Six Philosophical Characteristics

1. *Atomic* means the man is a cog in machine. He is different and away from his co-workers.
2. *Mechanical* means that organisation is a machine where organisational behaviour has no importance.
3. *Motionless*. This approach is not dynamic and called traditional approach.
4. *Voluntary*. Working member of organisation remains free from his colleagues and social control.
5. Rationality means work takes place in organisation as per rational way.
6. *Material based*. This approach assumed that personnel of organisation are motivated by material incentives only. Non-material incentives are not important.

Six Independent Activities of Industrial Undertakings: These are as follows (According to Henry Fayol):

1. Technical including production, manufacturing and adaptation.
2. *Commercial* – buying, selling and exchange.
3. *Financial* – provision of capital and optimum use of capital.
4. *Security* – protection of property and persons.
5. *Accounting* – stock taking, balance sheets, costs and statistics.
6. *Managerial* – planning, organising, commanding, coordinating and controlling.

Basic Qualities: Henry Fayol also observed that for each group of activities certain basic abilities are necessary to carry them out. These are:

1. Physical qualities
2. Mental qualities
3. Moral qualities
4. General education
5. Special knowledge of the task assigned.
6. Experience

Principles of Administration and Management

Fayol emphasised on the functional approach regarding administration and management. He has given the following principles:

1. *Division of Work*: According to Fayol, the major responsibility of organisation is to develop competent personnel for carrying out activities (technical, commercial, financial, security, accounting and managerial) of organisation. This needs specialised task skills which allow a member of organisation to perform better in his particular branch of activity, thereby facilitating increased production so, employees should be placed as per their talents and abilities in every organisation whether big and small.

2. *Authority and Responsibility*: Authority is the right to give orders and power to exact obedience. Authority can be official authority which is legally given to person and personal authority which a person acquires through his ability, knowledge, experience and intellect.

The member of organisation's authority must commensurate with responsibilities so steps must be taken to induce persons to accept responsibility for the accomplishment of the objectives of organisation as per his position.

3. *Discipline*: Discipline is needed for proper exercise of authority and it has two facets i.e. employees would obey orders only when administration plays its role well by providing good leadership.

4. *Unity of Command*: In order to reduce conflict and confusion, each employee in an organisation should have only one direct superior from whom he would receive directives.

5. *Unity of Direction*: There should be a single head and a uniform plan for a group of activities having the same objectives.

6. *Subordination of Individual Interest to General Interests*: The goals of organisation should remain supreme for individuals and interest of one employee or group of employees should not dominate over the organisational interests.

7. *Remuneration of Personnel*: The policies of compensation and practices should be fair and bring maximum satisfaction to both employers as well as employees.

8. *Centralisation*: The balance between centralisation and decentralisation should be maintained as per competencies of people of the organisation.

9. *Scalar Chain or Hierarchy*: Scalar chain refers to the authority from superior to subordinate as well as channel of authority for communication and decision making. It should not be broken and any employed should not approach to his superior's superior directly.

10. *Equity*: In an organisation, justice and kindness towards employees should prevail.

11. *Stability of Tenure of Personnel*: For the purposes of improving the

morale of employees, sustenance of experience and expertise in organisation and continuance of policies of organisation, stability in tenure of personnel is essential.

12. *Order*: This principle maintains that there is a place for everything and everyone. It applies on both human as well as material resources and reduces wastage of time as well as material resources.

13. *Initiative*: This should be encouraged by administration at all levels of organisation. Administrators must share some decision making authority with their subordinates. This will generate initiative on the part of subordinates.

14. *Esprit de corps*: It is described as the prevalence of harmony among employees of organisation. For this administration must encourage interpersonal cooperation as well as reward each man for his merit without any malices.

Limitations

This approach suffers from some limitations. These are as follows:

1. The principles enunciated in this approach have been labelled as sayings since the problem is whether and to what extent these principles really serve as definite principles. For example, concepts such as centralisation, decentralisation and delegation suffer from superficiality and over simplification.
2. It has limited outlook since it sees that individual and organisation are different.
3. It over emphasises 'structure' and 'formalism' and negates the importance of human relations.
4. Here, organisation is closed unit which is not affected by external environment which is not correct.
5. It views organisations as power centred and does not provide for underpinning the elements of democratic form of organisation.
6. It gives importance to material incentives and formalism only which is not the holistic view.
7. The members of organisation are not cog of machine, they have sentiments and emotions also which are also important for the enhancement of productivity.

Contributions

Besides these limitations, this approach contributed much in the fields of organisation, administration and management.

1. This approach has established a separate identity of administrative organisations from the point of view of study and practice.
2. It has exercised a role in the enhancement of productivity in the organisation.

3. It started an independent thinking regarding authority and responsibility in organisations.
4. It has established administration as discipline of study.

II. The Neo-Classical Approach of Organisation of Human Relations Theory

This theory came into existence due to—

(a) Over emphasis on mechanical variables in classical approach,
(b) non-recognition of human relations in administration; and
(c) findings of Hawthorne Studies which concluded that social and psychological factors are more important than financial incentives in influencing productivity of any industrial concern.

Main contributions of Hawthorne investigations have been:

1. Realisation of existence of phenomenon of informal organisation in every society.
2. Importance of informal social groups in increasing the levels of output has been recognised.
3. Worker is no more an 'economic man' only and motivate by pay packet.
4. Importance of role of superior in the equation of morale and productivity has been demonstrated.
5. Human relations approach in personnel administration has grown and developed.

Important proponents of this approach have been Elton Mayo, Kurt Lewin, Douglas Mc-Gregor, Rensis Likert, Mary Parker Follett, Bernard, Roethliberger and Dickson.

The main features of this theory are as follows:

1. *Organisation As Social System*: The situation of organisation is viewed as social as well as economic and technical.
2. *Human Nature Perspective*: Employees should be recognised as individuals having importance and worth and problem of administration should be approached from human nature perspective.
3. *Influence of Informal Groups*: Employees should be encouraged to form cohesive groups which can act informally leading to change the behaviour of employees.
4. *Use of Informal Groups*: Informal groups should be used as supplementary forces to the formal administrative structure.
5. *Adequate Channels of Communication*: For effective functioning both formal and informal channels of communication with employees and their groups should be used and for this administration must modify their formal communications channels by authorising bypasses for certain types of message.

6. *Importance of Non-Economic Rewards and Incentives*: Administrators should provide non-economic rewards and incentives for changing the behaviour of employees in addition to economic incentives. These non-material rewards may be more effective than the economic rewards.
7. *Professionalisation of Administration and Management*: Mary P. Follett maintained that the exercise of professional judgment and professional's importation of outside value systems into organisation may certainly affect the actual processes of decision making.
8. *Organisations Should Develop Their Own Policies*: Organisations should not merely act as neutral instruments for carrying out the wishes of external sponsors but they themselves help to develop and decide on policies. So, administration should contribute towards policy making as well as influence policy by making operational choices on the use of resources. This leads to involvement of a larger number of administrators and programme staff.
9. *Distribution of Decision Making Functions*: These functions should be largely distributed among members of organisation instead of remain concentrated at the top level.
10. *Acceptance of Organisation Authority*: The members of organisation should accept the organisational authority. This enhances the effectiveness of organisational authority. These should be reciprocity between leaders and led for the understanding of exercise of authority.

Thus, this approach emphasises on the importance of human factor in organisation and demands for establishment of organisational relationships based on reciprocity between leaders and led leading to alternative of autocratic administration to democratic or participative administration. This enhances satisfaction among employees which ultimately increases organisational effectiveness.

Limitations

The human relations theory of organisation has been developed as reaction to classical theory. Thus,

1. This theory overemphasised those factors which were ignored by classical thinkers such as informal organisation, informal leader, non-economic reward, social and psychological aspects of the organisation. This is short-sighted perspective, since formal organisation and economic incentives play an important role in contemporary organisations also.
2. This theory failed to mention the interconnection between formal organisation and informal organisation as well as between economic incentives and non-economic incentives.

In this way, this theory has been labelled as organisational modification rather than organisational transformation.

III. Modern Organisation Theory

(a) Behavioural Theory

This theory is an improved version of human relations theory. The main proponents of this theory are: Douglas McGreger, Maslow, Kurt Lewin, Chester Bernard etc. The main features are as follows:

1. This theory prefers more flexible organisational structure and jobs designed as per abilities and aptitudes of average employees.
2. Participative and group decision making have been emphasised in this theory.
3. This theory envisages for the encouragement of self-direction and control instead of imposed control in the organisation.
4. Introduction for positive and reformative measures not punitive measures for under performer of work.
5. These scientists made studies of groups and leadership.
6. This theory is of the view that no two people are exactly alike and manager should organise his attempts to influence people according to their individual needs.

(b) The Systems Approach

In this theory, an organisation is considered as a system of mutually dependent variables. The organisation consists of five parts i.e. inputs, process, outputs, feedback and environment.

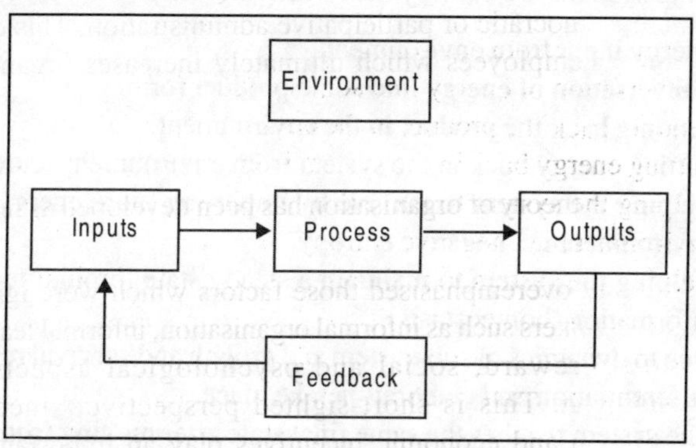

It is believed that:

1. A system is composed of certain strategic elements.
2. These elements share mutual dependency and relatedness.

3. There should be such processes in the system that they link the parts together and interact in an unitary whole.
4. Each system must have a set of goals.

Thus, system refers to an organised unitary whole composed of two or more interdependent parts, components or subsystems and delineated by identifiable boundaries from environmental supra system. (Cast and Resenzewing)

Administrative and Management Point of View

From this point of view system involves both general and specialised systems and closed as well as open analysis

System		*Concerns*
General System	-	Formal organisation, technical and socio-psychological as well as philosophical concepts
Specific System	-	Organisation structure, job design, computerised information, planning and control mechanisms.
Closed System	-	Self-contained without external inputs (In real sense this exists in theory)
Open System	-	Environment (system influences and is influenced by environment)

All living systems are open system which characterised by:

(a) Energy input from environment.
(b) Conversation of energy into some product form.
(c) Sending back the product in the environment.
(d) Putting energy back in the system from environment sources.
(e) Helping the system to survive by importing more energy from the environment i.e. negative entropy.
(f) Helping the system to maintain a steady state through feedback of information (homeostasis).
(g) Due to dynamics of sub-system and growth and survival relationship differentiation and elaboration take place.
(h) The system reaches the same final state after moving from different initial and paths of development i.e. the existence of equi-finality.

When Organisation is Taken as a System

1. It consists of several sub-systems and sub-sub-systems.

2. The organisation itself is a part of larger system i.e. environment, society, governance, etc.
3. As a system, organisation is partly economic, partly political, partly technical, partly social and even in some cases partly spiritual.
4. Every system has objectives to be achieved and activities to be performed; on the basis of which evaluation of system takes place.
5. There are inter-relationships and inter-dependency among elements/ parts of each sub-system, among the different sub-systems, between the different systems and between the organisation and the environment.

It is the function of administration and management to integrate (a) different elements/parts of each sub-system, (b) different sub-systems within the organisation, (c) among the different sub-systems themselves, and (d) between the system and the environment.

Sub-Systems in the Organisation

These are as follows:

Formal Part	Technical Sub-system Consists of	Elements Structure Rules Procedures Decision Communication Action Balance processes – Roles assigned to Personnel
Non-formal Part	(a) Social Sub-system	Individuals and groups in interaction. Informal organisation status, role, value and norm.
	(b) Power-sub-system	Formal and informal position Hierarchy of power centres

In this way, systems approach undoubtedly has unified organisational theorists, to view the organisation as a whole made up of interrelated and interdependent parts leading to the concept of synergism as well as this approach has an element of dynamism since structure changes with change of technology and vice-versa.

But, this theory is too abstract to be of much use for solving problems of administration and management. The possibilities suggested easily but difficult to achieve and its models may feature elegance rather than enlightenment.

Application of Systems Theory by Social Workers

This theory is helpful for social workers since they interact with four types of social systems through their professional system.

These four types of systems are as follows:

(a) *Client System.* People, when they ask for or agree to accept social work services, became part of client system.

(b) Target System.

1. This system includes the people or social systems that change agents "need to change or influence in order to accomplish their goals".
2. When agreed upon goals for service involve change in client system is simultaneously the target system as well.
3. If social worker approaches a person at the request of someone else or a person comes to social worker because he or she is required to do so, the change efforts done by social workers with them, they are target system not client system.

(c) Change-Agent System

1. Social workers are change agents employed for the purpose of planning and working with other systems.
2. Agency or organisation is taken as change agent system.
3. The system strongly influences social workers' professional behaviour through policies, procedures, constraints and resources.

(d) Action System

1. This system consists of those with whom the social worker participates in problem solving efforts.
2. Social work routinely collaborates with numerous action systems such as neighbourhood or community groups, advocacy organisations, family groups, self-help and support groups or interdisciplinary professional team.

For the purpose of interaction with these systems, the social workers have following professional system.

1. This system includes social work associations, schools and departments of social work, social work accreditation and licensing bodies and the values, ethics, laws and sanctions that pertain to social workers and they practice.
2. The knowledge, values and culture of the professional system strongly influence the nature of the actions of social workers.
3. This system largely determines what social workers must do and what they may do – what is required and what is permissible.

(c) The Contingency Approach

This theory was developed out of some significant researches conducted at Tavistock Institute by Joan Woodward and Burns and Stalker. These findings are different but one key aspect is that all researches relate the environment to the organisational structure.

This theory assumes that there cannot be universal applicability of management principles and concepts developed by different schools of management. They can be applied as per situation demands. This theory has following features:

1. Striving for organisational designs and managerial actions appropriate for specific situations.
2. Technology and environment also affect the organisational structure because technology and environment keep on changing, so structure is dependent on these changes.
3. Organisation shapes and adapt environment which is helpful in meeting the objectives of organisation.
4. According to this theory, organisations interact with environment so that they cannot freely take absolute actions. Their actions are affected by social, political, technical, cultural and economic factors.
5. Modern organisations are facing changing circumstances as well as environmental conditions, so organisational design should be flexible.

TYPES OF ORGANISATIONS AND ORGANISATIONAL STRUCTURES

Advancements in technology and experiences as well as knowledge about human behaviour have brought out the following paradigm shift:

(a) From commanding the organisations to consensus based self-control.
(b) Classical mechanistic forms of management systems into organic ones.
(c) Specialisation and requirements of coordination brought out issues and choices related to product versus function and matrix organisation.

These paradigm shifts have created different types of organisational structures. These are as follows:

(a) Formal and Informal Organisation

Formal organisations are concerned with the:

(a) development of formal procedures,

(b) regulation of relations between members, among members and their organisation,
(c) bestowing status to members of organisation,
(d) laying down of norms,
(e) prescription of relationships, and
(e) flowing of communications – horizontally or vertically among members.

In social administration, formal organisation is a structure of agency with officials of management, supervisors and practitioners.

Informal organisation contains: (a) unstructured informal relations, (b) unprescribed relationships, (c) unofficial norms evolved through consensus in informal organisations, (d) voluntary interaction, and (e) flow of communication in any direction.

In social administration, informal organisation refers to arrangements and operations outside the observed, regular, charted and planned structure of the agency, it includes the arrangements "underneath the table" and at the "coffee hour" (Skidmore).

Difference between Formal and Informal Organisation

	Formal	*Informal*
1.	Relationships are structured	Relationships are unstructured
2.	Positions with status	Status is earned by persons
3.	Norms are official	Norms evolved through consensus
4.	Prescribed relationships	Relationships are not prescribed
5.	Rules/roles determine interaction	Voluntary interaction
6.	Horizontal or vertical communication	Multi-directional communication

(b) Vertical and Horizontal Organisational Structures

Vertical or tall organisational structure refers:

1. A series of narrow span of control.
2. Control and close supervision on subordinates.
3. Hierarchical structure of control, authority, communication and feedback.
4. Relationships are usually formal.
5. Dominance of rules and regulations.

Horizontal or Flat Organisational Structure

1. Concerns a particular level within the structural hierarchy that goes sideways and involves numerous workers in variety of ways (Skidmore).
2. Has wide spans and limited layers of control at horizontal levels.
3. Provides decentralisation, individual initiative and self-control.

Differences between Vertical and Horizontal Structures

Vertical	*Horizontal*
1. Narrow spans	Wide spans
2. Closed control	Self-control
3. Hierarchical structure	Flat structure
4. Centralisation	Decentralisation
5. Initiative as per rules and regulations	Individual initiative

Centralised and Decentralised Organisational Structures

Centralised structure envisages the following in organisation:

1. Establishment of central authority.
2. Central authority takes all major decisions.
3. Central authority regulates the functioning of organisation
4. Subordinate units of organisation remains attached with main unit.
5. Unified and integrated system within organisation.

Decentralised Structure calls for:

1. Division of authority among different levels and units of organisation.
2. Authority remains attached with responsibility.
3. Some fixed authority at central level.
4. Decentralisation has following aspects/bases:
   (a) Administratively, subordinate officers are given the opportunity to work on their own, only few matters are sent to central authority.
   (b) Politically, more power and authority to direct are handed over to subordinates for the purpose of involving people's representatives more and more.
   (c) Geographically, more freedom is given to units which are more close to masses.
   (d) From the point of responsibility, local units have more

responsibility to complete the work, so authority is given to them which is commensurate with their responsibility.

(e) For the purpose of seeking cooperation, this system may be helpful to take cooperation from outside organisation also.

Distinction between Centralisation and Decentralisation

Centralisation	*Decentralisation*
1. Centralised authority	Decentralised authority
2. Command given by centralised authority	Initiative taken by local units
3. More responsibility at the centre/top	Less responsibility at the lower level
4. Lack of participation in activities of lower levels	Participation of lower levels.

Integrated and Disintegrated Structure

Integrated structure of organisation calls for the following:

1. No independent status of any unit, all units function as one integrated unit.
2. All responsibilities are vested in main executive.
3. Authority is vested in one person.

Disintegrated Structure makes following arrangements:

1. All institutes, offices and units remain free from main executive.
2. They work independently and have different responsibilities.
3. Every institution work as an unit.

Difference between Integration and Disintegration

	Integration	*Disintegration*
1.	No independent unit in organisation	Independent unit in organisation
2.	Responsibilities vested in one executive.	Responsibilities are vested in different units.
3.	One executive exercises the authority.	Authority is exercised at unit level.

Product and Functional Structures

This form of organisation can be chalked out on the basis of activities performed by group whether primarily by product or by function.

In product structure, all functional specialists working on a single product are grouped together under the same person who exercises the authority.

In functional structure, all specialists in a given function are grouped under common boss even if they deal different products.

Difference between Product and Functional Structure

	Product	*Functional*
1.	Single products	Different products
2.	More effective integration	Less effective integration
3.	More successful in improving capacities of plant	Less successful in improving capabilities
4.	Less effective in stable production	More effective in stable production

Mechanistic and Organic Structures

Mechanistic Organisational Structure (a) is primarily pyramid shaped, (b) has centralisation of authority at the top, (c) consists of departmentalisation of jobs, (d) has hierarchy of command, (e) is made up of narrow span of control, and (f) has division of labour.

Organic Organisational Structure: (a) has wide spans of control, (b) more general supervision, and (c) more decentralisation.

The shapes of both type of structures are shown in Fig. 1:

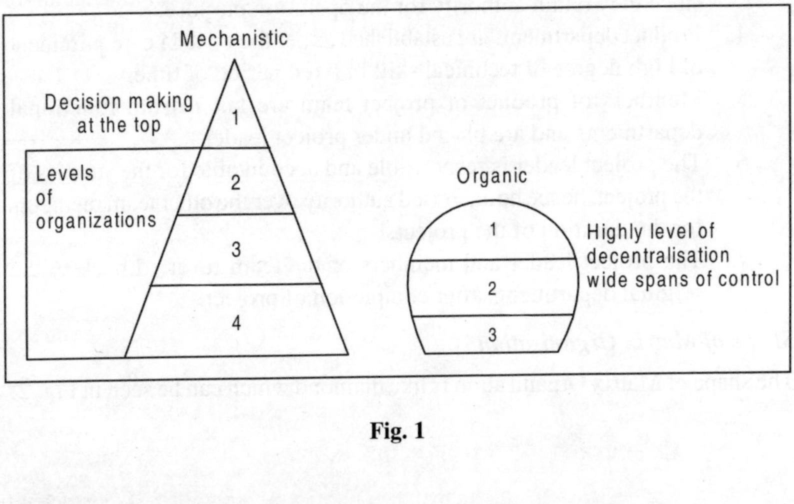

Fig. 1

Difference between Mechanistic and Organic Structures

	Mechanistic	*Organic*
1.	Distance from top to bottom	Less distance from top to bottom
2.	Extended communication lines	Less extended communication lines
3.	Narrow spans of control	Wide spans of control
4.	Centralisation	Decentralisation
5.	More hierarchy	Little hierarchy
6.	More command	Less command
7.	More specialisation	Little specialisation

Matrix Organisation

This type of organisational structure was originated with the United States Aero Space Programme of the 1960s. The need of this type of organisational structure arises when: (a) there are two or more critical sectors in terms of functions, products, services and areas which organisation is supposed to cope; (b) uncertainty, complexity and interdependency of the tasks of organisations and (c) existence of economies of scale.

The main features of this structure are as follows:

1. This involves dual chain of command.
2. There are two types of departmentalisation – functional and product. They exist simultaneously.
3. Functional departments remain permanent fixture of this organisation since they retain authority for the operation purpose.
4. Product departments are established as per their need i.e. requirement of high degree of technical skill in fixed period of time.
5. Members of product or project team are taken from functional departments and are placed under project leader.
6. The project leader is responsible and accountable for the success of the project, hence he exercised authority over the other team members for the duration of the project.
7. The project leader and members of the team reverted back to the original departments after completion of project.

Shape of Matrix Organisation

The shape of Matrix Organisation is like diamond which can be seen in Fig. 2:

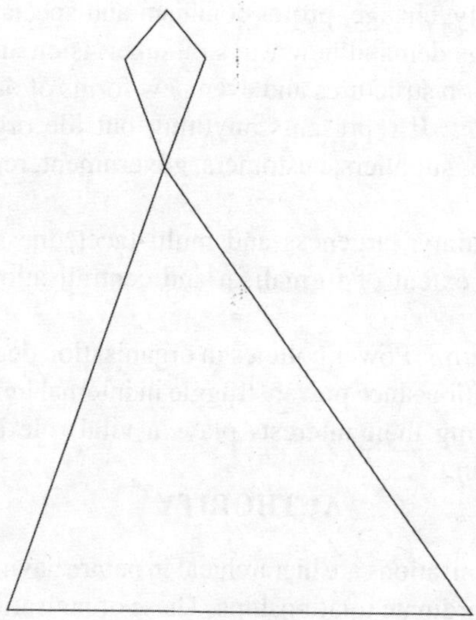

Fig. 2

Top of the diamond represents top of the management.

Two arms of diamond symbolise dual chain of command.

The left arm shows functional specialist groups (resource or input side of organisation)

The right arm shows the various products, projects, markets, clients, services or areas (output side)

Beneath the matrix is manager having dual bossism.

FACTORS DETERMINE THE STRUCTURE OF ORGANISATION

These are as follows:

1. *Size*: Size of organisation influences the structure since with increase in members of organisation. There are increases in: (a) horizontal differentiation, (b) vertical differentiation for coordinating horizontally differential units, (c) spatial differentiation, (d) complexity of organisation leads to formalism in organisation and, (e) use of formal rules and regulations.

   These increases force management to decentralise the structure.
2. *Technology*: It is a body of peculiar knowledge consisting of equipments, machines or tools, sets of activities, methods of processes, arrangements or pattern.

   Technology has features of specialisation, integration,

discontinuity, change, professionalism and specialised work force. These things demand new ways of supervision and guidance, new compensation structures and even new forms of organisation.

3. *Environment*: It represents anything outside organisation which incorporates suppliers, customers, government, regulatory agencies and so on.

   Uncertainty, largeness and multi-facetedness of environment decide the extent of formalism and centralisation in organisation structure.

4. *Power Control*: Power policies in organisation decides the structure of organisation since power struggle in internal units of organisation for furthering their interests plays a vital role in controlling the organisation.

AUTHORITY

Administrative organisations are hierarchical in nature having formal structure of superior and subordinate relationships. These organisations strive for their objectives through team work which is secured through 'authority'. So, authority is essential in administrative organisation.

Definitions of Authority

Mooney and Railley: "Authority is the principle at the root of organisation and so important it is that it is impossible to conceive of an organisation at all, unless some person or persons are in a position to require action of others".

H.A. Simon: "Authority may be defined as the power to make decision which guide the action of another. It is a relationship between two individuals, one "superior", the other "subordinate". The superior frames and transmits decisions with the expectation that they will be accepted by the subordinate. The subordinate expects such decisions, and his conduct is determined by them".

Henri Fayol: Authority is "the right to give orders and power to exact obedience".

Max Weber: Authority is "where orders are voluntarily obeyed by those receiving them".

Davis: "Authority is the right to take decision and giving order".

Different Angles to Explain the Meaning of Authority

(a) *Formal or Legal Angle*: Authority means (a) the giving of orders by superior to subordinates, (b) these subordinates are expected to obey these orders legally and follow the commands of the superior, and (c) law limits the scope and boundaries of authority.

(b) *Status Angle*: Authority refers that (a) it is vested in the hierarchical position; and (b) it is exercised by virtue of his position.

(c) *Human Relations Angle*: Authority is the capacity to evoke compliance in others, since authority depends on its acceptance by people due to the loyalty to the common goals of the organisation.

Approaches to Explain the Concept of Authority

(a) *The Traditional Concept*: In the opinion of Schell, "If we are to control, we must provide avenue through which it can function easily and directly. The avenues we speak of are paths of authority. They pass from administrators who determine policy to the executive who are responsible for the performance of the policy, and then to the employees who perform the actual operations". The basis of authority is legitimacy.

(b) *The Functional Concept*: According to this approach, authority is vested only in the particular job to be done. Authority belongs to the job and stays with the job.

(c) *The Behavioural Concept*: According to this concept, authority refers to the actual patterns of behaviour of individuals as they influence others and are being influenced. Authority is accepted by persons and groups since it is related to the human relations in administration.

(d) *Integral Concept*: Fayol has been the supporter of this concept and maintained that concept of authority can best be explained by combining all these three concepts.

Characteristics of Authority

After reviewing above definitions, angles and approaches, the following characteristics of authority can be brought out:

1. Authority is an administrative right exercised from the above.
2. It has power and mandate to take decision.
3. Decisions are communicated to the subordinates for implementation.
4. It influences behaviour pattern of subordinates
5. Capacity and judgment of superior determine the extent of acceptance of authority
6. It is exercised for achieving the objectives of organisation.

Thus, authority in administration and management is the right to guide and direct the actions of others and to secure from them responses which are appropriate to the attainment of the purposes and goals of the organisation.

Perspectives regarding Sources of Authority

According to Theorists, there are different perspectives of sources of authority. These are as follows:

1. *Formal Authority Perspective*: According to this perspective authority is the power transmitted from basic social institutions to individual administrators and managers. Administrative authority remains vested in constitution, legislative and masses and appointed persons in administrative structure.
2. *Acceptance Perspective*: This perspective envisages that merely having authority to give orders is insufficient until unless it is accepted by the person to whom these orders have been given. This acceptability is dependent upon the understanding of instructions received, ability to implement these instructions and the belief that instructions are to see that ends of organisation are served.
3. *Capacity Perspective*: This authority flows through technical competence, experience, moral wealth and ability to lead, it is the combination which ensures acceptance of the authority by the subordinate.

Types of Authority

Max Weber divided authority into (a) traditional authority which is exercised by person due to his/her inherited status; (b) charismatic where personal abilities of person make him/her leader, (c) legal rational in which authority is exercised as per certain rules and regulations for achieving specified ends. However, from the point of administrative organisations, the authority may be classified as follows:

1. *Line Authority*: It is heart of relationship between superior and subordinate, since it is (a) the ultimate authority to command, (b) to act or to decide in matters affecting others, (c) the authority which sanctions or approves actions which take place in the organisation, (d) the authority which channels and directs responses of others and requires them to confirm to decisions, plans, policies and procedures.
2. *Staff Authority*: Staff refers to those activities which provide advice and service to line. This authority is not supposed to take decisions for others. It moves horizontally not vertically as in case of line authority.
3. *Functional Authority*: This authority stands in between line and staff. It is related to a particular activity or action. Here decisions can be taken but in a limited fashion.

Functions of Authority

These are as follows:

1. Authority develops feeling of responsibility.

2. It inspires for special capacity to take decisions.
3. It coordinates different activities of the organisation.
4. Supporters of legal view of authority are of the views that authority establishes uniformity between individual works and norms established by society or organisation.
5. Decisions taken by authority encompasses wisdom, ability and skill, so it brings effect.
6. Authority is means of establishing control, direction and discipline.

Limitations of Authority

The following factors are responsible for limiting the authority:

1. *Legislative Control*. Authority can only be exercised as laws and regulations made by legislative.
2. *Executive Control*. Authority is regulated and controlled by executive orders, code of ethics, position in hierarchy, etc.
3. *Judicial Control*. Authority is dependent on the interpretation of legislative provisions enunciated by legislature as per constitution.
4. *Mass Opinion, Pressure Group and Media*. These things also determine the exercise of authority and its boundaries.
5. *Extent of Acceptability on the Part of Subordinates*. To what extent subordinates accept the authority is vital for its exercise. It decides boundaries of authority also.
6. *Personality of Persons Exercising Authority*. The nature of personality and its qualities determine the exercise and acceptance of authority.
7. *Technical Limitations*. The extent of knowledge, understanding and skills determine the nature and exercise of authority. Mere vesting authority is not sufficient, knowledge and skill involved in it should also known to the person responsible for the exercise of authority.
8. *Biological Limitations*. The physical and mental capacities of person determine about the understanding and acceptance of a decision or giving of order to subordinates.
9. *Psychological Limitations*. These are fear, tension, depression, concern etc. which determine the mind set of person who accepts the authority as well as who exercises the authority.
10. *Leadership Limitations*. The person at the top provides leadership to the organisation and its members. But it depends on the capacity and cooperation.
11. *Economic Limitations*. In contemporary administrative structure, finance is the central point which decides the implementation of activities. So, authority is also influence by these limitations.

12. *Environmental Limitations*. Authority is influenced by geographical, social and political environment in which people are functioning.

SPAN OF CONTROL

The span of control refers the number of subordinates an administrator can direct effectively. If span is wide, the administrators will have a number of subordinates reporting to them. In case of narrow span, administrators have few subordinates. It is related to the hierarchical system and unity of command principle of organisation.

Appropriate span of control should be determined mainly because (a) it affects the efficient utilisation of administrators and effective performance of their subordinates, and (b) it determines the structure of organisation because narrow span results in tall organisation with many levels between top administrator and lowest subordinate and wide span creates a flat organisation with few or levels of administrative channels.

Appropriateness of Span. What should be an appropriate span for an administrator or what should be the ideal number of subordinates directly reporting to an administrator has been a subject of discussion among administrative thinkers which is evident from the following:

Urwick suggested the 5 or 6 persons should be directly supervised by one executive or an administrator while for Hamilton the ideal number should be 3 to 6 subordinates. But J.C. Worthy believed that one executive can directly supervise as many as 20 subordinates. Ernest Dale in his study of 100 large companies has brought out that median number of executives reporting to company presidents is 8 and in some cases it was found as 20 or more.

V.A. Graicunas has suggested these various kinds relationships are involved in determining the appropriateness of span of control.

1. Direct one to one relationships. Relating superior directly and individually with his immediate subordinates.
2. Direct group relationships exist between the superior and each possible combination of subordinates.
3. Cross relationships which are created when subordinates consult one another.

Factors Governing the Span of Control: These factors are: (a) nature of work, (b) capability of administrator, (c) abilities of employees, (d) proper or improper definition of authority and responsibility, (e) geographic location, (f) availability of information and control system, (g) period of establishment of organisation, (h) financial position of organisation, (i) status of delegation of authority in organisation, (j) control mechanism of organisation, and (k) hierarchical status of organisation.

DELEGATION AND DECENTRALISATION

Organisation has a chain of superior-subordinate relationships which is interlocking. These relationships exist from top to bottom. Delegation is the formal mechanism through which a network of superior and subordinate relationships are established and maintained. Some definitions of delegation are as follows:

Louis Allen. It is "the dynamics of management, the process a manager follows in dividing the work designed to him, so that he performs that part which only he, because of his unique organisational placement, can perform effectively and so that he can get others to help him with what remains".

McFarland refers it "as that part of organising process by which a manager makes it possible for others to share the work of carrying out the company's purpose.

Thus, delegation refers as process of:

(a) conferment of some authority or discretionary powers on individuals for taking decisions in order to meet their obligations,
(b) transferring powers from higher to lower level or from superior to subordinate,
(c) this transfer of power can be revoked and modified as per demand of the situation,
(d) the superior retains the power to hold subordinate responsible for his/her actions, and
(e) it is the duty of superior to see that the job is performed properly.

Steps in Delegation

1. Assignment of duties by an administrator (superior to his immediate subordinates).
2. Permitting them to exercise authority where they can use resources and take necessary action.
3. Giving responsibilities or obligations to subordinates for satisfactory performance of duties assigned.
4. Retaining of accountability with himself for the performance of subordinates.

(a) Advantages to Superior

1. Relieves the superior of many routine duties and saves his/her valuable time.
2. Improves the quality of decision and performance of superior.
3. The superior can devote his time for his/her personal growth and development.

(b) Advantages to Subordinates

1. Increase of feeling of belongingness and responsibility towards superior and organisation.
2. Getting opportunities to test their capacities.
3. Developing potentials, skills and abilities.
4. Opportunities for getting higher position.
5. Development of feeling of respect and confidence.

(c) Advantages to Organisation

1. Helping in creating formal organisational structure.
2. Develop and train superior to be a better successor in case of departure of senior person.
3. Establishment of a sense of belonging and morale among members of organisation leading to enhance their commitment towards organisation.

Barriers or Reluctance in Delegation

These are as follows:

(a) Administrator's Point of View

1. Administrator may have psychological desire to dominate and control.
2. There exists fear of loss of power.
3. Lack of confidence in subordinates.
4. There is fear on the part of administrator to be exposed before subordinates.

(b) Subordinates' Point of View

1. Avoid involvement in decision-making due to the fear of criticism.
2. Lack of information and resources also promote reluctance to accept authority.
3. Lack of self-confidence and initiative.
4. Sometimes lack of personal gains avoid acceptance of authority.

Measures of Effective Delegation

1. Clarity in nature and scope of task.
2. Assigning authority as per responsibility.
3. Clear understanding on the part of subordinate regarding limits of authority.
4. Rendering positive incentives for accepting responsibility.
5. Proper training and guidance to subordinates before delegating authority.

6. Mutual trust and mutual confidence and goodwill should be created.
7. Subordinate should remain accountable to one person.
8. No overlapping or splitting in delegation of authority.
9. Clarity in understanding why to delegate what to delegate, how much to delegate, how to delegate successfully.

Decentralisation

Everything that goes to increase the importance of the subordinate's role is decentralisation and everything that goes to reduce it is centralisation (Fayol). In decentralisation, the authority is delegated to the levels where the work is performed. According to Ernest Dale, criteria to measure the extent of decentralisation in an organisation depends on the following:

When decentralisation is greater:

1. The greater is the number of decision made at lower levels.
2. The more important are the decisions made at lower levels.
3. The more is the number of areas in which decisions can be made at lower levels.
4. The fewer are the people to be consulted and less is the checking required on the decisions made at the lower levels.

Dimensions of Decentralisation

These are as follows:

1. *Administrative*: Authority is transferred to subordinate officers for doing work. Only few subjects are referred to top officer.
2. *Political*: Elected units are given more powers for giving directions leading to the participation of masses.
3. *Geographical*: Freedom is given to units which are near people and far away from central units.
4. *Functional*: Freedom is given to local units for performing different functions at local level.
5. *Responsibility Dimension*: If local units are responsible for performing work, then these units should be given proper authority.

Difference between Delegation and Decentralisation

	Delegation	*Decentralisation*
1.	It is a process.	It is the end result.
2.	Superior remains responsible for dele-gated authority.	Superior is relieved from the authority.
3.	Delegation is compulsory for running the organisation	Decentralisation is voluntary.

Advantages of Decentralisation

1. Quick and better decision making.
2. Problems related to communication and red tape are reduced.
3. Human element is recognised.
4. Creation of competition among members of organisation.
5. Development of more competent administrators.
6. Diversification of activities.

Factors Affecting Decentralisation

1. *Size of organisation*: Decentralised operations are needed in case of very large and complex organisations.
2. *Values and philosophy of administrators*: Belief in democratic values on the part of administrators lead for decentralisation.
3. *Abilities of lower level administrators*: If organisation has competent lower level executives then there is possibility of more decentralisation.
4. *Nature of management function*: Function related to quality control and engineering need decentralised operations.

7

Staffing

Every organisation strives for the fulfilment of objectives. These objectives are met by conducting certain activities. For these activities, persons at different levels of organisation are required which is known as staff.

Staffing refers to the filling and keeping filled positions in the organisation structure through identifying workforce requirements, inventorying the people available, recruiting, selecting, placing, promoting, appraising, planning the career, compensating and training or otherwise developing both candidates and current jobholders to accomplish their tasks effectively and efficiently (Koontz and Weihrich).

In social administration, staffing is a major administrative process involving social welfare organisation/agency in order to locate and obtain staff and maintain its working and its separation from organisation.

The activities performed in an organisation can be divided into three types as per their importance and staff can also be divided in three types for the performance of these activities. This is as follows:

- Most important activities — Top level staff
- Ordinary important activities — Middle level staff
- Less important activities — Lower level staff

FUNCTIONS OF TOP LEVEL

These are as follows:

(a) Direction: involves running of organisation by directing activities clearly.

Functions related to this direction are:

1. *Planning:*
   (a) Plan for the implementation of administrative policies
   (b) Meeting definite objective at various levels of organisation.
   (c) Clarity in the duration of completion of work.

(d) Attainment of efficiency.

2. *Coordination*:
   (a) Coordinating the functions of subordinate authorities.
   (b) No duplication of work.
   (c) Avoiding extra labour.
   (d) No leniency in work.
   (e) Successful coordination of plan
3. *Programming*: Making programming for implementing administrative policies
4. *Research*:
   (a) Continuous research for enhancing efficiency.
   (b) Maintaining quality of activities.
   (c) Innovative measures are introduced in organisation.

(b) Controlling: Responsibility is established in the implementation of policies. Functions are:

1. *Organisation*:
   (a) Establishment of mutual relationships among different staff members.
   (b) Authority is exercised and transferred.
   (c) Boundaries of responsibility are established.
2. *Supervision*:
   (a) The behaviour of members of organisation is made static.
   (b) Morale of subordinate employees is boosted.
   (c) Generate interest in work.
3. *Documentation*:
   (a) Writing of organisational functions, behaviours, achievements and problems.
   (b) Officer gets initiative from the organisation.
   (c) Restructuring failures and meeting the problems.
   (d) Cooperation is established through information sharing.
   (e) Other organisations also take interest.
4. *Reporting*:
   (a) This makes top officers familiar to actions and progress.
   (b) It brings out problems and successes of organisation.

FUNCTIONS OF MIDDLE LEVEL

These are as follows:

1. Organisation of team.
2. Keep the level of work static.

3. Protect volume of work and attributes necessary for performing work.
4. Development of efficiency among workers.
5. Supervision and inspection of work of subordinates.
6. Making communication effective at top level.
7. Link between lower and top level.
8. Making line staff and organisation effective.

FUNCTIONS OF LOWER LEVEL

1. Real execution of functions of organisations.
2. Obeying orders, instructions and directions.

IMPORTANCE AND NEED OF STAFFING

Proper staffing is required since it:

1. discovers talented and competent employees and develops to move upward in the organisation;
2. ensures greater production by putting the right man in the right place;
3. helps to avoid sudden disruption of an enterprise's production run by indicating shortage of personnel, if any in advance;
4. helps to prevent under-utilisation of personnel through over-manning and the resultant high labour cost and low profit margins; and
5. provides information to management for internal succession of managerial personnel in the event of an unanticipated turnover (Tripathy and Reddy).

LOGIC OF STAFFING IN SOCIAL ADMINISTRATION (SOCIAL WELFARE ADMINISTRATION)

Social administration is usually used in two senses, i.e. it is the administration or management of social welfare/service programmes and agencies/organisations and as a method and technique of social work. Due to the uniqueness of this administration proper and efficient staff is important for administration and management of social welfare programmes and organisations managing these programmes.

The staffing patterns are different in governmental and non-governmental organisations.

In governmental organisation, staffing is governed by general principles of administration i.e. hierarchy, scalar chain of command, unity of command, span of control, delegation and decentralisation. But, in case of non-governmental organisation, logic of staffing is related to three levels of staff.

1. Administrative and senior supervisory level which exists at headquarter level and staff is supposed to exercise duties of policy making, planning, programming, research, etc. The main concern of this staff is to direct and supervise.
2. Intermediate supervisory level where staff is supposed to implement the policies and programmes. Staff is engaged in supervising and controlling at programme level or a particular unit of organisation.
3. Field level staff is supposed to carry out programmes at field level.

APPRAISAL AND DEVELOPMENT OF STAFF

Appraisal of Staff

For the purpose of professional development, appraisal of work of staff engaged in the practice of social work takes place. Through this, competence in service activities with individuals, groups, communities and society at large are assessed as per pre-determined standards.

Purposes of Appraisal

Carlisle suggests these purposes as follows:

1. Keeping subordinates informed on how they are doing.
2. Determining merit pay increases.
3. Uncovering training needs.
4. Identifying candidates for promotion.
5. Recognising barriers or problems to improved performance.
6. Discussing ways in which performance can be improved both in relation to the individual and the work unit.

Methods of Appraisal

These are as follows:

1. *Ranking Method*: Here, each man in group is compared with all other members of group and placed in simple rank order. Order is maintained from best to worst of all individuals comparing the group.
2. *Rating Scale Method*: This method brings out some kind of scale for measuring absolute differences among individuals. Two types of scale are generally used:
   (a) *Discrete*: Here, two or more categories are provided. These categories represent the discrete amounts of ability or degrees of the characteristics. Of these categories one can be ticked mark showing best to desirable person being rated. For example: commitment to job may be rated as very good, good, average, bad, very bad.

(b) *Continuous*: Here, categories are linked with a line either from best to worse or worse to best and later is supposed to tick at any point.

Very Good   Good   Average   Bad   Very Bad

3. *Paired Comparison*: Every individual in group is compared with every other member of the group. During this comparison choices are found by every member in the group. These choices are counted and converted into percentage scores leading to the fair idea as to how each individual in the group is judged by rates.
4. *Grading*: In this, meaning of certain categories of abilities of performance is pre-conceived and then as per their traits and qualities persons are put in particular category. These categories may be outstanding, good, average, poor and worst. They may be termed as A, B, C, D and E also where A indicates the best and E as worst.
5. *Forced Distribution Method*: In this method, the assumption is that the performance level of employees conforms to a normal statistical distribution curve, that is, ten percent may be best, 20 percent above average, 40 percent as average and 20 percent below average. So, the person who appraises, is forced to appraise the person being appraised as per the pattern of normal curve.
6. *Forced Choice Method*: This method contains a series of items or statements normally depicting degree of proficiency. The rater examines the extent of effectiveness of statement describing each individual being rated.
7. *Check List Method*: In this method, the rater prepares report of appraisal by answering a series of questions concerned with persons being appraised. Usually prepared by HR Department, these questions are related to the behaviour of persons to be appraised. Normally, each question has two alternatives i.e. Yes/No.
8. *Graphic Rating*: The appraiser is provided categories with boxes or with an uninterrupted line placed just below the category notations on which he indicates his rating by means of a check mark.
9. *Free from Essay Method*: This method seeks the superior to write note or essay containing his views regarding his subordinate.
10. *Critical Incident Method*: In this method, firstly, a list of critical requirements of job should be prepared. These requirements are vital for the success or failure on the job. Secondly, after the identification of these factors, the supervisors may then observe and record instances and events of on-the-job behaviour falling under any of these factors as they take place.

11. *Group Appraisal Method*: Here, employees are rated by an appraisal group consisting of their supervisor and three or four supervisors who have some knowledge of their performance.
12. *Field Review Method*: In this method, appraisal of employees are based on interviews with their immediate supervisor who answers the questions covering the progress of subordinate and his level of performance. The interviewer consolidates the detailed notes he has taken the interview. It is then placed for the approval of the concerned supervisor (interviewee) and an approval placed in the employer's personal folder.
13. *Assessment Centre Method*: Here a number of evaluators join together for judging performance of employee in different situations by using criteria such as paper and pencil test, interviews and situational exercises.
14. *Management by Objectives* (*MBO*): First used by Peter Drucker in 1954 and since adopted by management theorists and administrators. Odiorne interpreted and popularised MBO, describes the basic premises of MBO as follows:
    A. Business management takes place within an economic system that provides the environmental situation for the individual firm. This environment, which has changed drastically over the past 30 years, imposes new requirements on companies and on individual managers.
    B. Management by objectives is a way of managing aimed at meeting these new requirements. It presumes that the first step in management is to identify, by one means or another, the goals of organisations. All other management methods and sub-systems follow the preliminary step.
    C. Once organisational goals have been identified, orderly procedures for distributing responsibilities among individual mangers are set up in such a way that their combined efforts are directed towards achieving that goals.
    D. Management by objectives assumes that managerial behaviour is more important that manger personality and that this behaviour should be defined in terms of results measured against established goals rather than in terms of common goals for all managers, or common method of managing.
    E. It also presumes that while participation is highly desirable in goal-setting and decision-making its principal merit lies in its social and political values rather than in its effects on production. Though even here it may have a favourable impact, and in any case seldom hurts.

F. It regards the successful manager as a manager of situations, most of which are best defined by identifying the purpose of the organisation and the managerial behaviour best calculated to achieve that purpose.

15. *360 Degree Appraisal Method*: It is the process of systematically gathering information on a person's skills, abilities and behaviours from a variety of sources – The manager, peers, subordinates and even customers and clients (Millman and Others). Here, appraisal of an employee is done by his superior, his peers, his subordinates and clients or outsiders with whom he interacts in the course of his job performance.

Factors Affecting Performance Appraisal

These are as follows:

1. The condition and constraints of environment.
2. The leadership of the organisation.
3. Mutual and interdependency of sub-systems of organisation.
4. The nature and type of organisational structures

Kahle presents a comprehensive statement of factors to be covered in evaluation of staff:

I. The purpose of evaluation.
II. Responsibilities assigned and carried.
III. General aspects of practice (strengths and weaknesses).
IV. Specific (qualitative) aspects of practice (strengths and weaknesses)
   A. Service to the board or governing body.
   B. Service to the staff.
   C. Service to community.
   D. Service to agency programme.
V. Summary and recommendations (This section should provide a condensation of total evaluation)

Development of Staff

Development refers to the nature and direction of change induced in employees. Development activities and programmes have substantial influence in changing the capacity of individual to perform his assignment better and in doing so are likely to increase his potential for future assignments (National Industrial Conference Board).

Approaches to Development

These are as follows:

(I) Traditional Approach

This approach is based on the assumption that how people learn and grow and bringing changes in employees as per requirements of an organisation. This approach may be divided into two forms:

(A) On-The-Job Training Programmes

These are:

(a) *Coaching* – Day-to-day performance is observed by senior person.
(b) *Rotation of position* – Training and development of skills in different jobs.
(c) *Assigned to special projects* – Assignment given outside the scope of person's routine areas of responsibility.
(d) *Committee assignment* – This assignment is continuous.

(B) Off-The-Side Training Programme

(a) *Special training course* – It consists of lectures, group discussions, brain storming sessions, etc.
(b) *Management games and simulations* – Assignment of individuals to team which interact as competing companies in a simulated industry.
(c) *Role playing* – Emphasises on human relations skills.
(d) *Sensitivity training* – It is particularly concerned with self-awareness and self-knowledge as a key to developing social sensitivity.

(II) Social Psychology Approach

This approach believes that no change is brought about in an individual unless he is motivated or ready to change. The change is brought out in three stages:

(1)	Process of opening up	Individual gets rid of his inhibitions.
(2)	Process of changing	Here, individual emulates the person who has these attitudes.
(3)	Process of integration	Here, the individual integrates these activities with the rest of his personality.

GENERAL PROBLEMS OF STAFF

Staff may face a variety of problems inside and outside the organisation in which they are the part. These are as follows:

1. Faulty placement of employee without knowing his/her interests, sentiments and attitudes.
2. No opportunity to participate in decision-making.

3. Autocratic attitude of seniors.
4. Lack of respect of employees as well as their feelings.
5. Suspicion and distrust in the minds of employees.
6. Fear of authority.
7. Inability of employees to express their viewpoints.
8. Lack of opportunity to employees to express their views.
9. Difference in knowledge and understanding between employees and their superior.
10. Unwillingness of superiors to get and to give information.
11. Deliberate efforts made by superiors to maintain spatial as well as social distance with the lower level employees.
12. Undue preferences given by superiors to some employees.
13. No reward system for good work.
14. No proper human relations programme.
15. Unfair supervision.
16. No proper opportunities for development.
17. Repetitive and routine work.
18. Feeling monotony and boredom.
19. Inadequate light arrangement at the work place.
20. Lack of safety equipment.
21. Insufficient facilities at work place.

PROBLEMS OF STAFF IN WELFARE AND DEVELOPMENT SECTOR

Programmes of welfare and development sector are being implemented through public and private agencies. These agencies are manned by social activists, social administrators and in some cases political leaders also. In general, staff working in this sector has following problems:

1. Staff of this sector has lower status in the eyes of masses as compared to staff of government sector.
2. Working environment of this sector is challenging since it involves work in field.
3. Working in this sector involves skilfulness which is difficult to imbibe.
4. Service conditions in this sector are not good since there are low pay packet, lack of security of job, lack of standardisation of activities, individuality in rules and regulations etc.
5. Problems in mobilising resources in voluntary sector.
6. Commercialisation of voluntary sector.
7. Suspicion and mistrust in masses towards the staff of this sector.
8. Absence of cadre of social welfare and development personnel.

9. Problems of future development of staff.
10. Problems of fixation of unrealistic targets of work.
11. Untrained and unqualified staff.

RECRUITMENT AND SELECTION PROCESS

Recruitment

Basically, recruitment refers attracting persons as applicants for different positions of the organisation. The main aim is to employ those persons who have competence and ability to deal with clients/customers and other senior and junior members of the staff as the case may be.

Recruitment is important to people or persons seeking employment since it is the first step for employment and person is able to search the job as per his/her aptitude.

It is important to organisation since it gets right person for the right job and is able to get adequate, competent and skilful human resource.

It has vital importance for the whole society since through recruitment employment markets are organised and equitable distribution of employment can also be achieved.

Sources

The main sources of recruitment are as follows:

1. *Advertisement*: Clear and to the point advertisement usually sent in newspapers.
2. *Brief Announcements*: These announcements having clear details of positions may be sent to professional organisations, teaching and training institutions, persons or institutions working in the field, etc.
3. *Private Employment/Placement Agencies*: These agencies may be contacted for getting suitable persons by sending the requirement of the organisation.
4. *Campus Recruitment*: Educational/Training institutions can be contacted through their placement cells for recruiting students for job in the campus itself. This is generally done for filing the vacancies at entry level.
5. *Employment Exchanges*: These exchanges have been established by governments; through them also recruitment can be made.
6. *Deputation*: The person may be called on deputation from other organisation or from within organisation for filling a position.
7. *World-of-Mouth*: This is known as 'Employee Finding' also. Here, persons already employed are given an attractive offer by another organisation.

Selection

This is usually referred as negative process i.e. rejection of candidates for a position. It is the process of differentiating between applicants in order to identify (and hire). Those with a greater likelihood of success in a job (Thomas H. Stone).

Difference between Recruitment and Selection

	Recruitment	*Selection*
1.	To attract maximum number of applicants	To choose best out of them
2.	Process of creating application pool as large as possible (positive process)	Process through which more and more candidates are rejected (Negative Process)
3.	Here, techniques are not intensive	Here, specialised techniques are needed
4.	Outcome is the creation of application pool	Finalisation of candidates who are competent to do the job

Thus, recruitment acts as input to selection process.

Selection Process

This process involves several steps:

1. Application Pool	This is developed by recruitment process which acts as base for selection process.
2. Screening of Applications	Perspective employees have to fill up an application form having personal bio-data, qualifications, achievements, experiences, etc. Applicants are screened to locate qualified applicants for the job.
3. Selection Tests	These tests provide information about the aptitudes, interests and overall personality of the applicant.
4. Interview	These tests are followed by personal interview of applicant.
5. Checking the References	These references provide additional information about the applicant. These references may

	provide employers, persons associated with educational institutions of applicants, etc.
6. Physical Examination	Physical standards and fitness of perspective employees are ascertained through this examination.
7. Approval by Appropriate Authority	After recommendation of selection committee, the appropriate authority approves the recommendation of selection committee.
8. Final Selection	After this approval, the selection becomes final and selected candidate is informed accordingly.
9. Employment Contract	That employment contract between employer and employee establishes relationship between selected employee and organisation.
10. Evaluation	(a) During the Selection Process. The evaluation tries to measure the reliability and validity of various steps used in the selection process. (b) After the Process, the evaluation measures the outcomes of selection process in terms of performance of selected persons.

Brief Description of Selection Tests

(a) *Achievement Tests*: These tests measure what the applicant can do. Trade tests are a type of achievement test which measures the trade knowledge and skill of applicants.

(b) *Aptitude Tests*: In order to test particular talent, these tests are conducted. These may be learning or reasoning of mechanical. Several types of standardised tests are available.

(c) *Intelligent Tests*: These tests measure varied lands of mental ability which includes verbal, quantitative, spatial and reasoning aptitudes. Intelligence test, is normally referred as aptitude test. The score of this test is usually explained in the form of intelligent quotient (IQ) which can be calculated as follows:

$$IQ = \frac{\text{MentalAge}}{\text{ActualAge}} \times 100$$

(d) *Interest Tests*: These tests identify interest patterns of employees through interest inventory.

(e) *Personality Tests*: Individual value system, emotional state and maturity are measured through these tests. Questionnaire or projective can be used for conducting these tests.

In social administration, the professionals should be selected having competence, caring and commitment. Competence derives from professional training and previous successful experience. Caring is manifested in both verbal and non-verbal communication. Commitment involves person's desire to make a contribution to agency services and willingness to utilise his or her time and talents to do so, even if it means working time (Skidmore).

PERSONNEL POLICY OF ORGANISATION

The dictionary meaning of "policy" is a "plan of action". Policy is a man made rule of pre-determined course of action established to guide the performance of work toward the organisation objectives (Flippo). It is a pre-determined, selected course established as guide towards accepted goals and objectives (Yoder).

Personnel policy refers to principles and rules of conduct. These principles and rules of conduct formulate, redefine, break into details and decide a number of actions governing the relationship with employers in getting the objectives of organisation fulfilled.

Importance

The personnel policy (a) keeps the individuals on right direction for the fulfilment of personal objectives, (b) provide proper directions for a wide variety of employment relationships in the organisation, (c) translates the organisational objectives into selected routes, (d) provides general guidelines for healthy organisational procedures and practices, (e) brings out improvements between employee and employer relationships, and (f) indicates actions of an organisation.

Aims and Objectives

The general aim of personnel policy is to express top administrator's philosophy of human resources and to bring out convictions regarding worth and dignity of people in an organisation. The specific objectives are as follows:

1. Prepares organisation for the fulfilment of main objectives of policy of employment.
2. Provides information to employees regarding these objectives for securing their cooperation in fulfilment of these objectives.
3. Chalks out such conditions and procedure of employment which can enhance the belongingness of employees to the organisation.
4. Develops competent and trained staff for every level of organisation.
5. Gives protection to every member of organisation and recognises the role of employees' organisations in the organisation.
6. Makes arrangement for consultative participation.
7. Gives consultative service for the purpose of generating mutual faith among employees of organisation.
8. Develops bold and imaginative leadership.
9. Enforces discipline in organisation.
10. Provides security of employment to employees.
11. Gives an opportunity for growth in organisation.
12. Prevents waste of energy.

Sources of Personnel Policies

These are as follows:

1. Organisational practices prevailing in an organisation.
2. Prevailing practices in other connected organisations.
3. The philosophy of organisation.
4. Knowledge and experience governed from day-to-day practices.
5. Suggestions and complaints of employees.
6. Programmes of collective bargaining.
7. Legislative enactments.
8. Nature of economy of country.
9. International pressures.
10. Technology and environment of organisation.
11. Unionisation and values of employees.
12. Organisational objectives and goals.
13. Ethical background and considerations in and outside organisation.
14. Pronouncements of judgments by courts as well as awards of tribunals.
15. Social, political and cultural background of employees.

Coverage

In Indian organisations, personnel policy usually covers the following subjects:

1. Manpower planning and development.

2. Recruitment of hiring of employees.
3. Conditions of employment.
4. Working conditions.
5. Employer-employee relations as well as management-employee relations.
6. Communication system of organisation.
7. Maintenance of discipline and harmony in organisation.
8. Welfare, training and development of members of organisation.

Parts of Personnel Policy

First part is stated objectives showing commitments and convictions of top administration towards members of organisation.

Second part is the procedures for the attainment of these objectives.

Third part is rules and regulations arising from the policy and procedures for the purpose of indicating omissions and commissions to be observed by all levels of employees.

POLICY FORMULATION

This is a complex process involving different types of persons including experts.

First step: is to identify the problem area or situation involving all levels of organisation by involving existing personnel staff by studying documents, knowing the community and industry practices, review of prevailing conditions, etc.

Second step: is initiation of policy based on the details of identified problem area or situation.

Third step: Circulation of policy to the concerned members of organisation as well as sending it to top administration for their observations, comments, criticisms and suggestions.

Fifth step: Finalisation of policy draft in writing.

Sixth step: Adopting and launching it.

Seventh step: Sending and communicating it to all levels of organisation.

Eighth step: Administering it.

Ninth step: Follow-up action.

Tenth step: Evaluating it.

Eleventh step: Changing or modifying or reformulating policy.

ORIENTATION

It is a process of introducing new employee to the organisation, its activities and the overall environment. In case of social welfare organisation, the in-charge of the organisation (may be Director/Secretary/Chairman) should take the new employee to the whole building. He may explain the following things to the employee:

1. Historical background and activities/services of the organisation.
2. Rules, regulations and policies of organisation.
3. Structure of organisation and employee's position in the structure – employee's dealings with other members of organisation.
4. Facilities available to new employee regarding his/her conditions of work and working conditions.
5. Fringe benefits available to new employee.
6. Opportunities and challenges to be faced.
7. All information pertaining to key persons, clientele and community should be given to new employee in friendly and warm manners.

Besides this, the new employee may be asked to give his/her views or impressions regarding organisation and its activities.

MOTIVATION

It is an inner state of mind of employee which energises and activates those behaviour patterns among employees which directs or channelises to fulfilment of goals of organisation. For motivating employees, the social work administrators should do the following:

1. Understand what motivates employee and how this motivating force can best be harnessed.
2. Know the needs and wishes of employee and meet them in day-to-day functioning.
3. Practice or apply humane as well as sympathetic approach towards the solution of needs and minimisation of problems.
4. Establish policies for participation of the employees in decision making and its implementation.
5. Provide clear and full information to employees regarding their areas of work and interaction.
6. Assign responsibilities in such a way that each employee can contribute to a maximum extent.
7. Contribute in the professional development of employee.
8. Maintain a positive attitude towards employees.
9. Establish an atmosphere of cordiality leading to get maximum feedback from employees regarding executive policies and action.
10. Introduce proper scheme of incentives for good work.
11. Recognise the worth and dignity of individual employee.
12. Develop a feeling of belongingness in employees.

TRAINING

It is an investment in employee. Training refers to any process through which aptitudes, skills and abilities of employees are increased and updated in order to perform the jobs in an efficient and effective manners.

The main objective of training is to induce suitable change in the individual concerned and bridge the gap between existing performance ability and desired performance.

Levels of Training

Training is required for different levels of employees i.e. for unskilled workers, semi-skilled workers, skilled workers, office staff, supervisory staff and managerial personnel.

In social welfare/development organisation training is needed to persons involved in the management of organisation, officials running the office and field workers.

Methods of Training

These are as follows:

1. General Methods

(a) *The telling method* incorporates lectures in the form of classroom lectures. This method is suitable for giving information quickly.

(b) *The showing method* involves the actual demonstration of dramatization of lesson or content of training through playing the role by trainer himself.

(c) *Role playing* involves the participation of trainee in the activity of learning process. In reality he is made to do so.

(d) *The discussion method* involves participant in his training and allows him/her to interact with trainer by asking questions and making observations and bringing issues for discussion.

2. Specific Methods

(a) *On the job training*: This is conducted on the job since employee is supposed to learn things while doing or working.

(b) *Off the job*: This training is conducted on specific subject away from the job may be through conferences or case studies.

(c) *Understudy method*: Here, employee is given an understudy or assistant who, in addition to his day-to-day functions, is supposed to get some familiarity with the tasks and practices of his superior.

(d) *Role playing*: An employee learns by playing a role in dramatic setting which corresponds to his work.

(e) *Case study*: Content for reflection of practical interest is given by trainee in this method. It presents a diagnosis of situation and deals with real life difficulties.

Steps in Organisation of Training Programme

1. Need-assessment which involves discovering and assessing the needs of training. This needs identification of job aspects which need training.
2. Locating trainees refers the identification of employees to be trained.
3. Preparation of learner incorporates the things known to learner and things to be needed to learner.
4. Presentation of operations and knowledge. Here, the trainer should clearly inform, show, illustrate and question in order to put over the new knowledge and operations.
5. Testing and evaluating the programme which is done by (a) giving written tests to trainees, (b) observing trainee on the job, (c) finding out the reaction of individuals about training programme, and (d) knowing the opinion of senior level personnel about the performance of trainee.
6. Follow-up for knowing the effectiveness of training programme.

TERMS AND CONDITIONS OF SERVICE

These terms and conditions are necessary part of personnel policy. Each employee is supposed to work under these terms and conditions. Normally, a manual is developed having these conditions. These conditions contain hours of work, pay and allowances, probation, promotion, resignation, retirements, punishments, appeals, leaves and holidays (vacation leave, casual leave, sick leave, earned leave, general leave, personal leave, medical leave, special leave, etc.).

Probation Period

This period is the period which starts after joining the job by an employee. It may range from one year to two years. During this period the employee is:

(a) watched for his/her activities on the job,
(b) examined regarding his/her conduct, and
(c) evaluated overall performance of the employee.

Confirmation

After the completion of probation period, conformation of employee takes place. This makes employee full-fledged member of organisation and enjoys all facilities, i.e. provident fund, deductions, pension, bonus, etc. Confirmation of employee takes place after getting positive recommendation from the superior.

PROMOTION

Promotion provides flexibility and mobility of workforce to suit the requirements of organisation as well as fulfils the desires or aspirations of members of organisation.

Importance of Promotion

Promotion is important in the career of an employee due to following factors:

1. *Individuals are dynamic* so they want change in their jobs towards higher position due to their hard and devoted work.
2. *Investment consideration*: The employee invests his energy, skills and time in his job daily during a position of his life. Naturally, he rightly expects increasing returns from his job as time advances.
3. *Social responsibilities*: As the man grows, his individual, familial and social responsibilities also increase. For the fulfilment of these responsibilities he needs additional resources which individual can get through his job.
4. *Promotion as incentive*: Promotional opportunities in the organisation motivate the employee to work as devoted and dedicated matter. He puts his full efforts on the job and gets promotion. This enhances his belongingness to the organisation.
5. *Less labour turnover*: The system of promotion retains employee in the organisation, so frequent recruitments became out of question.
6. *No personnel hiring*: The competitive organisation fails to lure the employee if he gets proper advancement in his job in the organisation in which he is presently serving.

The Meaning of Promotion

The definitions given by writers are as follows:

1. *L.D. White*: Promotion means "an appointment from a given position to a more difficult type of work and greater responsibility accompanied by change of title and usually an increase in pay".
2. *Scott and Clothier*: "A promotion is a transfer of an employee to a job which pays more money or one that carried some preferred status".
3. *Pigors and Myres*: "A promotion is the advancement of an employee to all better in terms of greater responsibilities, more prestige a status, greater skill and specially increased rate of pay or salary".

Characteristics

These are as follows:

1. Promotion is upward advancement of employee in an organisation.
2. Involves change from one job/position to another.
3. Job/position normally has better status, pay and perks as compared to present job/position.

Types of Promotion

1. *Horizontal Promotion*: In this type, promotion enhances the responsibility, pay with change in designation.
2. *Vertical Promotion*: This type of promotion involves change in status, responsibility, job classification and pay. Here, the nature of job may completely be changed.
3. *Multiple Chain Promotion*: Here, employee gets several promotional avenues in the organisation.
4. *Dry Promotion*: It refers to change in status and responsibilities without any increase in pay or other financial benefits.

Purpose of Promotion

Promotion is generally given to:

1. put the employee in a position where he will be of a greater value to organisation and where he may derive increased personal satisfaction and income from his work.
2. recognise the performance of individual and reward him for his work so that he may have an incentive to forge ahead.
3. increase an organisational effectiveness.
4. build up morale, loyalty and sense of belonging on the part of employees when it is brought home to them that they would be promoted if they deserve it.
5. promote job satisfaction among employees and give them an opportunity for unbroken continuous service.
6. attract good employees.
7. ensure long service of employee to the organisation.
8. impress upon others that opportunities are open to them also in the organisation, if they performs well.
9. develop competent internal source of employees ready to take jobs at higher levels in changing environment.
10. develop competitive spirit among employees.
11. promote interest in training and development programmes of the organisation.
12. promote employee self-development.

Bases or Principles of Promotion

Promotion is based on seniority or merit or seniority-cum-merit. The details are as follows:

(A) Promotion Based on Seniority

Seniority refers to length of service in the organisation or in its various parts or in its departments or in a particular position.

Arguments in Favour of Seniority

These are as follows:

1. It is an objective test, since seniority is a matter of fact which is apt to be accepted.
2. Senior man is more experienced. Hence, more experience ordinarily should be enough qualifications for promotion.
3. It is a fair and just basis of promotion as everybody gets an opportunity for promotion.
4. Interference by influential persons can be avoided if this system of promotion is adopted.
5. It keeps the morale of employee boosted as they are sure of promotion at their turn.
6. Better type of persons may be attracted to the jobs when they are certain of promotion.
7. The seniority basis of promotion leads to automatic promotion.
8. The old employees, in particular stand for this system of promotion since young ones has no chance of promotion before them.
9. This principle/basis leads to an optimum utilisation of existing workforce by training and development.
10. This system is much more economical.

Defects or Demerits

1. It does not lead to the selection of best among eligibles.
2. No effort for self-improvement on the part of employee.
3. This system does not generate a feeling of competition among employees.
4. It does not attract competent people towards organisation.
5. It does not ensure the reaching to the higher positions by every person.
6. The work of individual is not recognised.
7. Due to fast changes in technology and communication systems, organisation needs new young blood having enthusiasm.

(B) Promotion on the Basis of Merit

Merit denotes an individual employee's skills, knowledge, ability, efficiency and aptitude. This basis of promotion considerations for promotion are employee's competencies irrespective of their length of service.

Arguments in Favour of Promotion Based on Merit

1. It brings rewards for meritorious work, extra competence and initiative.
2. It encourages employee to work hard so that he may get an opportunity for advancement.
3. It leads to increased productivity.

Defects

1. Measuring of merit is not an easy task.
2. Existence of feeling of distrust about judging of merit.
3. The techniques of measuring merit may be subjective.
4. It ignores the maturity of employees since with advancement in age; some emotional related competencies also increase.
5. The system also reduces the sense of belongingness to organisation.

(C) Promotion on the Basis of Merit-Cum-Seniority

Due to defects in both bases i.e. seniority and merit of promotion, some organisations adopt the policy of promotion on merit-cum-seniority basis in which following combinations of merit and seniority can be used.

1. Employee can be promoted out of all senior most employees having above the cut-off point in terms of merit.
2. Employee can be promoted on the basis of merit who has minimum length of service.
3. Employee can be promoted on seniority basis after excluding really incompetent senior employees.

An organisation can choose any combination. However, factors to be considered for promotion may be: (a) personal judgments of supervisor, (b) service records, (c) examination and interview, (d) seniority, (e) age, (f) skill, (g) initiative, (h) leadership, (i) loyalty towards organisation, and (j) cooperative nature of the worker.

Promotion Policy

Every organisation should have promotion policy. This policy should be linked to overall human resource policy. This promotion policy should have the following elements:

1. *Statement of Promotion Policy*: This statement should consist of procedure and sources of filling the positions of organisation.
2. *Routes of Promotion*: The organisation must decide about the channels of promotion at different levels of organisation having a

clear cut guidelines for the ladder up to which one particular position holder can go.

3. *Procedure of Promotion*: This policy should incorporate the procedure for initiation of promotion and person involved in taking decision about promotion.
4. *Basis of Promotion*: This policy should spell out the criteria of promotion i.e. seniority or merit or merit-cum-seniority.

After formulation of policy, it should be communicated to personnel concerned.

Criteria of Good Promotion Policy

1. It should have framed and implemented systematically.
2. It should be consistent and applied to all concerned personnel.
3. It should be fair and impartial.
4. It should be positively correlated with career of employee.

PERSONNEL RECORDS

Records are document of activities of organisation providing ready information and preserving for future reference or use. Personnel records are meant for the preservation of information regarding personnel in files and documents. These personnel records contain information on job analysis, evaluation and description of personnel, recruitment process, training, development, appraisal, promotion, transfer, discharge, dismissal, lay-off, disciplinary actions, wages, bonus, social security benefits, settlement of disputes etc. These records are important since—

1. These records make available the necessary information about personnel.
2. Information is preserved for future use.
3. These records help in preparing training and development programmes for personnel.
4. In case of revision of pay, perks and activities, these records are needed.
5. These records help in the advancement of employee in service.

Contents of Personnel Records

Name, Father's name, Date of birth, Place of birth, Age, Sex, Height, Weight, Nationality, Marital status, Language known, Present address, Permanent address, Designation, Date of appointment, Date of confirmation, Date when increment due, Department in which posted, Date of joining, Pension and

Provident Fund, Monthly contribution, When payable (in case of death), Members in the family, Ages of children (Sons/Daughters), Educational qualifications, Professional qualifications/Technical qualifications, Promotion (To… With effect from…), Transfers (To… From…), Leave records, Medical examination, Performance appraisal, Warning, Date, Remarks, etc.

Essential of Good Records

1. The objective of records should be clear.
2. Consistency in preparation and maintenance.
3. Records should be kept at secured place.
4. Records should be easily accessible.
5. Easily identified and differentiated.
6. Sufficient information should be collected and maintained.
7. Duplication of entries in different records should be avoided.
8. Records should be kept under a person.
9. A procedural manual should be maintained.

Social welfare agencies are supposed to maintain personnel record for each employee. This record should have application, references, academic and experience documents, appointment process, pay perks, leave record, correspondence, periodic assessment etc.

PERSONNEL EVALUATION

The performance of people is a complex product of personnel interest, qualifications, commitment and expectations on the one hand, and of the employment environment, working conditions, supervision, leadership, opportunity and challenge on the other (Mamoria).

Personnel evaluation refers to examination and evaluation of personnel staff as well as employees. For this, following things are necessary:

1. The evaluation is related to job performance.
2. It should be conducted periodically.
3. Employee should take part in this process.
4. Proper recording should be done regarding all aspects of evaluation.
5. It should be a part of confidential record of agency/organisation and be remained available to employee concerned.
6. It should be used for the development of personnel.

Kahle presents a comprehensive statement of factors to be covered in evaluation of staff.

1. The purpose of evaluation explaining why, for whom and for what purpose evaluation is being conducted.

2. Responsibilities assigned and responsibilities carried out.
3. General aspects (strengths and weaknesses)
   (a) Extent of possession of professional expertise, tendency of keeping himself informed of new developments as well as increasing of existing knowledge.
   (b) Working knowledge of the problems and structures and of key groups and individuals in his community.
   (c) Qualitative aspects of the performance.
   (d) Manner of organisation and preparation of work.
4. Specific (qualitative) aspects (strengths and weaknesses)

(A) Service to the Board or Governing Body

1. Wellness of relating to the board members.
2. Ability of communicating of ideas clearly and receipt of communication from others.
3. Capacity of employee to evolve members of board meaningfully in planning, policy making, interpretation and overall operations of the agency.
4. Ability to inform board adequately.
5. Acceptance by board the general attitude of employee.
6. Extent of providing leadership for the competition of activities of board.

(B) Service to the Staff

1. How well does he relate to staff?
2. Does he understand their work and the problems that arise from their work?
3. Does he use personnel appropriately?
4. Does he delegate authority and responsibility appropriately?
5. Does he communicate well with staff?
6. Does he encourage and use staff participation in planning, policy making and operations?
7. Does he contribute to staff development?
8. Is he fair in actions relating to personnel practices?

(C) Service to Community

1. How effective is he in his relations with funding bodies?
2. How effective is he in his activities with planning bodies?
3. How effective is he in his relations with other public voluntary organisations?
4. How effective is he in community and social action?

5. Is he effective in public relations and community education?
6. How is he viewed by his peers in other agencies?

(D) Service to the Agency Programme

1. Does he play soundly?
2. Is he creative and innovative?
3. Does he assume the appropriate responsibility by making decisions?
4. Does he organise well?
5. Does he use agency resources well?
6. Is he effective in keeping the agency's programme related to current community needs?
7. Does he demonstrate effective leadership of the agency staff?
8. Does he understand and use the budgeting process effectively?
9. Does he demonstrate ability in developing physical and financial resources?

Summary and Recommendations (Overall Evaluation)

Evaluation Form: Carlisle has given following sample graphic form for evaluation of staff:

Name .... Job Title ....
Department .... No. of Months/Years in
Position .... Circle Appropriate Rating

	Unsatis-factory	*Fair*	*Good*	*Supe-rior*	*Exce-llent*
Knowledge: Extent of knowledge and practical know-how that relates to the job	1	2	3	4	5
Judgment: Capacity to analyse facts and to make responsible decision	1	2	3	4	5
Attitude: Cooperative and willing. Loyal to company and enthusiastic about job	1	2	3	4	5
Leadership: Sets goals and motivates others to achieve them	1	2	3	4	5
Initiative: Works independently and strives to improve plans and follows through	1	2	3	4	5

(Contd.)

	Unsatis-factory	Fair	Good	Supe-rior	Exce-llent
Dependability: Trustworthy and reliable in carrying out assignments.	1	2	3	4	5
Interpersonal relations: Gets along well with associate cooperative.	1	2	3	4	5
Quality of work: Is accurate and through. Work requires little checking.	1	2	3	4	5
Quality of work: Accomplishes required work. Works quickly and achieve goals.	1	2	3	4	5
Comments and Recommendations					
Signed by Rater…….	Employee Signature…….				
Date………………………………	Date………………………………				

8

Directing

Directing is an important managerial function since for the satisfactory completion of work, proper orders should be issued and subordinates should be motivated to accept those orders and complete their assignments accordingly.

MEANING OF DIRECTING

The definitions of directing are being presented here:

Haimann: "Directing consists of the process and techniques utilised in issuing instructions and making certain that operations are carried out on as originally planned".

Koontz and O'Donnell: "Directing is the interpersonal aspect of managing by which subordinates are led to understand and contribute effectively and efficiently to the attainment of enterprise objectives".

CHARACTERISTICS

1. Directing is a process.
2. In this process, instructions are given and orders are issued by superior.
3. Superior has to lead and motivate subordinate.
4. The purpose is the smooth and effective running of operations in organisation.
5. Fulfilment of objectives of organisation.
6. Establishment of effective communication network.
7. The subordinates are supervised for completing the operations of organisation.

Thus, directing is process in which orders are issued and executed by leading and motivating members of organisation.

FEATURES OF EFFECTIVE DIRECTING

These are as follows:

1. *Harmony of objectives*: The functioning of organisation becomes effective when goals of members of organisation are in complete harmony with organisational goals.
2. *Unity of command*: As per this principle, subordinates should receive orders and instructions from one superior only.
3. *Direct supervision*: Superior must have face-to-face direct contact with his subordinates.
4. *Efficient communication*: Communication is an instrument of directing since it is through this process, superior gives orders, allocate jobs, explain responsibilities and ensures performance.
5. *Follow-through*: Directing involves not only telling subordinates to do the things but seeing the doing of subordinates as per desired way also.

GIVING ORDERS

Order is a device employed by a line manager in directing his immediate subordinates to start an activity, stop it and modify it.

Basic principles of giving orders are as follows:

(a) Clear and complete order
(b) It should be compatible with the purpose of the organisation.
(c) It should be compatible with employee's personal interest.
(d) Order should be operationally feasible.
(e) Order should be prepared in advance.
(f) For long distance orders, face-to-face suggestions are feasible.
(g) Order should be integral part of the situation.

Mode of communication of order is either verbally or in writing. Written orders are appropriate when (a) subject is important, (b) varied kinds of details are involved, and (c) if there exists, geographical distance between order giver and recipients.

METHODS OF ENSURING COMPLIANCE OF ORDERS

1.	Force	–	Employee will be punished if he does not follow orders.
2.	Paternalism	–	Employee develops a feeling of gratitude toward the manager who provides reward first and expects compliance to follow.

3.	Bargain	–	Here, the control of manager is reduced gradually.
4.	Harmony of objectives	–	Here, complete compliance of order takes place, if there is harmony of objectives between order giver and order receiver.

LEADERSHIP

Administrative leadership is an important aspect in organisational structure, since in a welfare state this leadership has an urgent place in establishing a planned, democratic and socialistic society. The welfare state strives for the establishment of social welfare institutions in the field of health education, housing, nutrition, upliftment of weaker and vulnerable sections of society. This throws a lot of challenges to administration which can be met through effective administrative leadership.

Definitions

Some definitions are as follows:

1. Millett: "Leadership is often thought of as being primarily personal in character, as being founded upon individual pre-eminence or accomplishment in a particular field of endeavour, superior strength, superior cunning, superior intelligence, superior knowledge, superior determination – any or all of these may be means to the attainment of leadership".
2. Keith Davis: "Leadership is a part of management but not all of it. A manager is required to plan and organise, but all we ask of leaders is that they influence others to follow… Leadership is the ability to persuade others to seek defined objectives enthusiastically. It is the human factor which binds a group together and motivates towards goals. Management activities such as planning, organising and decision-making are dominant cocoons until the leader triggers the power of motivation and guides them towards goals".
3. Terry: "Leadership is the activity of influencing people to strive willingly for group objectives".

Characteristics

1. It is individual pre-eminence.
2. It indicates special talent or quality in individual.
3. It guides others who may become followers or being led to accomplish some goals.

4. Administrative leadership can be developed and learned.

Thus, leadership is an art and process of influencing people so that they will strive, willingly and enthusiastically with zeal and confidence, towards the achievement of the group goals.

Theories of Leadership

These can be divided into four categories: (a) Trait theories, (b) Behavioural theories, (c) Situational theories, and (d) Skill theory.

(A) Trait Theories

These theories stress on importance of personality traits as related to leadership. Here, traits are grouped into four categories, (a) physical qualities such as sound health, vitality, endurance, etc., (b) psychological qualities as enthusiasm, forcefulness, ability to inspire, tact etc., (c) intellectual traits such as high intelligence, sound judgment, scientific approach, ability to teach etc., and (d) qualities of character such as integrity, fair play, moral courage, etc.

This is known as 'Great Man' theory also.

(B) Behavioural Theories

These theories view that leadership is performance of those acts which help the group to achieve such preferred outcomes as improved quality of interaction, to build cohesiveness to make resources available to the group and to increase its effectiveness.

Three different schools, the Harvard School, the Ohio School and the Michigan School made attempts to measure what a leader actually does in a group. As a result, they came to the conclusion that there are two distinct styles of leadership, known as job-centred and employee-centred styles of leadership.

(C) Situational Theory

According to this theory, leaders are products of a given situation. This theory incorporates that people tend to follow these in whom they perceive a means of accomplishing their personal desires, and the leader recognises these desires and undertakes activities to fulfil these desires.

Fiedler's Contingency Theory

Fiedler and his associates at the University of Illinois have suggested this theory in which features of trait theory and situational theories have been combined to some extent. Here, it was maintained that people become leaders not only because of attributes of their personality but also because of various situational factors and interaction between the leaders and situation.

Critical Dimensions of Situation Affecting a Leader's Most Effective Style

These are as follows:

(a) *Power of positions* which refers the power inherent in the position of leadership. This power encompasses rewards and punishments related to positions, authority vested in position in hierarchical order of organisation, and the support leader get from his superiors in organisation.

(b) *Task structure* means extent of clarity in tasks leading to better control on quality performance and making group member more responsible for accomplishment of tasks.

(c) *Leader-member relations*: This refers to degree of confidence the subordinates possess in the person as leader. Loyalty towards leader and attractiveness of followers also determine the effectiveness of leader.

4. *Skill Theory*: It is said that leadership in business requires three kinds of skills:

   (a) *Technical skills*: Person having better technical knowledge and greater proficiency, command greater acceptability, respect, obedience and loyalty from his followers.

   (b) *Human relations skills*: This refers to understanding of people for better interacting with them as well as handling them for the fulfilment of their desires as well as organisational objectives.

   (c) *Conceptual skills*: These skills refer to the possession of vision regarding environmental, technological, economic and social developments, its impact on business and people and initiate actions accordingly.

LEADERSHIP STYLE

The style of leaders refers the perception of subordinates of the behaviour patterns consistency used by leaders while at work with other subordinates. These styles are affected by the (a) value system of an individual; (b) the degree of confidence in his subordinates; (c) personal inclination; and (d) feelings of security in situation of uncertainty (Tannenbaum and Schmidt).

These styles are as follows:

1. *Authoritarian*: In this style:

(a) everything including policy making is decided by leader;

(b) the leader does not take part in group activities; and

(c) rewards, punishments, praises, criticisms, etc. are done at personal level.

2. *Paternalistic*: In this style, leader:

(a) decides about policy, techniques, methods, activities with giving advice as per need;
(b) allots the task;
(c) participates occasionally/symbolically in group activities; and
(d) praises, criticises, awards and punishments at personal level.

3. *Democratic*: Here leader—

(a) makes policies after discussing with the group;
(b) finalises goals, techniques, activities etc. after group discussion having technical advice provided by him;
(c) leaves the division of tasks and manner of their execution on the group;
(d) remains objective yet involved with group;
(e) takes part symbolically in group activities;
(f) praises and criticises objectively based on facts; and
(g) provides awards publically and punishes privately.

4. *Autocratic*: Here,

(a) policies are decided by another person/group representing employer;
(b) existing rules and regulations are strictly followed in taking up techniques, methods and activities; as well as allotment of tasks and group activities; and
(c) participates in group activities, praises and criticises when rules and regulations demand from the leader for these activities.

5. *Laissez Faire*: In this style,

(a) complete freedom to group to frame policies with minimum interference from leader;
(b) supply of information takes place when leader is asked for;
(c) leader does not take active part in discussions and allotment of tasks;
(d) leader does not attempt to appraise or regulate activities of group; and
(e) leader makes spontaneous though infrequent comments.

6. *Authoritative*: In this style of leadership,

(a) policies are decided jointly by leader and group, but with final say of leader;
(b) targets, techniques etc. are decided by group discussion;
(c) leader leads the participation of group members in group activities and things are decided jointly;

(d) leader exercises his authority to guide and train; and
(e) he criticises/praises member objectively based on facts related to the performance of tasks.

In short, it can be maintained that there may be two styles of leadership i.e. directive and participative.

1. Directive style

Here, leader uses his authority and direct the group members for accomplishment of goals without their participation in policy and decision making.

Main advantages of the style are:

(a) central controlling and coordinative system;
(b) clarity and consistency in policy making, interpretation and implementation;
(c) quick decision-making process;
(d) strong leadership; and
(e) more emphasis on formalism.

The limitations are:

(a) low level of motivation and morale among employees due to closed supervision;
(b) lack of opportunities for people to their capacities;
(c) lack of understanding due to one-way communication; and
(d) feeling of inflexibility and alienation.

2. Participative style

In this style, group members participate in deciding policies and decisions of the organisation under the guidance of leader.

The advantages are:

(a) high level of motivation and morale of employees leading to fulfil their psychological needs; (b) skill and knowledge of the group are effectively used; (c) more commitment among employees towards their activities; (d) worth and dignity of individual are recognised; (e) more information to people; (f) two-way communication is established; and (g) more belongingness of employees towards organisation.

The limitations are:

(a) it is time consuming in decision-making;
(b) inaction on the part employees;

(c) lack of feeling of creativity and innovativeness on the part of leader due to fear of non-implementation or resistance from employees; and

(d) successful under the condition when employees have equal or approximately equal knowledge and expertise as compared to their leader.

Skills of Leadership in Social Administration

For effective leadership in social administration, the leader should have following skills:

1. The leader should have skill of persistence which involves thoughtfulness, planning, making appropriate proposals through making decisions. He should try again and again for getting his proposals approved and implemented.
2. The leader should have skill of time management which involves respect for the value of time and utilise it effectively and perfectly.
3. Leader should be equipped with skill of compromise which refers that he should have open mind and discuss openly with group members and reach an agreement in case of disagreement within group.
4. Skill of soft touch should be exercised by leader which refers that he should allow each worker as much freedom as possible within the framework of goals, needs, policies of organisation.
5. Skill of creativity which calls for a leader to think and act in original manner by spending time for contemplating and planning new, effective ways of improving organisational services (Skidmore).

COMMUNICATION

Communication acts as a blood circulation in organisation. In social work administration, communication is important since, (1) it is basis for social interaction which is fundamental to all human activity in organisation; (2) it is the primary means for people to obtain and exchange information , since quality and quantity of information affect the decisions and functioning of administrator/manager; (3) it consumes most of the time of manager/ administrator shows its importance; (4) it gives power and importance to person in the organisation, since who have more information he/she is bound to contact by many and several times; (5) it enhances effectiveness of organisation because effectiveness depends upon sharing information, views and feelings among staff members; (6) it improves efficiency of staff members since through communication they can openly share, think and feel about procedures, methods, policies, goals of organisation and their aspirations; and (7) it boosts morale in organisation since the leader and employees come on same wave length through communication.

Meaning of Communication

The word communication has been derived from the Latin word 'communis' which means 'to share or to make common'.

The following are some definitions of communication:

1. *C.W. Redfield*: "By communication we mean here the broad field of human interchange of facts and opinions and not the working of the telephone, telegraph, radio and the like".
2. *V.P. Shintre*: "Communication includes all methods of transmitting information and opinions. The term also is used to refer to a particular message".
3. *Dale Yader*: "Communication means the exchange of thoughts, ideas, information and opinions".
4. *M.L. Blum*: "Communication, therefore, must be regarded as two way process in which employer and employee has equal opportunity to convey their meaning, their feelings and their actions to each other".
5. *Batty*: "This function is the transmitting of instructions and information to all interested parties – employers, customers, suppliers, shareholders and general public".

Characteristics

A review of the above definitions brings out following characteristics of the concept of communication:

1. Communication is a two-way process.
2. There are two or more persons.
3. It has contents.
4. It has media and methods.
5. It directs actions and guides interactions.

In this way, communication is the process and capacity of an individual or group to convey information, ideas and feelings to another individual or group and where necessary to evoke discriminatory response.

Types of Communication

It can be divided into verbal and non-verbal communication

(a) *Verbal Communication*: It refers to the spoken word, that is, what one says and another person listens. In social work administration this communication can take place in meetings, conferences, interviews, face-to-face instructions/orders involving two or more persons. In informal situations such as tea breaks, canteens, informal discussions, it also exists.

(b) *Non-verbal Communication*: It involves body gestures, that is, movement of eyes, posture, gait, speaking style, pitch of voice, clear (specially readiness) of cheeks, tears and movement in lips.

(c) *Written Communication*: In this information is shared in writing in variety of ways that is, in the forms of messages, instructions, orders, circulars, etc.

Communication Process

This process involves three elements.

1. *Sharing* refers the sending and receiving information which happens verbally, non-verbally or in written form. The information can travel from top to down and from down to top and sideways.
2. *Understanding* involves the exactness of the receipt of information, that is, whether information has been received or understood or heard exactly as it has been sent.
3. *Clarifying* is the element which contributes in establishing effective communication in the organisation.

Components of Communication Process

These have been given by different writer:

1. Shanon and Weaver

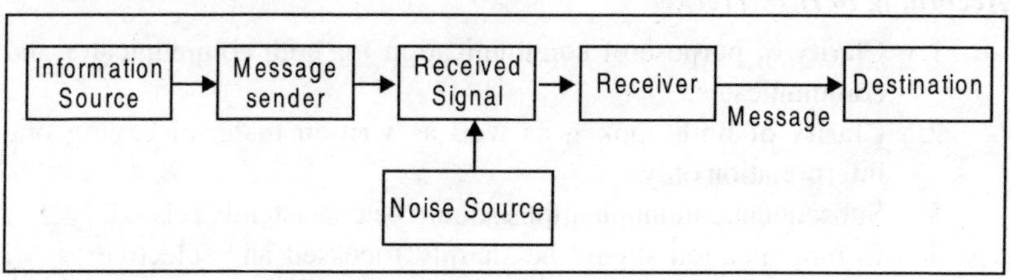

2. D.K. Berlo

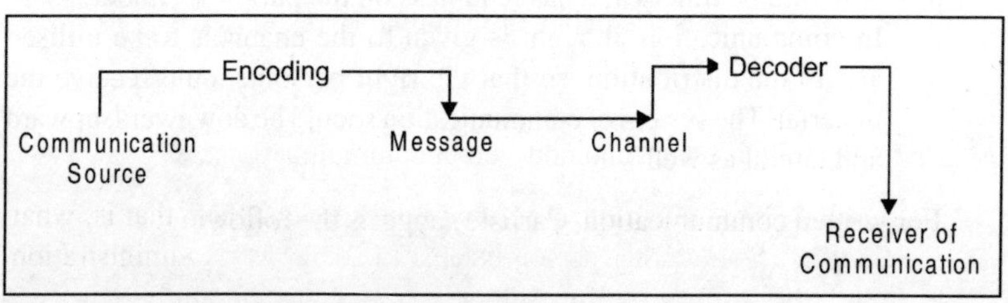

3. Fulmer

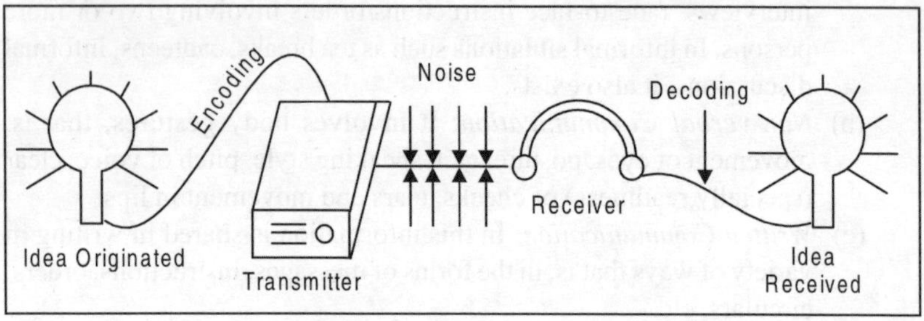

Thus, it can be concluded that communication process has following elements:

1. *Communicator.* For making communication there may be a speaker, sender, issuer, information giver, feedback maker, gossiper etc.
2. *Transmission.* There is transmission in the forms of sayings, sending, suggesting, objecting, gossiping etc.
3. *Communicatee.* To whom transmission is done, may be respondent, audience, addressee, receivers. The purpose is to influence the behaviour of communicatee.
4. Response in forms of reply, reaction, reporting, etc. (C.E. Redfield).

Effectiveness of Communication Process

Several suggestions have been offered for making communication process effective. Some of them are as follows:

According to H.B. Trecker

1. Clarity of purpose of communication for both communicator and communicatee.
2. Clarity of both spoken as well as written material having one interpretation only.
3. Subsequent communications should be consistently related.
4. Communication should be sharply focussed and selective as per content as well as adequately accomplish the purpose.
5. It should be timely and has readiness on the part of recipient.
6. In communication, thought is given to the channels to be utilised and to the distribution, so that the right person should receive the material. The system of communication should be downward, upward and lateral as well.

For written communication, Carlisle suggests the following:

1. Outline the message beforehand to be sure it has been logically thought through.
2. Draft the message with the receiver or audience in mind.
3. Give the message a concise title and use subheadings where appropriate.
4. Use simple words and short, clear sentences.
5. Attempt to summarise the content or significant of the message in first few sentences or paragraphs.
6. Back-up your opinions with facts.
7. Avoid "oversell" and flowery language.
8. Summarise your major points at the end.

To conclude, five Cs given by Fulmer can be quoted. These are as follows:

1. *Clarity*: Ambiguity makes it possible for people to give different signals and directions, even at the same time. Messages should be simple and clear. Only one idea or feeling should be presented at a time.
2. *Completeness*: An instruction that is only partially complete is difficult to follow. Effective communication includes a beginning, a middle and an end.
3. *Conciseness*: The shorter a presentation, the better, as long as it covers the subject. Both executives and workers are more likely to read one paragraph statement than a twenty page document; they are more likely to read a one-page than a ten-page memorandum.
4. *Concreteness*: Communication should be on target. It should be very specific, citing names and expectations, so that no misunderstanding arises.
5. *Correctness*: If false information is reported, difficulties ensue from the outset. Accuracy is essential (quoted by Skidmore).

Media and Methods of Communication

Communication is the transmitting of information and instruction to all interested parties which incorporates media and methods of transmitting information by anyone with a view to making oneself understood (Shintrey).

(a) Visual Media

In usual written media, the methods are used namely (1) personal message; (2) circulars; (3) manuals; (4) handbooks; (5) bulleting board notices and announcements; (6) newsletters; (7) pamphlets; (8) signs; (9) employee publication; and (10) standard forms.

In visual-pictorial media, the methods are (1) pictures; (2) photographs; (3) diagrams; (4) maps and pictographs.

In written pictorial media, the methods are: (1) posters, (2) silent films, (3) film strips and (4) cartoons.

In symbolic media, methods used are (1) insignia, (2) flags, (3) lights, and (4) other signals.

(b) Audio Media

In face-to-face situation, the methods are (1) conversation, (2) interviews, (3) committees, and (4) conferences.

In intermediate contacts, the methods have been: (1) telephone, (2) radio, (3) public contact system, and (4) intercom.

In symbolic media, the methods may be: (1) buzzer; (2) bells and (3) other signals.

(c) Audio-Visual media

Here comes, (1) television, (2) demonstration and (3) other signals.

Communication Barriers

These are as follows:

1. There is always some difference in experience and background of communicator and recipient.
2. The communicator is sometimes not able to communicate at a time when it is needed by recipient or in the manner in which the recipient wants.
3. The beliefs and attitudes influence the message.
4. Emotional state of mind and way of thinking may influence the message.
5. Lack of recipient's faith in communicator mars the effectiveness of communication.
6. Sometimes, respondents are unable to understand the meaning of message.
7. Different people may take the same word differently owing to their socio-cultural and personality differences.
8. Symbolic meanings can be assigned to messages.
9. Symbolic communication (through gestures) is difficult to understand.
10. Fear of authority in subordinates and authoritarian attitude of superiors.
11. Lack of opportunity to express view point of subordinates.
12. Over-business of communicator with multifarious activities in organisation.
13. Lack of feeling of cooperation, system of coordination and collaboration in organisation.

14. Absence of suitable media and methods of communication in organisation.
15. Difficulty in getting feedback from subordinates.

MOTIVATION

The thinking, values, goals, meeting of biological and social needs as well as capabilities of individual determines action, reaction and inaction in a person. The drive and motivation determine the behaviour patterns of individual in organisation and this act as base for effective functioning of the organisation.

Meaning of Motivation

Derived from Latin word 'emovere' meaning 'to move', motivation acts as driving force for initiating action as well as its continuation by a person. Few definitions of motivation are as follows:

1. *Leavitt.* "Motivation is a concept which is linked to the three basic assumptions that human behaviour is caused, human behaviour is goal oriented and human behaviour is motivated".
2. *Stanley Vanace*. "Motivation influences any motion or desire which so conditioned one's will that the individual is propelled into action".
3. *Berelson* and *Steiner* have defined the term motives as "an inner state that energies, activates or moves (and hence motivation) and that directs or channels behaviour towards goals".
4. *Dale* and *Beach*. Motivation is "a willingness" to expand energy to achieve a goal or reward.
5. *Shartle*. Motivation is "a reported urge or tension to move in a given direction or to achieve certain goals".

Characteristics

A review of above definitions brings out the following characteristics:

1. The motivation is psychological rather than logical, it is primarily on emotional process rather than thinking process;
2. the motivation is fundamentally an unconscious process or at least very important part of it;
3. not only do motives differ from person to person, but in any individual they vary from time to time;
4. motivation is a social process since our actions and needs are influenced from the moment of birth by people around us,
5. in most of our daily actions we are guided by habits established by motivational processes that were active many years earlier; and

6. motivation is individual in nature since knowledge of needs common to people in general maybe used only as a point of departure in dealing with individual.

Objectives of Motivation

Some writers have given their views regarding these objectives:

1. *Skinner* said motivation makes individual to learn positive behaviour which is known as desirable behaviour also.
2. *Maslow* maintained that motivation always generates need for individual since satisfaction of one need creates another higher need.
3. *Herzberg* reported that motivation provides opportunities to individual to be a better expert on his/her job, more demanding assignments, a feeling of control on his/her work rather than to be supervised.
4. *Maclelland* presented an opinion that the objective of motivation is to create a strong desire in a person through which he/she enjoys the accomplishment of work and facing of challenges in place of monetary or other awards.
5. *Victor Vroom* opined that motivation acts as a means of communication for establishing positive values in the personality of employees resulting into enhancement of efficiency by good performance.

Thus, motivation generates a positive attitude in person and drives his/her forward towards accomplishment of goals.

Types of Motivation

Two types of motivation:

I. Negative Motivation

Traditionally, this type of motivation assumes that man basically has an attitude of pleasure seeking of laziness and wants to keep away from work, so efficiency can only be improved through fear and direct him/her in pre-determined way. Thus, the motivation consists of use of force for taking work from people. This involves close supervision and fear of firing in case he/she fails to deliver as per norms set beforehand.

However, this type of motivation may get success for sometimes but in the long run it creates hostile attitude among people resulting into unfavourable attitude towards job.

II. Positive Motivation

Adoption of good human relations in the organisation is the crux of this type of motivation. It established an atmosphere in which individual talent flourishes and enhances informal communications. This motivation is basically reward oriented and either extrinsic or intrinsic.

The extrinsic motivators are related to the situation which comes after completion of work and intrinsic motivators are related to the performance of work.

Theories of Motivation

These theories are as follows:

(A) Content Theories

1. *Traditional Theory*. This theory has been evolved from the work of F.W. Taylor. This theory is based on the assumption that money is the primary motivator of people, so financial rewards are directly related to performance. The reward is great enough, employees will produce more. Here, the fallacy that all men were identical units in the production process.
2. *Need Hierarchy Theory*. Abraham H. Maslow has developed this theory. According to him, five basic needs are related to one another and constitute a hierarchy in terms of motivation, starting with
   - (i) physiological or physical needs which are compelling needs such as food, sleep, water, exercise, clothing, shelter and so forth and progressive through—
   - (ii) safety and security needs which are concerned with protection against danger, threat or deprivation;
   - (iii) affection or belonging needs which include love, affection, belonging, respect and acceptance;
   - (iv) self-esteemed needs which include both self-esteem and the esteem of others; and finally
   - (v) self-fulfilment needs which are the highest order needs in Maslow's hierarchy, the needs of people to read their full potential in terms of their abilities and interests. These needs are concerned with the will to operate at the optimum and thus receive the rewards that are the result of that attainment. The rewards may be not only economic and social but also mental.
3. *ERG Theory*. Clyto Alderfer has given the concept of existence, relatedness and growth (ERG) which condenses Maslow' hierarchy of needs into these three main areas. Here, existence is equivalent to physiological and safety need-levels, relatedness to social level and growth to esteem and self-actualisation levels (Emse).
4. *Motivation and Hygiene Theory (or Two Factor Model)*. The researches, conducted by Herzberg, Mausner and Syderman, have

propounded this theory which envisages the following:

(a) There are factors surrounding employment that tended to satisfy the employee and thus produce positive motivation. These factors have been labelled as 'satisfiers' or 'motivation factors'. These factors include (i) achievement in a task; (ii) recognition for task; (iii) advancement; (iv) the challenging nature of task; (v) responsibility for the task; and (vi) professional growth and advancement in task responsibility. The last three are important and related to work itself.

(b) There are other factors that produce negative motivation and these factors tend to override the positive motivational factors if they produce a negative response in the individual or group. These factors have been labelled as 'dis-satisfiers', 'maintenance factors', 'hygiene factors'. These factors include: (i) incompetent and cold supervision; (ii) poor company policies and administration; (iii) criticism or blame (negative motivation); (iv) poor working conditions; (v) pay, fringe benefits; and job security. These factors do not produce motivation but can prevent motivation from accruing.

(c) Herzberg believes that for solution of motivation problem is to adopt a meaningful approach to positive motivation of employees is through 'job enrichment' which involves upgrading the job by adding motivator factors.

This theory was criticised on the grounds that it is not universally acceptable since it was concerned with white collar employees only, and it ignores environment factors. But, it is pertinent to note that this theory has thrown new light on the content of work motivation.

5. *Achievement, Affiliation and Power Motivation Theory* Developed by David McClelland, this theory holds that all people have three needs. They are as follows:

1. The need for achievement – to drive, to excel, to achieve in relation to a set standards, to strive to succeed.
2. The need for affiliation – the desire for friendly and close interpersonal relationships, need to belong, to be close to people, to be friends.
3. *The need for power – which seeks to influence people and events.* These needs are not arranged in progression. As per this theory the most of the people have a degree of each of these needs but that the level of intensity varies. These needs are learned through experience.

The administrator is supposed to recognise the dominating

needs in both themselves and their employees and to effectively integrate these differences.

6. *Theories X and Y.* Professor Douglas McGregor propounded the idea that managers appealed to either their employees' lower level needs or higher level needs, depending on what the manager visualised their employees' needs to be. McGregor has given theory 'X' and theory 'Y'.

   Theory 'X' is based on authoritative management approach in which a harsh attitude based on the following belief is taken by manager.

   1. The average human being inherently dislikes work and will resort to all kinds of self-serving and disruptive tactics to avoid it.
   2. Due to this inherent dislike of work by the people, they have to be coerced, directed or made to work by threat of punishment if the desired work is to be accomplished.
   3. The average person responds to these threats and controls because he wants security above all to other factors in his job.

Theory 'Y' is based on the fact that employees have feelings and they should be treated as human being. The assumptions underlying theory 'Y' are as follows:

1. Employees can have the opinion that work is as natural as rest or play.
2. If employees are committed to the goal of organisation, then self-direction and self-control may be exercised by them.
3. Average person want and accept learning and even ready to accept responsibility.
4. Employees may also be involved in creativity; it is not the sole domain of managerial functions.

The role of administrator in the application of theory 'Y' is to establish work conditions that promote cooperation and enthusiasm.

Process Theories

1. Expectancy Theory

This theory was originally developed by Edward Tolman as a part of purposive psychology of behaviour. Victor Vroom was first to relate the theory of motivation in the work environment which was expanded and refined by Porter and Lawler and others.

According to Vroom, motivation is the product of three factors: (1) how much one wants a reward (valence), one's estimate of probability that effort will result in successful performance (expectancy) and one's estimate that performance will result in receiving the reward (instrumentality). This is the form formula.

$$\text{Motivation} = \text{Valence} \times \text{Expectancy} \times \text{Instrumentality}$$

$$M = V \times E \times I$$

Valencerefers to the strength of an individual's preference for particular outcome. Value, incentive, attitude and expected utility are other terms for valence. The valance may be both positive and negative.

Expectancy	it is the strength of belief that an act will be followed by particular outcomes. Expectancies are stated as probabilities.
Instrumentality	represents the employees' belief that reward will be received once that task is accomplished.

This theory is relevant for administrator since it explains what that administrator should do to motivate employees. The administrator must be able to identify employee's goals, must be able to offer rewards which are attainable and must be willing to help the employee by providing him or her with the training, facilities, tools and other support necessary to achieve favourable performance.

The Porter-Lawler Model

This model points out the effort (motivation) does not directly lead to performance. More important is what happens after the performance. The rewards that follow and how these are perceived will determine satisfaction. Thus, in this model of motivation, satisfaction and performance are all separate variables.

2. *Equity Theory*

This theory says that people are motivated by the desire for fair and equitable treatment. Equity can be seen in operation when employees complain about doing more work than others at less pay. It is always subjective and relative and it involves more than one person. First, an employee is hired into the organisation based upon a ratio of outputs to inputs.

Inputs variables are age, sex, social status, organisational pattern and how hard the person works. Outputs are rewards such as pay, status and promotion. The ratio is based upon the person's perception of what the person is giving (inputs) and receiving (outcomes) versus the ratio of what the relevant other is giving and receiving. If the person's perceived ratio is not equal to the others, he will strive to restore the ratio of equity. This striving to restore equity is the work motivation.

3. Attribution Theory and Locus of Control

According to Kelly, it is mainly concerned with the cognition processes by which an individual interprets behaviour as being caused by (attributed to) certain parts of the relevant environment. It is concerned with the why questions of motivation and behaviour.

4. Stimulus-Response Theory

This is known as 'Reinforcement Theory' also. As per this theory, human behaviour can best be understood by studying the relationship between stimuli and response. Stimuli have been defined as events or activities that modify behaviour. This is also believed that future responses (new behaviour) will depend upon how a person reinforces for the real responses. There are two types of reinforce as: (a) positive reinforcers are actions following the desired outcome that strengthen the behaviour, and (b) negative reinforcers are actions that strengthen the desired behaviour by removing the undesirable consequences.

5. Core Job Theory

The theory identifies three critical psychological states, that is, experienced meaningfulness of the work, the experienced responsibility for the outcomes and the knowledge of actual results. These three critical psychological states are affected by five core dimensions namely, skill variety, task identity, task significance, authority in work and feedback from the job itself. The more of these five core dimensions that are present in a job, the higher the probability that the person doing the job will experience the personal outcomes.

6. The Global Theory

This theory believes that goals influence behaviour and if an administrator helps an employee in setting of clear and meaningful goals, he brings about motivation.

Conclusion: There are several things that an administrator can do to affect employee motivation. Some of the most useful of these are to (i) make the work interesting, (ii) relate rewards to performances; (iii) provide valued rewards; (iv) treat employees as individuals; (v) encourage participation and cooperation; (vi) provide accurate and timely feedback; (vii) establish a democratic, participatory climate conducive for developing and enriching personal interests; (viii) provide opportunities to mediate, evaluate, justify, plan and create to the advantage of organisation; (ix) help in resolving the problems; (x) clarify responsibility and authority; (xi) provide approval and appreciation for good work; and (xii) make available the opportunities for achievement.

TRANSACTIONAL ANALYSIS (TA)

This analysis was originally propounded by Eric Berne in 1950 for psychotherapy. Harris and Jogneward popularised this analysis by applying it to ordinary interactions. For better understanding of TA, structural analysis (ego states), life position and analysis of transactions should be understood.

(A) Ego States

These are individual's way of thinking, feeling and behaving at any time. These ego states are related with the behavioural aspects of age and any person can possess these states, but there are differences of degrees. These states also based on real behaviour. These are as follows:

1. Parent Ego

Main features of this state are as follows:

(a) This state encompasses the attitude and behaviour of all significant people serving as parent figure when a person was a child.
(b) In the mind of person, the value and behaviour are recorded making them basic values of personality.
(c) Overprotection, distantness, indispensability and uprightness are the characteristics of person with parent ego.
(d) Wagging finger to show unhappiness, quoting rules, laws and regulations and reliance on past ways of success are some aspects of behaving of person with this ego state.

Two types of parent ego states:

(a) *Nurturing*. This behaviour is not with the children but also with people who are in interaction.
(b) Critical or evaluative behaviour in course of interaction with others.

2. Adult Ego

This ego state has following characteristics:

(a) This ego state is based on rationality.
(b) Thoughtful focus and discussion based on facts are physical as well as verbal signs.
(c) This ego state is formed through one's own experience and this experience is continuously updated through the verification of parental ego.

3. Child Ego

It contains the following:

(a) Creativity, conformity, dependence, fear, anxiety, depression, hate etc. are the characteristics of this state.
(b) Silent confidence, seeking of attention, temper tantrums, coyness, etc. are physical and verbal clues.
(c) It shows early childhood conditions and experiences perceived by individuals in early life of childhood.

Three parts of child ego:

(a) Natural child does the things naturally. He/she remains affectionate, impulsive, sensuous but at the same time fearful, self-centred and aggressive and may perform unwanted roles.
(b) Adoptive child performs his/her tasks usually at the instance of parents. He/she is trained but overtly inhibited turns into troublesome personality.
(c) Rebellious child has experiences of anger, fear and frustration.

Life Positions or Psychological Positions

At a very early age in childhood, experiences generate a dominant philosophy in individual which encompasses specific assumptions determining his/her behaviour towards others as well as his/her identity, sense of worth and perceptions of other people. Such positions are labelled as life or psychological positions.

There are four categories of such positions:

1. I am O.K. you are O.K. This position is:

(a) chosen rationally, (b) based on adult ego, (c) based on large number of O.K. experiences with others, and (d) helpful in solving problems constructively.

Implications for Administrator/Manager

The position brings out consistent pattern of confidence as well as competence on the part of administrator, manager; generates ability to express freely and delegate authority with feeling of goodness.

2. I am O.K. you are not O.K. This position is:

(a) taken by those who have been too much ignored in his/her childhood and have feeling that they have been victimised or prosecuted, (b) based on rebellious child ego and operation of parent ego, and (c) based on feeling on the part of individual that they are always right.

Implications for Administrator/Manager

Persons having this position usually give critical and oppressive remarks, point out shortcomings and rarely maintain any warm as well as genuinely carrying feelings. They do not delegate authority since they lack trust and confidence towards the competence and loyalty of subordinates.

3. I am not O.K. you are O.K. This position is:

(a) carried out by those persons who have a feeling of inability to do things as others around him/her are able to do leading to powerlessness; and (b) instrumental in generating feeling of grumbleness for one thing or other.

Implications for Administrator/Manager

They give and receive bad feelings. Their behaviour remains unpredictable and erratic.

4. I am not O.K. you are not O.K. This position is:

(a) taken by those who lose interest in living, (b) taken a desperate life position, (c) instrumental in general suicidal tendencies, and (d) created due to serious neglect of persons during their upbringing.

Implications for Administrator/Manager

Persons having this life position do not take decisions in time, do stupid mistakes, get negative reactions and lack competence as well as depend on others to take final decisions.

Every person is dominated by one of these positions but desirable position is an adult-adult transaction i.e. 'I am O.K. you are O.K.' Showing acceptance of self and others. Education can be instrumental in learning this position.

***Transactions*:** Interaction between people involves transactions. Verbal and non-verbal stimulus from a person is being responded by another person, a transaction takes place. There may be three types of transactions.

(A) *Complementary Transactions*: This incorporates:

1. Stimulus and response patterns from one ego state to another are parallel.
2. There are nine types of complementary transactions (i) adult-adult, (ii) parent-child, (iii) adult-parent, (iv) adult-child, (v) parent-parent, (vi) parent-adult, (vii) child-parent, (viii) child-adult and (ix) child-child. Among these transactions, adult-adult and parent-child transactions are most accepted and desirable.
3. In adult-adult transactions, the administrator/manager in the state of adult-ego: (a tries to reason out issues, (b) classifies and informs issues, (c) concerns for facts and figures and human needs, and (d) contains 'I am O.K. and you are O.K.' life position.

4. This transaction is ideal transaction and solution is achieved in which both parties become satisfied. This is depicted as follows:

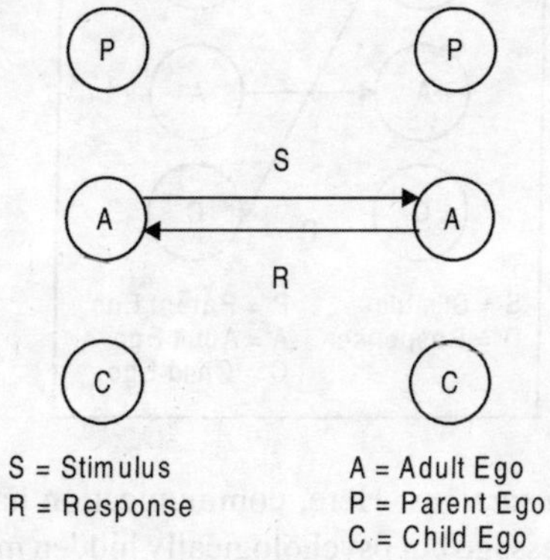

5. Parent-child complementary transaction becomes ideal if Administrator/Manager interacts with employee with parent ego and employee responses with child-ego. Here, employee remains burdenless, has less responsibility, no conflict and easy operation.
6. However, in the long run this situation is not good for employee since employee has to surrender his adult ego resulting into non-development of personality. This is presented as follows:

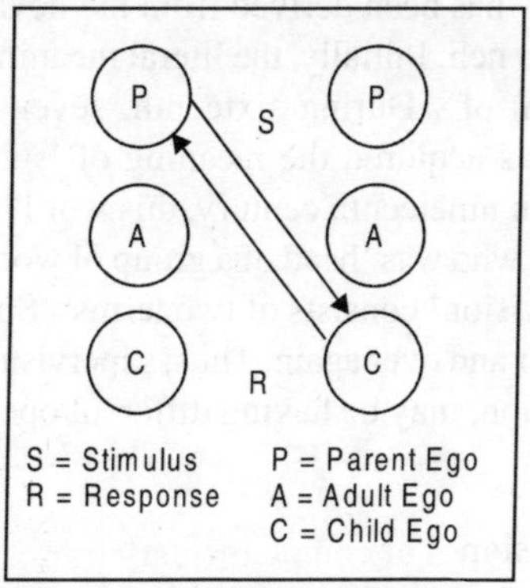

(B) *Non-Complementary Transactions*: These are known as cross transactions also. These transactions occur when:

I. Stimulus and response lines are not parallel, and
II. The person initiating transaction does not get response as expected.

Here, communication becomes faulty or sometimes blocked since manager/administrator deals with employee an adult-adult basis but employee responds on child parent basis. This can be depicted as follows:

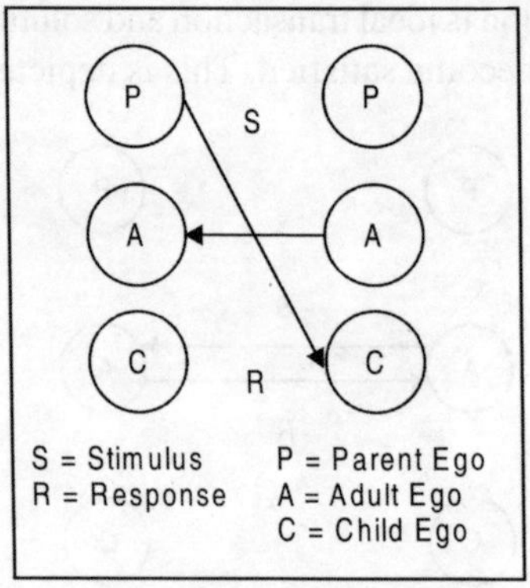

(C) *Ulterior Transactions*: Here, communication has dual meanings – socially clear adult message but psychologically hidden message. This makes this transaction complex and undesirable.

Uses of T.A. It is useful since it: (a) increases positive thinking by changing negative feelings, (b) makes interpersonal relations better and effective, (c) motivates personnel, and (d) develops the organisation.

SUPERVISION

The term 'supervision' has been derived from medieval Latin 'Supervidore' came to English via French. Initially, the literal meaning of the term has been 'to have the oversight of'. During sixteenth, seventeenth and eighteenth centuries, this term has acquired the meaning of 'surveyor'. But, after the industrial revolution in nineteenth century, this word has acquired a specific meaning of somebody who was 'head of a group of workers' (Verma, R.B.S.).

The word 'supervision' consists of two terms: 'Super' and 'vision', that to look into things over and over again. Thus, supervision involves overseeing of one cohesive function, may be having different operations and performed by a group of persons.

Purposes of Supervision

(a) Teaching — helping employees to increase the knowledge and understanding for deepening the professional attitudes among employees. It also develops skills in them through learning by doing.

(b) Administration — directing, instructing and guiding employees in administering the work operations, that is, giving assignments, promotions, functioning of committees, personnel work etc.

(c) Enablement facilitating the work of the employees (supervisors) so that they do their work in the delivery of social services.

Approaches to Supervision

These are as follows:

1. *The 'Hard-Nosed' or Formal Approach*: Proponents of formal approach believe that management has a right to manage and that it should do just that. Thus management is to decide to manage, and however much it may consult with workers or delegate to them, it always has and retains the right to give orders and requires that they be obeyed. This leads to 'hard-nosed' attitude (Sartain and Baker).

2. *The 'Sentimental' and 'Happiness' Approach*: This approach is based on happiness philosophy in which it is believed that the happy employee is a productive employee. This added impetus to growing fringe benefits. This also believes in manipulation, that is to doing things for employees not because they are being loved but because they could give more that way. Thus, supervisor was exhorted to demonstrate an interest in his people. He was to call them by name, to praise in public and to reward suggestions for improvement (Sartain and Baker).

3. *The 'Sensitivity' or 'Sweatness-and-Light' Approach*: Here, the supervisor, instead of being 'decider' as to how work is to be carried out when it is to be carried out, and how much it is to be carried out, becomes a 'linking pin' or a connector between the group of operatives and the appropriate higher group or other groups of organisation.

Attributes of Effective Supervision

These are as follows:

1. Knowledge about organisation, people, environment, clients as well as programmes carried out by organisation.
2. Equipped with professional attitudes which require skilful handling of problems based on scientific and rational thinking.
3. Have practice skills developed by doing and handling situations.
4. Have open mind and give supervisee chance to remove doubts and suspicious without any barrier leading to practice of an open door policy.
5. Possession of strong conviction and commitment towards organisation, its members-particularly supervisee for effective functioning.
6. The worth and dignity of supervisee should be recognised.
7. Establishment of a system of appreciation and commendation in case

of good work at the same these should be positive, developmental and corrective view towards members who are not upto the mark.

8. The supervisor should have capacity to transmit knowledge, assess performance and professional development of the staff and understand authority and use it appropriately (Scherz).

Thus, an effective supervisor should have competence of doing things in a scientific and democratic manner based on positive thinking.

Principles of Supervision

1. Sharing and transmitting of knowledge, principles and skills.
2. Allowing the employees to govern themselves.
3. The employees can govern themselves by selecting goals and objectives consistent with the principles of supervision.
4. Supervisors should always keen a helpful attitude and remain available for help when needed to supervise.
5. Employees should have motivation enough to call their supervisors in case they need their help.
6. Employees should give their progress of work as well as accent of activities periodically to supervisor.

Models of Supervision

According to Watson, these are as follows:

1. *Tutorial model*: Where supervisor and supervisee remain one-to-one relationship.
2. *Case consultation*: Involves an employee and a consultant, may be having one-to-one position or other staff with purpose of benefiting their learning or seeking their contributions or both.
3. *Supervisory group*: Involves a superior and a group of supervisees, this is in a way, an extension of tutorial model.
4. *Peer-group supervision*: Here, no designated supervisor and all group members participate as equals.
5. *Tandem supervision*: Two employees functioning themselves for the purpose of supervising each other.
6. *The team*: Deliberately varied membership, decision is taken through peer interaction.

Supervisory Process

It is concerned with (According to Cohen and Rhodes)—

1. Setting individual and group objectives for task allocation and implementation.

2. Implementing shared decision making.
3. Directing group process.
4. Planning work.
5. Developing communication networks.
6. Evaluating performance.
7. Motivating employees.
8. Consultation and professional support.
9. Team building.
10. Advocacy of employee and beneficiary.
11. Conflict management.
12. Planned change at dyadic, team and inter-group levels with particular attention to coalescing separate interests into collective interests on behalf of employees and clients (Quoted by Skidmore).

In supervisory process, supervisors are in a position to influence employees since supervisor:

(a) has administratively assigned and sanctioned authority over the supervisee,
(b) mediates the relationship between the supervisee and the organisation,
(c) has a role to play in hiring and firing of supervisee,
(d) controls the supervisor's salary increases and promotions and determines the kind of entries that will appear in his record,
(e) expects from the supervisee to reveal much about himself in supervisory relationship, and
(f) extends beyond the tenure of supervisee on the job (Levy).

HUMAN RELATIONS IN SOCIAL WELFARE/ DEVELOPMENT AGENCIES

Social welfare/development agency refers to an organisational structure which contains staff at various levels, committee arrangements, board structure, chain of command and other factors related to the agency. These social welfare agencies should remain dynamic, alive and renewed. This can be done by—

1. an effective programme for the recruitment and development of talent since people are the ultimate source of renewal;
2. establishing a hospitable environment for individual;
3. having built-in provision for self-criticism;
4. having fluidity of internal structure in forms of division, branches, departments, etc.;
5. keeping adequate system of internal communications;

6. having some means of combating the process by which men become prisoners of their procedures;
7. finding out some means of combating the vested interests that grow up in every institution;
8. concentrating wheat is going to become and not what it has been; and
9. running the organisation on motivation, conviction and morale (John Gardner).

Human relations are vital for social welfare agencies mainly due to following factors:

(A) Social Welfare Development Agency Serves the Clients

The functioning of agencies should be based on human relations because:

1. The major resource of these agencies of human in the form of specialists through them services reach to clients.
2. Agency personnel work directly with clients on a day-to-day basis, the service function of the agency as a whole demands a broader and longer-term approach to the meeting of the need. Not only existing clients be served but unmet needs must be diagnosed and planned for.
3. These agencies provide services to the clients the mediation of 'professionals' which strives for human relations.

(B) The Bases of these Agencies are Social Values

They are relevant to relation not only between workers and clients, but between social workers themselves as professional colleagues, and indeed between all those who share the work of agencies. This demand for—

1. Creative use of human resources which is possible through establishing good human relations.
2. Doing things in democratic way.
3. Establishment a professional culture in the agency not a bureaucratic structure (Joyce Warham).

(C) Agency personnel are required to cultivate 'empathy' for people under stress or in distress, for destitute, for the victims of vice, crime or disease and rehabilitate them.

In this way, these agencies have human relations mainly due to their involvement with the creative use of human resources based on democratic and professional authority.

9

Budgeting

From nineteenth century, the functioning of state has increased manifold in all directions. In order to standardise financial allocations and expenditures, several developments in financial administration has taken place including introduction of budget system. Presently, the budget has now become a vital tool of financial administration.

Importance of Budget. Budget is important for administration since it acts as a tool for it and as an instrument for social and economic policy as well as planning.

As a tool of administration, the budget is important since—

1. budget is schedule of activities;
2. it is means of financing these activities;
3. it brings out estimate of anticipated revenues and proposed expenditure together;
4. it executes efficiently the functions and services of organisation;
5. it helps in attaining economy and efficiency; and
6. it acts as a tool of control in democratic process.

As an instrument of social and economic policy, budget is vital for the formulation and implementation of policies, specially economic policies, production policies, distribution policies and taxation policies.

As an instrument of planning, budget is important for the preparation and execution of different plans.

MEANING OF BUDGET

The word 'budget' has been derived from a French word, namely 'Bougettee' meaning 'leather bag' or 'wallet'. The Britishers adopted this for the first time in 1733 in a satire known as 'opened the budget' which was pointed against Walpole's financial plan for that year. The chancellor of the Exchequer used to carry a leather bag containing papers on the financial plans for the country to the House of Commons, so when he set off to place his financial plans before the house, he used to open his 'budget', that is, bag and it is because of this association of financial plan with 'bouqette' that the financial statement, of a country has come to be known as 'budget'.

DEFINITIONS

Dimock: "A budget is a financial plan summarising the financial experience of the past stating a current plan and projecting it over a specified period of time in future".

Harold R. Bruce: "A budget is a financial statement, prepared in advance of the opening of fiscal year, of the estimated revenues and proposed expenditures of given organisation for the ensuring fiscal year.

Munro: "Budget is a plan of financing for the incoming fiscal year. This involves an itemised estimate of all revenues on the one hand and all expenditure on the other".

Rene Stown: "Budget is a document containing a preliminary approved plan of public revenue and expenditure".

Taylor: "Budget is a financial plan of government for a definite period".

Gross: Budget "represents the organisation's blueprint for the coming months or years expressed in monetary terms".

ELEMENTS OF BUDGET

The above definitions suggest the following elements of budget:

1. It is a statement of expected revenue and proposed expenditure.
2. It requires some authority to sanction it.
3. It is for a limited period.
4. It is equipped with procedure and manner for collection of revenue and administration of expenditure.
5. It acts as control mechanism of financial affairs.

Thus, budget denotes the document which contains estimates of revenue and expenditure of an organisation or whole country, usually for fixed period. It presents a proposed programme of action also.

TYPES OF BUDGET

Basis	*Types*	
1. Period covered	(a) Annual Budget	The budget is prepared for one year.

(*Contd.*)

	Basis	*Types*	
		(b) Long Term Budget	Preparing budget for three or four years, in case of long term planning.
2.	Number of times Budget Introduced in Legislature	(a) Single	When the estimates of all government undertakings find place in one budget.
		(b) Plural	There are separate department wise budgets which are passed separately by the legislature.
3.	On the basis of overall position	(a) Surplus	If the estimated revenue is in excess of estimated expenditure Anticipated Revenue > Proposed Expenditure
		(b) Deficit	If anticipated revenue falls short of the anticipated expenditure Anticipated Revenue < Proposed Expenditure
		(c) Balanced	This budget is one wherein the anticipated revenue is equal to proposed expenditure Anticipated Revenue = Proposed Expenditure
4.	On the basis of taking the items of income and expenditure in the budget	(a) Cash	This budget is one wherein the estimates of various items of income and expenditure include the amounts actually to be received or spent in one year.
		(b) Revenue	Here, the revenue and expenditure, accruing in one financial year are budgeted in that financial year, irrespective of the fact whether the revenues are realised or the expenditure is incurred in that financial year.

(Contd.)

Basis	Types	Basis	Types
5.	On the basis of Receipt and Expenditure	(a) Departmental	The revenues and expenditure of one department are grouped under it without giving any information as to the activity or performance for which money is budgeted.
		(b) Performance	It is prepared in terms of functions, programmes, activities and projects.

Social welfare/work agencies utilise following types of budget singly or in combination.

(A) *Line-Item Budget*. This budget shows that how the money is to be spent but does not depict what the agency does. It is not programme oriented. The proposed expenditures for each department or unit are listed for a specific period of time.

(B) *Programme Budgeting*. It is related to cost estimates and specifies of each programme and this budget may cover several years particularly as a programme is offered and approved for specific amount of time.

(C) *Functional Budgeting*. This budget lists all revenues and expenditures, particularly as they relate to management and general functions, fund raising functions and identifiable programme offered by the agency.

(D) *Zero-Based Budgeting*. This budgeting operates on the premise that an agency must start from scratch and each year justify financial request it makes. In other words, the agency starts with no money each year and describes and justifies all expenditures that are claimed for the ensuring year, whether they have existed before or not.

FORMULATING BUDGETS

Main steps involved in formulating budgets are as follows:

1. *Specific Goals related to the Needs of the Agency/Organisation*: According to the needs of agency/organisation specific goals should be chalked out. These goals and objectives can be observed and measured for the purpose of periodic evaluation of the performance of agency in the delivery of social services.

2. *Ascertaining Facts regarding the Operation of Agency*: Available basic information regarding current and past operations of agency must be collected

and studied. This should include both competition and non-completion of operations. The facts gathered should be seen for the whole agency as well as in terms of staff and professional workers.

3. *Looking at Specific Alternatives for the Operation of Agency/ Organisation, Particularly in Terms of Money*: The good and effective administrators try to look at alternatives for the utilisation of money to be sanctioned in the year. However, creativity and innovativeness should be linked with existing services.

4. *Deciding upon Priorities for the Agency*: This involves studying different alternatives and listing them in order of priority. The policies and goals of agencies should be kept in mind while finalising priorities.

5. *Finalising Decision regarding the Budget*: Final decision regarding budget should be based on facts gathered needs and potential of agency/ organisation as well as members of agency/organisation.

6. *Providing Adequate Interpretations and Public Relations*: After the adoption of blueprint of budget, it should be interpreted to persons who are in power. For this, public relations as well as interpretations can be made with those who play a major role in the sanction of the budget.

Thus, it can be concluded that total budget formulation process involves (a) pre-planning (gearing up for the process); and (b) launching (the planned budgeting process), data gathering and analysis, objectives setting, programming the objectives, preparing and testing the budget, modifying the budget and adopting a balanced budget (United Way of America quoted by Skidmore).

PRINCIPLES OF BUDGETING

These principles are as follows:

1. *Balanced Budget*: Budget should be balanced since it (a) provides financial stability, (b) enhances faith of investors, and (c) deficit budgeting is possible and feasible for certain period of time.

2. *Responsibility of Executive*: Executive is responsible for running the administration, so budget preparation should also be done by executive.

3. *Cash Basis Estimates*: The estimates should be made on cash basis. This implies that budget should be prepared on the basis of actual receipts and expenditure expected during the year and not on the basis of receipts which are to be realised in some other years or expenditure which is ordered in that year but is likely to be incurred in the next financial year.

4. *Budgeting Should be Done on the Basis of Gross Income Not on the Basis of Net Income*: The budget should present a clear picture of the gross income of the country. Both receipts and expenditure should be shown in the budget not barely the resultant net position.

5. *Estimating Should be Approximately Exact*: There should neither be overestimating since overestimating invites more taxes nor underestimating because underestimating will make the budget out of gear when it will be executed.

6. *Annuality of Budget*: The annuality of budget should be maintained. This implies that budget should be prepared and sanctioned by legislature to executive for one year only.

7. *Application of Rule of Lapse*: The principle of annuality also means the money left unspent during the year for which it was sanctioned must lapse to public treasury and the government cannot spent it unless resanctioned in the next year's budget. This rule is essential for financial control.

8. *Treasury Control*: The budget should be controlled by treasury which should be authorised to give directions in this matter.

9. *Executive Discretion*: Executive must be given some discretion in the matter of allotment of appropriation if it is to exercise supervision over the activities of spending department.

10. *The Form of Estimate Should Match with the Form of Account*: This means that heads of budget should be the same as those of accounts for facilitating budget preparation, budgetary control and the account keeping.

11. *Revenue and Capital Parts of the Budget Should be Kept Distinct:* This means that overall surplus or deficit may be found out by taking both into account.

12. *Single Budget*: This means that all revenues and expenditures should be presented in single budget which will give clear picture to the people.

FUNCTIONS OF BUDGET

1. Budget presents detailed programmes and activities of organisation.
2. It fixes priority among needs as per resources.
3. It shows details of sources available with the organisation.
4. It enhances efficiency of the organisation.
5. It provides systematic completion of goals of organisation.
6. It presents the whole picture of the organisation.
7. It acts as a means of control in organisation.
8. It paves the way for formulation of socio-economic policies.
9. It brings out progress in the organisation.
10. It is helpful in execution of plans and programmes.
11. It acts a guide to staff of organisation about the manner of spending money on various schemes and heads of account.
12. Budget is necessary for grant giving bodies.
13. Assessing financial requirements of organisation.
14. It brings out status of agency/organisation before masses.
15. It is vital for fund raising for organisation.

PROBLEMS OF BUDGETING

In social welfare agencies/organisations, administration has to face many problems regarding preparation of budget and its implementation.

(A) Preparation of Budget

1. The income is not fixed, consequently the budget is prepared purely on fluid and unrealistic estimates.
2. Budget has to be prepared as per rules and regulations of grant-giving agency which sometimes does not match with the policy objectives of organisation.
3. To fulfil the commitment of share of organisation in case of taking grants-in-aid, the budget is prepared unrealistic manner.
4. Resources, e.g. donations, etc. remain fluid and uncertain.
5. Due to lack of resources for taking the services of experts in making the budget, it is prepared without expertise creates problems.
6. The quantification of assets and liabilities is difficult.
7. Dominance of vested interests in these organisations so budget is prepared as per whims of executives of these organisations instead of rules and regulations.
8. Poor maintenance or not availability of records creates problems in preparing budget.
9. Dominance of target system or ad-hocism affects the preparation of realistic budget.
10. Problems arise in deciding nature/type of budget, i.e., for what period and whether it should be line-item budget, programme budget or functional budget or zero base budget or combination of all.

(B) Implementation of Budget

1. Problems due to unrealistic estimates of income and expenditure.
2. Release of funds from grant-giving agencies is not timely.
3. Not following the rules and regulations due to vested interests.
4. Absence of proper monitoring and evaluation of expenditure.
5. Lacks expertise in document things professionally.
6. Lack of proper control, direction and supervision.
7. Absence of criterion to measure efficiency and effectiveness of the budget.
8. Difficult to calculate outcome of the budget.
9. Emphasis on utilisation of the funds rather than their appropriateness and relevance.
10. Lack of transparency and accountability.

10

Controlling and Project Formulation

Control is the function of every administrator/manager. Controlling is the process of measurement and control of subordinates in order to ensure the conformity of their activities with pre-determined plans and objectives.

MEANING

Control activities generally are related to measurement of achievements. Following definitions are being presented for clarifying its meaning:

Henry Fayol: "In an undertaking, control consists in verifying whether everything occurs in conformity with the plan adopted, the instructions issued and principles established. It has for its object to point out weaknesses and errors in order to rectify them and prevent recurrence".

Goetz: "Management control seeks to compel events to conform to plan".

E.F.L. Brech: "Control is checking current performance against pre-determined standards contained in the plans, with a view to ensuring adequate progress and satisfactory performance".

George R. Terry: "Controlling is determining what is being accomplished, that is, evaluating the performance takes place according to plans".

Taylor: "In an undertaking, control consists in verifying whether everything occurs in conformity with the plan adopted, the instructions issued and principles established".

CHARACTERISTICS

These are as follows:

1. Controlling is a process.
2. It involves setting of standards and measurement of achievements as per standards set.

3. It brings out variation between set standards and actual performance.
4. It initiates corrective measures.
5. It is a continuous operation.

In nutshell, control maybe interpreted as a continuous process which helps an administrator to get performance of his subordinates as closely as possible to the objectives, goals or target fixed, to detect variation between them the actuals as soon as they occur and to take corrective and timely steps to prevent similar variations in future.

NEED OF CONTROL

Control is vital for organisations in general and for social welfare organisations in particular. In case of social welfare organisations control is needed, since—

(1) management of social welfare functions such as social policy, social planning, social development, social action etc. are dependent upon control system;
(2) the process of control remains in operation at every levels of organisation;
(3) it is exercised at different points of time;
(4) it involves in corrections ensuring positive results;
(5) it helps in designing new policy and action;
(6) it reports deviations from plans;
(7) it ensures objectivity with standards; and
(8) it is economical, understandable and intelligible.

TYPE OF CONTROL

In the scenario of social welfare administration, control is of three types:

(A) *Operational Control*: Social action as per norms for producing desired results.
(B) *Programme Control*: Ensuring the achievement of social welfare programmes as per anticipated results.
(C) *Social Control*: Ensuring suitability of social welfare programmes in context of social environment and getting maximum benefits for community in context of receipt of inputs from community.

STEPS INVOLVED IN CONTROLLING PROCESS

These are as follows:

1. *Establishment of control standards*: This involves the following:

   (a) Determination of goals, objectives or targets of every social programme for which actual performance is to be measured.
   (b) These standards may be tangible or intangible.
   (c) Setting of standards should be done at strategic control points since every operation cannot be standardised.
   (d) In order to adapt changing conditions standards need to be flexible.
2. *Measurement of Performance*: This can be done through personal obligation, as in case of the subordinates being observed while they are engaged in work and by a study of various summaries of figures, reports, charts and statements. However, this measurement should be clear, simple, rational, paid direct attention and effort, reliable, self-announcing and understandable without complicated interruption (P.F. Drucker).
3. *Comparison Between Performance and Standards*: The performance should be compared to set standards and in case of deviations it is suggested to be realistic and accept a range of tolerance within which normal performance should have been occurred.
4. *Determining the Reasons for Deviations*: This is an important step since it spells out causes of deviations to ensure fruitful action. The causes of low performance in social welfare administration may be:
   (a) improper working out of the standards;
   (b) inadequate design of machinery of administration;
   (c) unmotivated and untrained personnel engaged in social welfare activities;
   (d) unrealistic financial allocation;
   (e) rigid procedure;
   (f) lack of participation on the part of beneficiaries;
   (g) defective criteria for identifying the beneficiaries;
   (h) incompetent persons managing the institutions; and
   (i) non-participation of the community.
5. *Corrective Action*: The administrator/manager must take corrective action without wasting of time so that the normal position can be restored quickly.

CHARACTERISTICS OF GOOD CONTROL SYSTEM

These are as follows:

1. The control system should be as per nature and demands of activity.
2. The system should be as such that subordinates would be able to inform their superiors about the expected deviations and failures.

3. The feedback system should be as short and quick as possible.
4. The system should be objective and understandable.
5. It should be flexible to be adjusted towards changing condition.
6. The system should be less expensive and economical.
7. Detection of deviations from standards is not enough but solutions of problems that cause deviations should also be provided.
8. The central system should be acceptable to the members of organisation.
9. The system should be able to know the expectations of strategic points.
10. It should motivate people to high performance.
11. Control over one side/phase of operation should not lead to less attention to other aspects of organisation.

CONTROLLING AS THE LINKING PIN OF PRINCIPLES OF ADMINISTRATION

Control is exercised on human behaviour making any organisational structure and its functioning a model of control itself. Fayol has specified some principles of management and administration. These principles are linked through the process of controlling.

1. *Division of Work*: The tasks of organisation can be completed by competent personnel having capacity to perform different activities of organisation. For this use of specialised task skills is essential. This specialised division of work is carried out through the controlling process since it defines boundaries of each activity and exercise control to maintain these boundaries.
2. *Authority and Responsibility*: Authority is exercised through the process of controlling and responsibility is carried out through self-control as well as formal control which decides limits of responsibilities.
3. *Discipline*: With the process of controlling discipline cannot be maintained in the organisation.
4. *Unity of Command*: This principle demands the control of one person (superior) on another person (subordinate). In other words, subordinate is supposed to be controlled and commanded by one superior.
5. *Unity of Direction*: This principle envisages that there should be a single head or a uniform plan for a group of activities having the same objectives. Controlling process facilitates the application of this principle since single head or uniform plan used to carry out their activities through this process.

6. *Subordination of Individual Interests to General Interests*: This is done through the process of self-control. Formal Control mechanism is also used.
7. *Remuneration of Personnel*: In order to maintain fairness in compensation policies, controlling devices are needed.
8. *Centralisation*: Degree of centralisation or decentralisation is dependent on controlling the activities, authority and responsibility.
9. *Scalar Chain or Hierarchy*: Here, line of authority from superior to subordinate is maintained through channel of authority for communication and decision making. For this, the process of controlling defines the limits of both superior and subordinates.
10. *Equity*: The controlling process fixes duty of administration for ensuring justice and kindliness for members of organisation.
11. *Stability of Tenure of Personnel*: This is maintained by controlling devices of rules and regulations.
12. *Order*: This is maintained in organisation by controlling process since this principle revolves round the idea that there is a place for everything and everything has its place.
13. *Initiative*: This is generated in employee of superior shares some of his/her decision making authority with employees but initiative is subject to rules and regulations.
14. *Esprit-de-corps*: Prevalence of harmony among all members of organisation can be attained through healthy control practices.

Thus, controls are designed and exercised for varied thing—policies, wages and salaries, employee selection and training, research and development, product quality and cost, pricing, capital expenditures, cash and other areas where we wish performance to confirm plan (Koontz and Weihrich).

The following means of control make it as linking pin of principles of administration:

1. Structure of organisation and hierarchy.
2. Authority and responsibility.
3. Rules, regulations, processes and procedures of organisation.
4. Code of ethics and conditions of service.
5. Line authority.
6. Inspection, enquiry and supervision.
7. Internal discipline and regulatory rule.
8. Standardisation of work or service.
9. Evaluation of performance.
10. Grievance handling.
11. Provision prescribed in policy, planning, programme and orders.

12. Unity of command.
13. Report.
14. Budget.
15. Limitations of duties.
16. Auditing.

PROJECT FORMULATION

Project is a complex, non-routine, one time effort to create a product or service limited by time, budget and specifications designed to meet customer needs. The main characteristics of project are:

1. It has an established objective.
2. It consists of a pre-determined life span with a beginning and an end.
3. It involves several departments.
4. Some innovative thing to be done.
5. It has specific time, cost and performance requirements.

Project is different from programme, since 'programme is a series of coordinated, related, multiple projects that continue over extended time intended to achieve a goal'. Thus, a programme is a higher level of group of projects targeted at common goal.

MEANING PROJECT FORMULATION

Project formulation refers to take up a first look carefully and critically at project idea by an entrepreneur to build up an all-round beneficial to project after carefully weighting its various components. In this way, project formulation involves:

1. An entrepreneur.
2. Assistance by specialists or consultants.
3. A process of making an objective and independent assessment.
4. This assessment is related to various aspects of an investment proposition of a project idea.
5. The purpose is the determination of its total impact and also its liability.

AIM OF PROJECT FORMULATION

The main aim of project formulation is to meet project objectives with a minimum expenditure and appropriate resources. This means to extract maximum benefits from minimum expenses within short time as far as possible.

Some Preliminaries: These are as follows:

1. *Defining Objectives*: Project encompasses a series of actions for getting predetermined objectives fulfilled. This strives for defining the objectives into the following categories:
   (a) General objective which states in broad terms the expected achievements.
   (b) Operational objective specifically mentions results expected from the implementation of the project.

   The clarity of objectives leads to quantification of them in physical, financial, human or in other terms.
2. *Location and Size of Project*: After defining objectives, project site is located and size of project is determined which is influenced by (a) availability of resources, (b) existence of infrastructural facilities, and (c) opportunity exploit these resources and facilities.

STAGES OF PROJECT FORMULATION

These are in sequential order.

1. *Feasibility Analysis*: This is the stage of examination of project idea for getting answers of following questions:
   (a) Whether the project idea is feasible?
   (b) Whether this idea is not feasible?
   (c) Whether unable to reach any conclusion for want of adequate information?

   If idea is feasible we proceed further, if not feasible the project idea is dropped. In case of third, more efforts are made to get the information and go ahead accordingly
2. *Techno-Economic Analysis*: At this stage, project demand potential is estimated and choice of optimal technology is made. Market analysis regarding produced goods and services is also needed at this stage. Thus, this stage sets for detailed design development of the project.
3. *Project Design and Network Analysis*: Here, individual activities constituting the project and their inter-relationship with each other are defined and interpreted. A detailed work plan of the project is prepared. Time is allocated for each activity. After this the project is presented in network drawing.
4. *Input Analysis*: In this step, requirement of inputs of each activity is decided and sum total of these requirements on qualitative and quantitative terms is taken. Input consists of material as well as human resources. Recurring and non-recurring requirements of resources of the project are also considered in input analysis. Evaluation of feasibility of the project from the point of view of availability of these resources is also conducted. This helps in assessing the cost of project itself leading to financial or cost-benefit analysis.

5. *Financial Analysis*: This stage is mainly concerned with project and its operation costs as well as requirements of funds. This analysis helps the decision maker to compare different project proposals on a common scale. Here, discounted cash flow, cost volume-profit relationship and ratio analysis are used as analytical tools.
6. *Cost-Benefit Analysis*: This analysis sees the project from the national viability point of view. Here, also design of project forms the basis of evaluation. In this analysis both direct costs and direct benefits of project as well as costs of all entities connected with project and benefits to be enjoyed by all such entities are taken into account.
7. *Pre-Investment Analysis*: In this final stage, all the results obtained in the above steps are consolidated and various conclusions arrived at for the purpose of presenting a clear picture. The project is presented in the shape that project sponsoring authority, project implementation authority and external consulting agencies may be in a position to decide the viability of project for its acceptance or not.

PROJECT MANAGEMENT

Project management is the application of knowledge, skills, tools and techniques to project activities to meet the project requirements. Thus, it refers meticulous planning, effective implementation, and professional organisation to achieve the management of cost, time and performance.

Aims and Objectives of Project Management

1. Completion of project within time.
2. Delays, technical flaws and drawing defects should be avoided.
3. Funds should be made available at proper time.
4. Use of proper tools and techniques.
5. Chain reaction activities should be properly controlled.
6. The project must be completed within allotted funds and allocated time well as to the satisfaction of users.

Components of Project Management

For successful project management, the following components can be mentioned:

1. Well and clear definition of objective.
2. An integrated project plan having (a) detailed project report, (b) tasks and activities, and (c) daily targets.
3. An integrated project team encompassing (a) representatives of owner

and/or executive authority; (b) consultant, (c) main contractor, (d) suppliers of critical equipment, (e) funding institutions, (f) central and state governments etc.

4. The needed resources.
5. An effective quick hitting control system.

Steps in Project Management

The successful implementation of project demands the constitution of project team having competent professionals such as engineers, techniques, managers, accountants with responsibilities. The team should be headed by a project manager. After this, the following steps and activities are undertaken:

Step I. Initiation and Defining: Activities to be performed here are:

1. Laying down objectives having pre-conceived meaning.
2. Seeking approval of relevant authority.
3. Identification of team and determining the training needs of the team.
4. Details of project: specification of project, authorisation, scope of project, communication strategy, control mechanism, control meetings, analysis of risk, time scheduling, cost of project, quality, fund flow, key issues of project, procedures for controlling etc. are the details.

Step II. Project Planning: Here, activities are:

1. What need be done, when, how and at what cost?
2. Clarity in plans and specifications having no confusion.
3. Team members of the project should understand.

The team organisation, key issues of project and demonstrating commitment which leads to harmonising the team efforts.

Step III. Project Execution: Main activities are:

1. Resource mobilisation for the project.
2. Fulfilling assigned work as per fixed targets.
3. Conducting control meetings, monitoring the actuals, review the progress as against the task set and take corrective actions.

Step IV. Completion of Project: Activities are as follows:

1. Handing over the project to relevant authority.
2. Project post-appraisal and report preparation.

Project Life Cycle

This denotes time-span between two points i.e. project mission and its completion. This cycle passes through different sequential phases which are as follows:

1. Defining Stage	(a) Goals of Project established
	(b) Specifications are defined
	(c) Team as per tasks is constituted
	(d) Major responsibilities assigned
2. Planning Stage	(a) Project schedule finalised
	(b) Budget is managed and allocated
	(c) Resources mobilised as per budgetary provisions
	(d) Analysis of risk is conducted
	(e) Staffing is arranged.
3. Executing Stage	(a) Preparation of status reports
	(b) Changes proposed as per report
	(c) Quality is assessed
	(d) Forecasts made
4. Delivering Stage	(a) Project product to customer is delivered
	(b) Training of customer
	(c) Resources are released
	(d) Staff is released
	(e) Lessons learned from the exercise
5. Commissioning, shut down or clean up stage	(a) Completed the project
	(b) Transferring the documents and material to relevant authority

Causes of Mis-management or Failure of Project

(A) Causes related to Physical and Technical Differences

1. Delay in location of site and getting of clearance.
2. Inadequate infrastructural facilities.
3. Insufficient funding arrangement.
4. Lack of arrangement of proper technology.
5. Underutilisation of resources.
6. Delay in execution of project.
7. Poor logistics.
8. Defects in establishment of project.
9. Lack of proper design, scheduling and specifications.
10. Procedural delays in securing material.
11. Lack of quality control equipment/measures.

(B) Causes related to Human Factors

1. Selection of incompetent staff and line staff which includes consultants and contractors.
2. Lack of timely execution of authority and planning.
3. Poor selection of manufacturers, vendors, suppliers etc.
4. Indecision and delay at different stages of project.
5. Weak project team.
6. Absence of personal accountability and commitment among team members.
7. General ignorance and non-implementation of sound project management practices.

(C) Environmental

1. No clearance or delay in clearance from environmental procedures/ formalities.
2. Political pressure and vested interests.
3. Law and order problems.

Qualities of a Good Project Manager

1. Adequate knowledge and skills.
2. Able to delegate authority.
3. Able to perform staff functions.
4. Possess inter-personal behavioural skills.
5. Good decision maker.
6. Possess leadership qualities.
7. Good communication skill.
8. Respect the subordinates and their views.
9. Able to motivate team members.
10. Act justily and fairly.
11. Able to praise, give rewards and make corrections in case of deviations.
12. Able to handle diverse team members.

PROJECT EVALUATION

Project evaluation refers to special investigations conducted by project managers or other concerned persons to help when decisions are made about the effect of various procedures, standards and policies on the achievement of desired outcomes in project.

Importance

Project evaluation is important, since:

1. It determines the utility of project.
2. It unfolds the project efforts and their achievements to sponsoring agencies, professional groups, clients, customers and to general public.
3. It tries to know the bottlenecks coming in the way of implementing the project.
4. It also tries to show the ways and means through which these bottlenecks can be removed.

Objective

1. It collects information about the type and quantity of project activities i.e. project efforts.
2. It provides information about the achievement of goals of current stage of project development i.e. project effectiveness.
3. It gives information about project effectiveness related to project effort i.e. project efficiency.

Basic Concepts related to Project Evaluation

(a) *Project Effort.* Evaluation of project effort refers to an assessment of the nature and kinds of project activities considered necessary for the accomplishment of programme goals within a particular stage of development. It refers to not only staff, time, activity and commitment, but also to the allocation and use of material resources – funds, space, equipment, etc.

(b) *Project Effectiveness*. Effectiveness refers to the extent to which the goals of a particular stage have been achieved.

(c) *Project Efficiency*. It focuses on the relationship between efforts and effectiveness. It is ratio of effectiveness to efforts and it is concerned with the relative costs for achieving programme objective. Costs include expenditure of manpower, time, money, physical facilities and so on.

Evaluation Techniques

These are grouped in four major categories:

(A) Management Information System (MIS)

All organisations/agencies/projects generate information in forms of income and expenditure records, case problem records, periodic reports, records of services provided/activities conducted, records related to beneficiaries/clients/customers etc. The expansion of information technology also necessitated every human services organisation to have an advanced management information systems characterised by the following:

1. Clear and operationlised statements of project objectives as well as the procedures and activities deemed necessary for the achievement of these objectives.
2. These systems are built around decision making or problem solving activities of actors at different points in organisation.
3. The design and operation of such systems necessitate the use of a standardised language to describe objectives, needs and activities.
4. More advanced systems are computer-based, i.e. data generated by the MIS are entered in a computer which permits a detailed and sophisticated analysis.

Thus, well designed and well implemented management information system is of great use.

(B) Monitoring Techniques

These techniques include those procedures which are used for direct review of project operation.

(I) Accountability audit which is used to review the consistency, dependability and accuracy of records pertaining to project expenditures, allocations of resources and processing project beneficiaries for the purpose of establishing project accountability. Two kinds of accountability records are generally reviewed:
   - (a) General accounting refers to the system of project for keeping track on project costs including pay roll, purchasing etc. This is done by an auditor or an experienced accountant.
   - (b) Social accounting refers to the methods used by the project evaluator for recording and keeping track of project beneficiaries. It is the source of project statistics on such things as how many persons were contacted by project staff and where contacts were made etc.

(II) Administrative audit refers to those methods used to evaluate the suitability of project policies and practices directed towards compliance of policies, adherence of staff practices to designated divisions of responsibility and function, and the organisational patterns of work in terms of preferred and efficient procedures within the project and/or between the project and other projects of similar nature.

(III) *Time and motion studies*. These studies refer to those methods which attempt to describe the use of time by project staff and administration in relation to the activities in which they are involved. Information in these studies may be obtained from samples of project activity during selected periods of time, it might also contain reports by staff members on written forms, observations of and interview with the staff and the relationship of descriptions of actual staff activity to planned staff functions.

(C) Social Research Techniques

These techniques refer to those procedures, exclusive of cost considerations, that are used for developing, modifying and expanding knowledge about the project which can be communicated and verified by independent investigators. These are generally of three types:

(i) Survey methods are those methods which aim to yield facts which are descriptive of project. Included among these facts are the accurate description of target population with respect to attitudes, opinions and reported changes in behaviour.

(ii) Experiments are done with the purpose of providing evidence as to whether or not programme efforts are related casually to the accomplishment of programme goals. Logical procedures are employed for setting up experimental arrangement and the collection of data so that inferences can be made about the effects of the programme.

These designs are of two types:

(1) *Classical Experimental Design*. This is the design in which objectives of the project and means to accomplish those objectives are specified and standardised. Criterion variable which is considered relevant to the effects of a project are defined precisely so that they can be measured. The target population is determined and representative sample of that population is secured through probability sampling techniques. The members of the sample are assigned randomly to experimental (one or more groups that receive project efforts) and control groups (one or more groups that are similar to the experimental groups with respect to all relevant characteristics except that they do not receive efforts of the project or efforts from other projects that are similar). Finally, the groups are measured before and after project activity and are compared with respect to change on criterion variable.

(2) *Quasi-Experiments or Approximation to Experiments*. These

experiments are done by experimentalists since in many instances they cannot use the classical experimental design because ideal experimental arrangements are not possible or practical, therefore, the experts may devise quasi-experiments or approximation of experiments. For example, instead of a control group as used in the classical experimental design, comparative groups such as the following may be used:

(a) A group that is similar to the experimental on many relevant variables is selected after the experimental groups have received project intervention.

(b) A group which is similar to the experimental group but receives less frequent project efforts rather than no project intervention.

(iii) The case study technique is concerned with the detailed description of social project as it unfolds in its process of development by employing both qualitative and quantitative data in an effort to develop hypothesis and new ideas explaining the progress or lack of progress in development of project.

(D) Cost Analytic Techniques

These are those procedures which are used to appraise the relative values of project in relation to its cost. These are as follows:

(i) Cost accounting technique relates project cost to the outcome of the project. Outputs are those project actions which can be measured. This accounting produces unit cost figures as a basis for analysing, budgeting and allocating resources. Objectives of cost accounting are the improvement in project budgeting and the procurement of information from determining project service priorities as a function of costs.

(ii) Cost-benefit analysis is a technique of evaluating the relative effectiveness of alternative programmes, strategies etc. in terms of cost. Its purpose is to ascertain the relationship of required resources (costs) in the attainment of specified goals (benefits). Essential elements in cost-benefit analysis are costs (financial costs of manpower and other resources), benefits (whether or not desired objectives have been achieved and the monetary value that can be ascribed to such achievements) and the specification of objectives, goals and values. Cost benefit analysists use accounting methods, economic methods of analysis along with graphic and tabular presentations to represent mathematical units of relationship.

(iii) Cost-outcome analysis is a modification of cost-benefit analysis because cost-benefit analysis attempts to relate project costs to the results of project activities in terms of monetary units, while cost outcome analysis relates project cost to project results (outcomes) without translating outcomes into economic indicators. The purpose of this analysis is to gauge the relative efficiency of costs of alternative project inputs with respect to the accomplishment of specified objectives of the project may be fixed but costs of project may vary. In this way, the essence of cost-outcome analysis is the determination of minimum costs that are necessary to produce a given outcome.

(iv) Operations research or systems analysis combines scientific experimentation, mathematics, statistics and computer technology in an effort to provide data on alternative ways of conducting and coordinating project activities within organisation, assignment of personnel, scheduling, allocation of resources, choosing among alternative programmes/projects etc. Though, it has goals which may be similar to those of cost-benefit and cost-outcome analysis, yet it differs from those techniques in its deliberate use of mathematical models to solve organisational problems.

11

Administration in Government and Voluntary Agencies

SOCIAL WELFARE/SERVICE AGENCY

A social welfare/service agency consists of an organisational structure. The structure includes staff at various levels, committee arrangements, board structure, chain of command and other factors related to agency framework (Skidmore).

According to Joyce Warham, 'social work agency' may be used as generic term for all agencies within which social work is practised, it is relevant to bear in mind that many of these have much broader purposes to serve than the provision of social work service to the clients. An autonomous professionally staffed, single purpose, voluntary family case work agency might serve as a prototype of a social work agency. A Local Authority Social Services Department on the other hand would be more accurately described as a social service agency, within which social work services are implemented but which is also required to serve socially determined purposes much wider than social work itself. To conclude, it can be maintained that all social work agencies are also social service agencies, the reverse is not always true.

COMMON CHARACTERISTICS OF SOCIAL WELFARE/ SERVICE/WORK AGENCIES

Joyce Warham has mentioned that all social welfare agencies, social service agencies and social work agencies have common characteristics.

(a) *Service to Clients*: These agencies are essentially service organisations (Blau and Scott) which by definition produce services not goods. The main features are as follows:

1. All agencies have human as their major resource in the form of specialist personnel through whom services reach clients and without whom these can be no service.
2. The service function of all agencies as a whole demands a broader and longer term approach to the meeting of the need.

3. There are difficulties in selecting objective of agencies, setting standards of performance or of output and evaluating the work both of individuals and of organisation as a whole.
4. All agencies have an in-built conflict between formal or bureaucratic methods of operation.

(b) *Service Based on Values*: The service to the client is based on values which include respect for individual worth, for the right of individual, to participate in the making decisions which will affect them, for individual capacity for growth, for freedom of access to right in general and for professional freedom as a value in itself.

(c) *Democratic and Professional Authority*: In these agencies authority of professional knowledge and skills assume significance. Traditional bureaucratic authority is unsuited to these agencies. Thus, the administrator should exercise authority democratically and professionally.

As an organisation, an agency: (a) has a formal structure: a set of positions through which members relate to each other 'officially', (b) is a social system composed of individuals whose interrelationships are not exclusively official but also personal, (c) was created to serve particular purposes, (d) cannot exist independently of the world outside itself, but is organically linked to its environment, (e) is subject to continuous change, and (f) both owns and requires resources for work it has to do.

CLASSIFICATION OF AGENCIES

Thus classification is based on different bases.

Bases	*Classification*	
(a) *Auspices*	(a) Statutory agencies	Operated as per legislative enactment, rules and regulations made by Government
	(b) Non-statutory agencies	These are managed by private resources
(b) *Size*	(a) Small organisation	Less bureaucratic or absence of bureaucratic structure
	(b) Large organisation	Bureaucratic and professional structure
(c) *Complexity*	(a) Simple organisation	Single activity performed in less expanded area
	(b) Complex organisation	Multiple types of activities expanded in larger area

However, the most popular classification of agencies is: (a) statutory of government agencies or organisations, (b) non-statutory or voluntary or non-government organisations/agencies.

Statutory or Governmental Agency

This agency has following characteristic features:

1. This agency operates under the mandate of a legislative enactment.
2. This enactment frames rules and regulations for the functioning of agency.
3. This type of agency implements pubic policy.
4. This agency is subject to the impact of major changes in structure and function over which they have no control.
5. These changes are politically motivated and have been implemented nationally.
6. The executive head of agency remains a statutorily constituted service cadre by Government.
7. The executive head remains responsible for the functions of agency as well as his/her functioning towards Government and for meeting the statutory obligations.
8. The executive head works as per sanctions of Government department under the strict system of financial control.
9. This type of agency contains bureaucratic structures of local government which has political overtones also.
10. This agency is largely governed and administered in a hierarchical system having principles of administration/management such as strict division of work, scalar chain, unity of command, span of control, etc.
11. Employees are formally employed and work mainly under line authority system supported by staff arrangement as per need of the organisation.
12. The agency has pre-determined system of working either with no flexibility or little flexibility.

In this way, the governmental agency works as a wing of government department. In case of social welfare organisations, it can be noted that since they are concerned with the upliftment of weaker and vulnerable sections of society, so they are generally the part and parcel of Social Welfare Department of Government which has now labelled as Social Justice and Empowerment Department.

Non-Statutory of Voluntary Agency

Non-statutory or voluntary agency is an organisation having 'voluntariness' and freedom from external control. The definitions are as follows:

Bourdillon. Voluntary agency is an organisation "initiated and governed by its own members without external control".

M.R. Malkani: "A voluntary agency is an organisation, whether its workers are paid or unpaid, initiated or governed by its own members without external control".

V.M. Kulkarni: "A voluntary worker is someone who gave unpaid services to a good cause and the group who was formed the running of good cause, came to be known as voluntary organisation".

D. Paul Chaudhury: "A voluntary agency is a group of persons who have organised themselves as a legal corporate body. It is initiated spontaneously and governed by its own members without external control or compulsion. It has a definite programme in fulfilment of its objectives with the funds raised by it from the community and grants received from Government, if any".

The following characteristics can be chalked out from above definitions:

1. Voluntary agency is a group of people.
2. It is established and maintained by private resources.
3. It can receive grants-in-aid from the government.
4. It has a definite objectives and programmes.
5. It provides services to people on non-profit no loss basis.
6. It is an organisation based on some legal enactment.

Thus, a voluntary agency is an organisation developed and maintained by private resources irrespective of getting grants-in-aid from government organisations and establishments.

VOLUNTARY AGENCY IN SOCIAL WELFARE

Understanding of voluntary agency/organisation strives for knowing the following concepts:

Voluntarism	For the welfare and development of the people and society, a spirit of action carried on by a person or group of persons or a community. It has institutionalised set of principles to give services to the people at large.
Volunteering	An innate human characteristic having its impact differently on different persons.
Volunteer	A person (male or female, belonging to any religion, caste, creed, having any kind of life styles) serves

	fellow being either independently or with an organisation/agency, full time or part time basis, engaged in long/short term activities. The person can serve with free will for different kinds of activities.
Voluntary action	The action or set of actions initiated by the volunteer. It may be formal and informal. Formal voluntary action may be in the form of organisation but not restricted to voluntary organisation. Voluntary organisation is formalised and legalised while voluntary actions can be in formal or informal shape.

EVOLUTION OF VOLUNTARY ORGANISATION

Voluntary organisation is comparatively recently originated, but voluntary action is as old as the history of human civilisation. Evaluation of voluntary action has taken place as per nature and pattern of society i.e. nomadic, agricultural, industrial and post-industrial. Voluntary action has evolved from different periods.

1. *Early to Medieval Period (Upto 1800)*: During this period, main features of voluntary action were as follows:

(a) Religion played an important role in emphasising the importance of charity, philanthropy as well as help on mutual basis.
(b) During this period, care of needy was carried out through institutional mechanism sanctioned by religion, such as giving alms and caring for destitute, infirm, elderly, handicapped etc. were taken as religious actions.
(c) The existence of joint family system used to take care of unproductive persons, sick persons, etc.
(d) In case of failure of family, caste, organisations, community councils used to take care of needy persons.
(e) The prevalence of 'jajmani system' (patron-client relationship) generally used to take care of the interests of weaker sections by affluent sections of society.

2. *British Period Phase I (From 1800 to 1900)*: During this period, the main features are as follows:

(a) More formalised and group efforts in the form of Christian Missionaries were emerged for providing health and educational services in remote areas such as remote villages, hill areas, border areas etc. The efforts have resulted in mass conversion also in many areas.

(b) As a defensive reaction, many social reformers among Hindus were emerged in different areas and took up different social reform issues such as widow remarriage, abolition of 'Sati Pratha', increase in age at marriage, improvement in the conditions of lower caste people etc. Few names such as Raja Rammohan Roy, Ishwar Chandra Vidyasagar, Keshab Chandra Sen, M.G. Ranade, Jyotibha Phule, Ramabai, Annie Besant can be mentioned.

(c) These reformers formed groups or associations for making their efforts effective. These organisations were Brahmo Samaj, Paramhansa Sabha, Sarvaganik Sabha, Prarthana Samaj, Arya Samaj, Widow marriage association, Arya Mahila Samaj, Rama Krishna Mission, The Theosophical Society, Indian Social Conference, Indian National Congress etc. These organisations tried to develop education, strived for improvement of the conditions of women and weaker sections of society and fought with social evils including practice of untouchability.

(d) Industrial revolution has brought rapid industrialisation, urbanisation and migration of people resulting into different kinds of problems, requiring different kinds of services leading to formation of organisations and groups. The number of these voluntary organisations and groups increased as well as these organisations was involved in different socio-economic issues. This resulted into the enactment of Literacy Scientific and Charitable Society Registration Act in 1860 which is still in operation.

(e) Since 1860, voluntary efforts, both formal and informal, remained continued their programmes related to welfare, relief, social action, social change with expanded programmes, actions and areas.

3. *British Period Phase II (1900-1946)*: The main features of this period are as follows:

(a) Social transformation at village level was linked with efforts of political freedom or emancipation leading to the attention of social figures like Gokhale, Gandhi and Tagore on the field of rural reconstruction and development. Consequently, the number of organisations engaged in rural development was increased.

(b) During the period of 1917-1940, a number of voluntary experiments were also initiated for improving the life and living conditions of people in rural areas at different places such as Sriniketan, Nilokheri, Gurgaon, Mrthandum, Baroda, Bombay, Hosangabad, Sevagram and Etawah. These experiments were conducted by well-intentioned individuals such as Tagore, Broyne, Spencer Hatch, Quacky groups and Gandhi belonging to both governmental and non-governmental organisations. These experiments were pioneering and experimental in character and conducted in remote places. These experiments also tried to develop both social and economic programme in balanced manner and focussed on leadership development and people's participation.

(c) These experiments have enhanced the dimensions of those organisations from mere social issues to economic issues also.

4. *The Contemporary Scenario*: With the beginning of decade of 1950, voluntary organisations were organising welfare activities also started to organise economic activities with the funding from Government and international organisations. The following features may be mentioned:

(a) In the early 1950s, the Central Social Welfare Board was constituted to provide financial and technical support to voluntary organisations.
(b) The constitution of the People's Action for Development (India) in the early 1970, was also a significant step in furtherance of voluntary organisations.
(c) From 1960s onwards, funds for activities of voluntary organisations became increasingly available from the International Funding Organisations including U.N. Bodies.
(d) The process of forming the organisations has been boosted mainly to get access to funding. In some cases, Gandhi and Vinoba both played as motivators for establishing these organisations.
(e) From 1965 onwards, the number of such organisations was increased mainly due to the bad conditions prevailing in rural areas, generation of feeling of resistance against suppression, especially in rural youth, impact of Naxalite and J.P. movement, realisation on the part of some people that association with these organisations brought prestige, power and money.
(f) Presently, these organisations are working at national, regional and local levels for the purpose of providing services at grass-root level.
(g) Rapid growth and development of servicing and consulting organisations have taken place in late 1960s and 1970s, mainly due to funding from international organisations having special programmes like watershed, development, technology transfer programmes etc. Mention may be made of Action for Food Production, Voluntary Health Association of India, New Delhi, Rural Development Consortium, Calcutta and Gandhi Peace Centre, Hyderabad. These specialised agencies have mostly been located in cities or towns.
(h) From the mid-1970s, the tendency to form network of servicing and consultancy organisations has emerged resulting into the formation

of coalition's alliances. Some examples have been Association of Voluntary Agencies for Rural Development, New Delhi. Voluntary Action Network of India, Joint Women's Programme and the Grain Niyojan Kendra, Ghaziabad. The coalitions may be for integrated programme or for the purpose of strengthening of a particular programme.

(i) In the late 1980s and beginning of 1990s, the new process of consultancy to grass-root level organisations has been developed in which highly qualified and skilled persons give consultancy to these organisations on charging the fees depending on nature of services and programmes.

(j) Presently, the voluntary organisations have started emphasis on right based approach for solving the problems of needy which involves generating and creating awareness among people regarding their rights and privileges, organising them (as per need) for solving the problems or meeting the needs of challenging the present circumstances. They also involve themselves with human rights and social justice issues.

Thus, it can be concluded that voluntary organisations started their activities based on charity with religious sanction, enhanced their domain to development and empowerment activities.

ROLE OF VOLUNTARY AGENCY IN SOCIAL WELFARE/ SOCIAL DEVELOPMENT

According to Study Team on Social Welfare and Welfare of Backward Classes, 1959, "The importance of role of voluntary organisations in a social welfare plan can be assessed on the basis of fundamental considerations. In the first place, there is an aspect of people's participation in the planning and execution of a national plan launched by a democratic government. The planners very often expressed their keenness not only to secure the willing assent of the people to a democratic plan, but also to seek their active participation in process of planning and implementation. In other words, it is no longer a question of 'associating' the people or their agencies through indirect representation with plan officially framed and administered, but of evolving a joint partnership in the entire process of development. It is, in fact, a step towards translating into reality the concept of participating democracy".

According to Seminar on Social Administration in Developing Countries, 1964 suggests the following services which can be rendered by voluntary organisation:

1. Organising and operating social welfare programmes.

2. Perceiving and publishing the changing social needs of a community.
3. Creating public opinion in favour of progressive social legislation.
4. Pioneering new services which statutory authorities are slow in recognising.
5. Experimenting with new techniques in bringing about changes in traditional attitudes or in organising social services.
6. Stimulating civic consciousness and public participation and enlisting voluntary assistance to improve state or voluntary services.

Thus, in the field of social welfare, voluntary organisations are involved in the welfare, development and empowerment of weaker sections of society. In the area of welfare and social development these organisations are involved in the following activities:

1. Educational activities such as organising adult literacy and non-formal education centres, mobile libraries, libraries in the communities, running of crèche, coaching centres, condensed courses for girls, balwadis, anganwadis, schools, organising camps on environment and ecology, discussions on issues related to human rights, social justice, health, nutrition, family planning, etc.
2. Training and skill enhancement activities for farmers, artisans, cooperative workers, youth, grass-root workers of different departments etc.
3. Health programmes/activities such as organisation of immunisation and nutrition services, availability of safe ad potable drinking water, organisation of games, sports and recreational programmes, as well as health and sanitation campaigns including blood donation, eye care, medicare etc.
4. Formation of cooperatives, children and youth clubs, beneficiary and target groups, women's organisation etc. Rendering positive contribution in Panchayati Raj Institutions.
5. Environmental and ecological activities consisting of afforestation, campaigns against pollution and waste of natural resources; legal education and awareness as well as generation of awareness for the conservation and protection of ecology and environment.

In the area of economic development, these organisations play an important role in the following activities:

1. Land and soil activities such as redistribution of land holdings, soil testing, soil conservation and reclamation, etc.
2. Irrigation and agricultural activities such as construction, depending and desalting of tanks and wells, sinking of tube wells and other water resources, lift irrigation, construction of small reservoirs and

bundies, supply of agricultural equipments, goods carriers, repair of equipments, etc.

3. Activities of khadi and village industries which include spinning, weaving, paper making, oil ghani, basket making, rope making, tailoring and embroidery, brick kiln, lime making, clay pipe making, bone made fertiliser, leather work, carpentry, printing, sericulture, etc.
4. Activities such as dairy, poultry, piggery, fisheries, sheep rearing, cattle breeding etc. strengthening of veterinary services, development of grasslands, etc.
5. Development of orchards, nurseries, community and social forestry, wasteland, etc.
6. Activities related to food preservation, food processing etc.

The voluntary organisations may also play an important role in the following:

1. Organisation and mobilisation of people for getting their rights.
2. Implementation of different schemes of government for upliftment of poor.
3. Monitoring of evaluation of government programmes.
4. Development of demonstration centres of effective activities.
5. Acting as watchdog for different activities of government particularly issues related to human rights violation, discrimination and deprivation.
6. Acting as service providers on behalf of government and international organisations.

ADMINISTRATIVE STRUCTURE OF VOLUNTARY AGENCIES

The constituents of administrative structure are as follows:

General Body

General body is the group of ultimate control. This body may be constituted by following types of members:

1. General members or paid members who have paid their membership or subscriptions for definite period.
2. Honorary members who have given membership due their contributions in their life.
3. Life members who have paid membership fee once for life.
4. Co-opted members who can be made members by Board or relevant authority for helping or guiding on the activities of agencies.

5. Ex-officio members are those who become members because of their official position and they ceased to be member when they relieve of their official position.
6. Institutional members are the representatives of member organisations.
7. Associate members may be the well-wishers of the agency.

Thus, general body may have membership from above types either single type or multiple.

Functions of General Body: These are as follows:

1. Policy making or legislative functions.
2. Control over fund raising and utilisation of funds.
3. Choosing of office bearers and members of executive through elections.
4. Approval of annual budget of the agency/organisation.
5. Appointing auditors of the agency/organisation's funds.
6. Considering annual reports of agency/organisation.
7. Approving annual plan of action.
8. Receiving and adopting audited statement of accounts.
9. Considering all matters related to changes in constitution, policy, budgeting, programme, accounting etc.
10. Any other matter undertaken by general body.

Managing/Executive Committee/Board

Every social welfare organisation/agency has a managing/executive committee/ board. The existence of this committee/board provides joint thinking as well as community participation in the activities of agency/organisation. It acts as supervisory body also. It provides guidance to the agency/organisation regarding community needs and how to satisfy them and help in other ways that can improve efficiency and effectiveness.

Functions: According to Trecker, the functions are as follows:

1. To establish the legal or corporate existence of the agency whether it be under the auspices of government or voluntary effort.
2. To take responsibility for formulating general objectives, policies and programme.
3. To inspire community confidence in the programme because of the competence and dedication of the board members as active trustees of the agency.
4. To assume responsibility for the provision of adequate finances and to be accountable for the expenditure of funds.
5. To provide conditions of work, personnel policies, and staff. The board is particularly responsible for the selection and evaluation of the administrator.

6. To understand and interpret the work of the agency to the community.
7. To study, know and interpret general community needs to the agency staff.
8. To relate the service of the agency to the work of other agencies and to concentrate upon the improvement of community condition.
9. To conduct periodic evaluations of agency operations with a view towards improving and strengthening the amount and quality of work that is done.
10. To improve the continuity of experienced leadership so that major staff changes will not weaken the agency.

Schmidt also gave following responsibilities of board:

1. Attaining the goals or purposes of the agency.
2. Creating the structure.
3. Providing the necessary facilities.
4. Employing the executive.
5. Fixing the policies.
6. Setting the budget and providing the finances.
7. Checking the operation.
8. Interpreting the services.
9. Participate in community planning.

In India, the functions of Boards of Social Welfare Organisation have been summed up by D. Paul Chowdhry.

1. A board of director is the legislative and judicial body of a social agency. The board members establish a legal and corporate existence of the agency.
2. A board ensures steady progress and continuity in the work of the agency.
3. The board members also help the agency in raising funds and determining how the funds raised will be utilised, for the best interests of community.
4. A board is a manifestation of public participation in welfare programmes. They inspire the community's confidence in the programmes.
5. The board members help in interpreting the programme of the agency to the community. In other words, the members work as liaison between the agency and the community.
6. The board members do not undertake any professional service but they are responsible for formulating the policy and general objectives of the agency.
7. A board is also responsible for engaging technical staff for the agency and determining terms and conditions of their work.

8. It is through the influential board members that effective coordination between various agencies in the community takes place.
9. The board members also help the agency to evaluate and review its work periodically in order to help the agency to become more useful and more effective.
10. The board members approach legislature for needed social legislation.

Qualifications of Member of Board/Executive Committee

Board members may pay nominal subscription. Besides this, they should have:

(a) genuine interest in the programmes of the agency;
(b) understanding and knowledge of the programmes;
(c) some influence and respect in the community;
(d) ability to discuss various issues in a free frank, congenial and cooperative manner; and
(e) able to work in partnership with the paid staff of the agency (D. Paul Chowdhry)

Office Bearers

The office bearers of these welfare agencies/organisations are normally designated as (a) President, (b) one or more Vice Presidents, (c) Secretary/General Secretary, (d) one or more Assistant/Joint/Associate Secretaries, (e) Treasurer, (f) Chief Executive (Direct/Organising Secretary) and (g) Auditors.

These office bearers are elected/nominated by members of managing/executive committee or Board of Directors whose members are elected/nominated by General Body.

President: Normally, elected by members of managing/executive committee, President performs the following duties:

1. Presides over meetings of General Body and Executive/Managing Committee/Board and other Financial and Standard Committees.
2. Operates accounts of agency/organisation.
3. Handles functioning of the agency.

Vice President: President can delegate his powers to Vice President. In the absence of President, Vice President performs the duties of President.

Secretary (General Secretary): The Secretary/General Secretary performs the following functions:

1. Convenes the meetings of General Body, Executive (Managing Committee/Board) under the direction of President.
2. Prepares the agenda for meeting in consultation with President.
3. Keeps information and documents.
4. Assists in conducting business of meetings.
5. Ex-officio Secretary/Member of all Committees.

6. Executes decisions of Executive/Managing Committee/Board.

Joint/Assistant/Associate Secretary: Normally functions in the absence of Secretary. In big organisations, they can function independently also.

Treasurer.

1. Responsible for the finances of the organisation.
2. Preparation and prosecution of the budget estimates to the General Body.
3. Regulation and supervision of fund raising and expenditure as per approved budget.
4. Proper maintenance of accounts books.
5. Arranges and helps in audit of accounts.

Chief Executive: Chief executive may be President, Secretary or any other person appointed by the Executive/Managing Committee. He/she performs the following duties:

1. Looks after day-to-day functioning of the agency.
2. Maintains continuity to the work.
3. Implements policy and decisions of managing/executive committee.
4. Provides professional services to the agency/organisation.
5. Report the progress of agency/organisation.
6. Prepares records and reports.
7. Provides administrative and technical leadership in agency/ organisation.

COMMITMENT OF ADMINISTRATIVE PERSONNEL

An administrative personnel in organisation, specially in social welfare organisation should have loyalty towards organisation and should identify with organisation as well as take active participation in the activities of organisation. The commitment reflects personnel's belief in the mission and goals of the organisation, willingness to expand effort in their accomplishment and intention to continue with the organisation.

Factors Stimulating Commitment

These are as follows:

1. Clarity of rules and policies define the working limits of administrative personnel in organisation and decisions should be taken and implemented accordingly.
2. Development of personnel through training may also stimulate commitment on their part since they will feel that their future is secured in the organisation.

3. Respect shown towards efforts of personnel develops a sense of belongingness to the organisation because respecting worth and dignity of an individual is an important value.
4. Participation and authority of personnel lead to commitment since personnel may be able to show their potential through participation as well as through proper authority. They may influence the other personnel of the organisation.
5. Personnel should be valued so that they may not feel neglected or side lined.
6. Bullying or showing of ego should not be done so that they may contribute in the activities of organisation fully.
7. Administrative personnel should be able to influence other personnel by making mutually benefit exchanges with them in order to gain their cooperation. This influence can be achieved or maintained the administrative personnel to (a) treat other personnel as potential allies; (b) specify their objectives; (c) learn about other personnel's needs, interests as well as goals; (d) inventory their own resources to identify something of value you can offer; (e) assess your current relationship with the other person; (f) decide what to ask for and what to offer; and (g) make the actual exchange that produces a gain for other personnel (Cohen and Bradford).

POLICY FORMULATION IN VOLUNTARY ORGANISATION

Voluntary organisations are governed by the group of ultimate control which is normally known as General Body. This body constitutes group of persons which runs the voluntary organisations which is normally known as Executive Board/ Board of Directors/Managing Committee etc. The following considerations are kept in view while formulating policy in voluntary organisations.

1. The specific circumstances of the area in which voluntary organisation is working.
2. The rules, regulations and policies of government.
3. The memorandum of association of the voluntary organisation (the mandate of organisation).
4. The needs and problems of people.
5. Human, technical and financial resources available.
6. The competencies and skills available with the organisation.
7. Networking with other organisations.
8. The rules, regulations, willingness and sensitivity of sponsoring agency, grant giving agency, donor, subscribers, etc.
9. Meeting the challenges of the situation.
10. Pressures from members of voluntary organisation.

The procedure for formulation of policy in voluntary organisation is as follows:

1. The issue which needs attention is discussed generally in managing committee of the organisation.
2. The necessary information is collected either by an executive of organisation or a committee constituted for the purpose.
3. This information is analysed and put into concrete proposal before the managing committee.
4. Managing committee discusses the proposal for policy making in detail.
5. The managing committee approves the proposal and keeps it in general body.
6. The general body approves the proposal.
7. After the approval of general body, the policy is declared or imbibed into the voluntary organisation.
8. The executive of the organisation implements the policy.
9. The results of policy is evaluated by the executive of organisation.
10. The needed changes may be brought out by managing committee with the approval of general body.

POLICY FORMULATION IN GOVERNMENT AGENCIES

The rules and regulations as well as mandate of government determine the policy formulation procedure in government agencies. The following procedure is normally put into action for policy formulation:

1. Concern expressed over an unmet need(s) or social problem(s) or gap(s) in social services by concerned people, social and moral innovators, advocates of change or new programmes, media, academics, social activists through discussions, conferences, appeals, movements, electronic shows and print media, articles and discussions, etc.
2. Development of formal and structured groups of people as well as of government officials.
3. Gathering of structured information related to need or problem or gap and people affected by this through academic sources, statistical organisations, professionals and their organisations, social planning organisations, independent or sponsored investigations, seminars, conferences, enquiries, etc.
4. Development of common policy solutions and determination of goals by (a) knowing the policy alternatives, (b) making attention to workable possibilities within the social reality and the value context of society, (c) taking into account objectives of a variety of allies that would offer support or resistance to the programme, (d) envisioning

both the manifest and expected functions of this general policy and the latent functions or unintended consequences, (e) estimating the numerical size and characteristics of the population on which this policy will be concentrated, and (f) assessing the cost of alternative solutions and of coverage of different groups in the need category.

5. Lobbying for change by concerned organisations through (a) gaining support from politicians and civil servants, (b) seeking out possible allies and gaining the help of general institutional groups.
6. Formulation of an operational policy and laws by (a) setting up task forces to put policy into operation and to write provisions of the law, possibly in research organisations or the research arm of agency or in a social planning council or planning division of a professional group, (b) shaping policy into operational guidelines, including the type of provision, the method of provision and degree of provision, organisational structure, financing and allocation of responsibility among different administrative levels such as federal, state and local, (c) adding or compromising on or deleting provisions, due to action of congressional or state legislature committees or reactions of overall board of national professional organisations or other enacting groups such as local community chest or local council.
7. Actual enactment of law as well as agency programme through (a) statement of agreed upon final provisions or programme structure; and (b) set up of agency or other structure to run the programme.
8. Implementation of the programme by (a) translating laws, executive orders or operational guidelines into provision of the services or benefits at the local level; (b) setting up an organisational structure and staffing its components; (c) structuring a delivery system at the agency-client level; and (d) facilitating access to the service through information, advocacy and accessibility mechanisms.
9. Evaluation and assessment of programme by (a) research to judge whether the programme meets the needs of intended target groups and reaches stated objectives and decreases the problem; (b) assessment of latent functions or impacts; (c) detection of bottlenecks in deliver; (d) integration of policy programme into overall social, political and economic institutions in the society, and (e) examination of alternative policies (Elizabeth D. Huttman).

FUND RAISING

For long time, voluntary social welfare agencies have been dependent on charity which has been based on the personal salvation and the satisfaction on the part of donor who used to feel that he/she has helped the poor people.

With passage of time, the philanthropy and charity have been affected mainly due to (a) weakening of religious forces, (b) abolition of zamindari and feudal systems, (c) charity from wealthy people often dictates the terms to agency to serve for special community, to appoint persons of their choice in the agency, to contribute in such programme which may serve them personally not socially, and (d) changes taken place in overall social environment and thinking that institutionalisation has been no more an important and effective method of fulfilling the needs of the needy.

Techniques of Fund Raising

In the contemporary period the following techniques are being used for fund raising by social welfare organisation:

(A) Preparation

The first technique is the preparation for fund raising which involves:

1. Defining the cause of activities for which funds are needed.
2. Correct estimation of funds to be required.
3. Time period during which funds to raise.
4. Proper communication of the cause of activity among people.
5. Proper demonstration of needs/problems of persons to be benefitted from these funds.
6. Transparency in utilisation of funds should be propagated for maintaining creditability of organisation.

(B) Location of Sources of Funds

The possibility of available resources have to be located. These resources may be as follows:

1. *Grants-in-Aid*. These grants can be taken from Government, autonomous and other international organisations.
2. *Donations*. These donations are being managed from general public. Sometimes, these donations are given as religious activities (donation to organisation based of religious philosophy).
3. *Subscriptions*. The members of organisation give annual/periodical/ life time subscriptions which become a source of earning of organisation. Sometimes, officials are also selected or appointed on the basis of their contributions or subscription.
4. *Interest*. There are certain agencies which operate on the interest accrued on fixed deposits and endowments.
5. *Fees*. There are organisations which run educational institutions, provide medical services, run art and craft centres, fees or service charges from beneficiaries, fees taken from families of unfortunate persons etc.

6. *Sponsorship*. Some beneficiaries are sponsored by resourceful persons for their overall development. In case #, this practice is more rampant.
7. *Sale Proceeds*. Some organisations run training-cum-development centres and produce some products which are sold in market. This process gives them some resources to the organisation.
8. *Building/Hostels*. Some organisations have building which gives them rent for accommodation and there are some organisations which run hostel and earn some resources out of these hostels.
9. *Literary and Recreational Activities*. There are another sources of fund raising in which fund raising is done through literary work such as writing books, publishing collection of poems, write-ups, autobiographies etc. as well as organising recreational activities in the forms of recreational programmes (dance, dramas, singing programmes, poetic meets, etc.) fairs, festivals, kitty parties, fates, shows, etc.
10. *Acceptance of Donations in Kind*. This may be in the forms of grains, clothes, food etc.
11. *Lotteries*. Organising lottery shows may also be used as a form of fund raising.
12. *Use of Politically Sanctioned Fund*. This fund is given to some social welfare agencies by elected representatives.
13. *Corporate Funding*. Emergence of big corporate and resultant responsibilities of these corporation known as corporate social responsibilities have provided another area of funding to welfare and development organisations. In order to fulfil these corporate social responsibilities, these corporate houses are supposed to be committed for sustainable economic development working with employees, their families, the local community and society at large to improve their quality of life.
14. *Help from Banking Sector*. Banking sector also makes provision for giving assistance to institutions working for social causes.

(C) Methods of Fund Raising

The following methods can be used in fund raising.

1. Advertisements in public dailies and electronic media by making appeals for funding.
2. Organisation of fund raising campaigns mostly by selling tickets.
3. Organisation of shows, exhibitions, rallies, fete, competitions, matches, stamps sale, etc.
4. Organisation of door-to-door fund collection programme.
5. Launching of movement for a cause.

6. Mobilisation of legislatures, religious and development organisations.
7. Organisation of religious meet, talks, preaching including building of religious places and sale of religious articles.
8. Organisation and mobilisation of volunteers for fund raising.
9. Organisation of alumni meet.

Strategies for Building and Maintaining Relationships with Donors

These strategies are as follows:

1. *Growth.* Maintain the relationship with those donors who have donated previously and motivate them to suggest other likeminded persons to be as potential donors.
2. *Involvement.* Donor should be treated well so that they should respond to the appeals of agency for participation in grassroots fund raising efforts.
3. *Visibility.* Relationships should be open and honest leading to generate good image in the public.
4. *Efficiency.* Donor should be responsive and loyal which can be obtained by recognising and appreciating their response.
5. *Stability.* The stability of organisation and its finances goes a long way in maintaining and sustaining relationship with donors.

Regulation and Supervision of Fund Raising

The organisation which is engaged in fund raising should be properly regulated and supervised and some of the regulations are as follows:

1. The organisation/agency should have a welfare programme for people/community.
2. It should function at non-profit basis.
3. Money should be raised for charitable purposes.
4. The organisation/agency should have proper registration.
5. It should be in operation for the last three years.
6. It should have proper and active governing board.
7. It should have community sanction.
8. It should have realistic budget and proper system of accounting and audit by properly qualified account and audit personnel.
9. It should have proper public relations.
10. It should prepare proper reports and returns and submit to proper authorities.

Problems Faced in Fund Raising

These are as follows:

1. Lack of tapping of new resources.
2. Lack of devoted and dedicated staff for activities of agency.
3. More emphasis on cash.
4. Absence of proper public relations.
5. Lack of creditability of organisation/agency.
6. Lack of devoted and dedicated volunteers for fund raising.

COMMUNITY CHEST

The concept of community chest came in 1913 in city Cleveland in America. This chest is an organisation based on the support of citizens and voluntary organisations. The main function of this chest is to collect funds from community and provides grants to agencies in welfare activities. The main conditions are as follows:

1. The chest should be registered under some legislative enactments.
2. It should have duly constituted working committee.
3. The funds should be collected and distributed as per rules and regulations.
4. The grant given by the chest should have central mechanism over its expenditure.

Benefits

1. Voluntary agencies can save time from collecting funds for their programmes. They get sufficient time to organise the programmes.
2. Donors used to give donations once a year which can be collected by this chest.
3. The fund raising is done by experienced people.
4. Through this chest, duplication of efforts can be avoided.
5. Efficient utilisation of resources.
6. Good access to donors.
7. Creditability of agency enhanced.
8. Savings in expenditure of agencies.
9. The grant is fixed and definite.

Constitution of Community Chest

This chest is constituted by representatives, volunteers, voluntary members, ex-officio members of different institutions for the purpose of mobilisation of resources for institutions in a geographical area. A community chest may have different committees such as Goal Determination Committee, Public Relations Committee, Campaign Committee, Distribution Committee, Account-cum-Supervision Committee, Budget Committee, etc.

PUBLIC RELATIONS

Public relations are an essential part of social work administration. It is responsibility of administrator that the work of organisation should be known to community in which it is working. It is through strong public relations, community participation in the working of social welfare organisation can be ensured.

Objectives

These are as follows:

1. Rendering information to community regarding: (a) the problems handled by social welfare agency, (b) services offered by the agency, (c) utilisation of money received by agency through donors, subscribers and general masses, (d) availability of benefits for perspective beneficiaries.
2. Keep on maintaining minimum standards of services in order to avoid public criticism.
3. Increasing donations, subscriptions, increasing effectiveness of fund raising.
4. Increasing the coverage of agency.

Principles

Elizabeth Haglund has suggested the following principles:

1. Know where and what your goals are. What are your targets?
2. Know who you want to reach. Who are your public?
3. Evaluate resources such as money, manpower and skills available.
4. Note how your benefits dovetail with those you reach. Give before you get.
5. Know specific techniques of public relations in regard to preparation and participation regarding advertising, publicity, and brochures. Ask the questions, who, what, where, why and how much. For example, brevity is important. Ordinarily 1½ -2 pages for newspaper is sample and probability ½ a page for radio and TV is optimal.
6. Be absolutely honest.
7. Thank people. Show appreciation (Quoted by Skidmore).

D. Paul Chowdhury has given the following broad principles which should be kept in mind while organising public relations work:

1. Focus should always be on various groups whom we are trying to approach.

2. While preparing any publicity material, we should have in mind a theme of each agency's work.
3. The attitude of the staff towards the general public is very important and quality of services is a fundamental aspect of public relations. If the clientele's needs are looked after properly, promptly and courteously, the news will spread in the community very soon.
4. Some of the influential people of the community may be very good for media and public relations because they are always in touch with the important and useful people in the community.
5. Public relations are a continuous process and as such there is no particular time to organise a campaign of publicity but there should be a regular time-table for using different media of public relations and approaching different groups at different time of the year.
6. A separate committee consisting of influential people of the locality, people with experience in journalism, members of the managing committee of the agency should be formed and this committee could be entrusted with public relations work.

Methods of Public Relations

These are as follows:

(A) *Personal Contacts*. Personal contacts made by members of Board, Managing Committee Members, staff of the community members, beneficiaries, donors and government and non-government agencies is a very effective method of public relations. This may be done by: (1) inviting people to visit agency, (2) organising seminars and conferences, (3) inviting selected people in annual meetings of the agency, (4) attending meetings and conferences organised by other agencies, (5) coordinating council, (6) making appeals and speeches, and (7) organising signature campaigns.

(B) *Visual*. This includes (1) newspaper, (2) magazine, (3) reports, (4) folders, (5) pamphlets, (6) photographs, (7) slides, (8) exhibition, (9) posters, etc.

(C) *Audio-Visual*. This encompasses (1) television, (2) dramas, (3) rallies, (4) demonstrations, (5) coordinating council, (6) making appeals and speeches and (7) organising signature campaigns.

(D) Networking with persons and agencies/organisations.

(E) Forming alliances with decision makers, bureaucratic etc.

(F) Forming and sustaining coalitions.

PROBLEMS OF VOLUNTARY AGENCY

These are few problems of voluntary agencies in India.

1. *Dominance of Vested Interests*: Voluntary agency functions under autonomous system having no external control system. So, sometimes these agencies are dominated by fulfilling the wishes and satisfying the whims of a person or group of persons without consideration of public good.

2. *Political and Economic Interests*: These agencies, sometimes, are organised for serving political and economic interest of few persons in the garb of public good.

3. *Lack of Resources*: A voluntary agency is financially managed by private resources, i.e. donations, subscriptions, etc. It can take grants-in-aid from the government. But, it may suffer from lack of resources, since regularity in funds procurement cannot be maintained.

4. *Lack of Creditability*: Due to private management and vested interests, these agencies have not been able to win the confidence of masses. People in general understand the formation of agency, now-a-days, leads to personal development rather than societal development.

5. *Lack of Trained Manpower*: Due to lack of resources as well as will of management, these agencies are mostly manned by untrained personnel rendering their duties not in scientific and systematic manner. Some agencies also do not have capacity to pay these trained personnel.

6. *Lack of Coordination Among Different Agencies*: There is lack of coordination among the activities of different agencies leading to duplication of efforts and waste of resources. Sometimes, same activities are conducted in the same area.

7. *Voluntary Work as Fashion*: Presently, the voluntary work has become a fashion of high status people.

8. *Lack of Supervision and Control*: These agencies work in an autonomous manner, so there are no arrangements for effective supervision and control either by agency personnel or from outside organisation.

9. *Problems in Fixing Standards*: It is very difficult to develop and fix standards of services to the people due to diversities of different actions.

10. *Lack of Existence of Sound System of Monitoring and Evaluation*: These agencies fail to establish a sound system of monitoring and evaluation so that strengths and weaknesses are not highlighted properly.

11. *Factionalism and Infighting*: Due to vested interests and keeping the control over the administration of these agencies breed factionalism and infighting adversely affecting the functioning of agencies.

12

Administration of Important Organisations

SOCIAL WELFARE DEPARTMENT AT THE CENTRE

The subject of social welfare existed at the central level either as an independent entity or a part of some allied department in the past. The main developments have been as follows:

1. Department of Social Security was established in June 1964 after pooling the subjects related to social welfare from different ministries like Education, Home Affairs, Health, Labour, Commerce and Industry
2. In January 1966, the Department of Social Security was re-designated as Department of Social Welfare.
3. Department of Social Welfare was elevated to Ministry in August 1979 and designated as Ministry of Education and Social Welfare.
4. Ministry of Education and Social Welfare was re-designated as Ministry of Social and Women Welfare in 1984.
5. The Ministry of Welfare was formed on 25th September, 1985 and subjects related to Welfare of Scheduled Castes and Scheduled Tribes, Minorities and Other Backward Classes from the Ministry of Home Affairs and Welfare of Disabled and Programmes of Social Defence from erstwhile Ministry of Social and Women Welfare and work relating to Wakf, from Ministry of Law were transferred to the Ministry of Welfare with effect from January 6, 1986.
6. The Department of Women and Child Development was placed under the new Ministry of Human Resource Development in 1986.
7. The name of Ministry was changed in May, 1998 to Ministry of Social Justice and Empowerment.

8. In October, 1999, separate Ministry of Tribal Affairs was formed after taking away Tribal Division from Ministry of Social Justice and Empowerment.
9. In January 2007 the Minorities Division along with Wakf unit have moved to form a separate Ministry.
   At the same time Child Development Division was made the part of Ministry of Women and Child Development.
10. On May 12, 2012, two departments have been created under Ministry of Social Justice and Empowerment. These are as follows:
    (a) Department of Social Justice and Empowerment (Samajik Nyay Aur Adhikarita Vibhag)
    (b) Department of Disability Affairs (Nishaktata Karya Vibhag)

SUBJECTS ALLOCATED TO TWO DEPARTMENTS

Subjects Assigned

A. Department of Social Justice and Empowerment (Samajik Nyaya Aur Adhikarita Vibhag)

1. The following subject which fall within List III - Concurrent List of the Seventh Schedule to the Constitution:
   Nomadic and Migratory Tribes
2. To act as the nodal Department for matters pertaining to the following groups, namely:
   (i) Scheduled Castes;
   (ii) Socially and Educationally Backward Classes;
   (iii) Denotified Tribes;
   (iv) Economically Backward Classes; and
   (v) Senior Citizens
   Note: The Department of Social Justice and Empowerment shall be the nodal Department for the overall policy, planning and coordination of programmes for the development of the groups mentioned at (i) to (iv) above, and the welfare of the group at (v) above. However, overall management and monitoring etc. of the sectoral programmes in respect of these groups shall be the responsibility of the concerned Central Ministries, State Governments and Union Territory Administrations. Each Central Ministry or Department shall discharge nodal responsibility concerning its sector.
3. Special schemes aimed at social, educational and economic empowerment of the groups mentioned at (i) to (iv) under entry 2 above, e.g. scholarships, hostels, residential schools, skill training, concessional loans and subsidy for self-employment, etc.

4. Rehabilitation of manual scavengers in alternative occupations.
5. Programmes of care and support to senior citizens.
6. Prohibition.
7. Rehabilitation of victims of alcoholism and substance abuse, and their families.
8. Beggary.
9. International Conventions and Agreements on matters dealt within the Department.
10. Awareness generation, research, evaluation and training in regard to subjects allocated to the Department.
11. Charitable and Religious Endowments and Promotion and Development of Voluntary Effort pertaining to subjects allocated to the Department.
12. The Protection of Civil Rights Act, 1955 (22 of 1955).
13. The Scheduled Castes and the Scheduled Tribes (Prevention of Atrocities) Act, 1989 (33 of 1989), (in so far as it relates to the Scheduled Castes, excluding administration of criminal justice in regard to offences under the Act).
14. The National Commission for Backward Classes Act, 1993 (27 of 1993).
15. The Maintenance and Welfare of Parents and Senior Citizens Act, 2007 (56 of 2007).
16. The National Commission for the Scheduled Castes.
17. The National Commission for Safai Karmacharis.
18. The National Commission for Backward Classes.
19. The National Scheduled Castes Finance and Development Corporation.
20. The National Safai Karmacharis Finance and Development Corporation.
21. The National Backward Classes Finance and Development Corporation.
22. National Institute of Social Defence
23. Dr. Ambedkar Foundation
24. Babu Jagjivan Ram National Foundation

B. Department of Disability Affairs (Nishaktata Karya Vibhag)

The following subjects which fall within List I - Union List of the Seventh Schedule to the Constitution:

1. Indo-US, Indo-UK, Indo-German, Indo-Swiss and Indo-Swedish Agreements for Duty-free import of donated relief goods/supplies and matters connected with the distribution of such supplies.

The following subjects which fall within List III - Concurrent List of the Seventh Schedule to the Constitution (as regards legislation only):

2. Social Security and Social Insurance save to the extent allotted to any other Department.
3. For the Union Territories, the following subjects which fall in List II - State List or List III - Concurrent List of the Seventh Schedule to the Constitution, in so far as they exist in regard to such territories: Relief of the Disabled and the Unemployable; Social Security and Social Insurance, save to the extent allotted to any other Department.
4. To act as the nodal Department for matters pertaining to Disability and Persons with Disabilities.
   Note: The Department of Disability Affairs shall be the nodal Department for the overall policy, planning and coordination of programmes for Persons with Disabilities. However, overall management and monitoring etc. of the sectoral programmes in respect of this group shall be the responsibility of the concerned Central Ministries, State Governments and Union Territory Administrations. Each Central Ministry or Department shall discharge nodal responsibility concerning its sector.
5. Special schemes aimed at rehabilitation and social, educational and economic empowerment of Persons with Disabilities, e.g. supply of aids and appliances, scholarships, residential schools, skill training, concessional loans and subsidy for self-employment, etc.
6. Education and Training of Rehabilitation Professionals.
7. International Conventions and Agreements on matters dealt with in the Department; The United Nation Convention on the Rights of Persons with Disabilities.
8. Awareness generation, research, evaluation and training in regard to subjects allocated to the Department.
9. Charitable and Religious Endowments, and promotion and development of Voluntary Effort pertaining to subjects allocated to the Department.
10. The Rehabilitation Council of India Act, 1992 (34 of 1992).
11. The Persons with Disabilities (Equal Opportunities, Protection of Rights and Full Participation) Act, 1995 (1 of 1996).
12. The National Trust for Welfare of Persons with Autism, Cerebral Palsy, Mental Retardation and Multiple Disabilities Act, 1999 (44 of 1999).
13. The Rehabilitation Council of India.
14. The Chief Commissioner for Persons with Disabilities.
15. The National Trust for the Welfare of Persons with Autism, Cerebral Palsy, Mental Retardation and Multiple Disabilities.

16. The National Handicapped Finance and Development Corporation.
17. Artificial Limbs Manufacturing Corporation, Kanpur.
18. Deen Dayal Upadhyaya Institute of Physically Handicapped, New Delhi.
19. National Institute for the Orthopedically Handicapped, Kolkata.
20. National Institute of Visually Handicapped, Dehradun.
21. National Institute of Mentally Handicapped, Secunderabad.
22. Ali Yavar Jung National Institute for the Hearing Handicapped, Mumbai.
23. National Institute of Rehabilitation Training and Research, Cuttack.
24. National Institute for the Empowerment of Persons with Multiple Disabilities, Chennai.
25. The Indian Sign Language Research and Training Centre, New Delhi.

ADMINISTRATIVE ORGANISATION

The Ministry of Social Justice and Empowerment is headed by Cabinet Minister followed by State Minister.

- After that there is Secretary of Ministry.
- Secretary has two Additional Secretaries – one looks after the all divisions of Ministry and another is Additional Secretary and Financial Adviser who deals with financial aspects of the Ministry.
- Additional Secretary is assisted by four Joint Secretaries (one of Scheduled Castes Development one for Backward Classes, Administration and Media, one for Social Defence and another for Disability Development and Chief Vigilance Officer), one Economic Adviser for Planning, Monitoring and Coordination, one Deputy Director, General Statistics.
- Additional Secretary and Finance Adviser is assisted by Director (Finance) and Under Secretary (Finance).
- Joint Secretary (Scheduled Castes Development) is assisted by four Directors.
- Joint Secretary (BC, Administration and Media) is assisted by Director/(Scheduled Castes Development), Joint Director (Raj Bhasha), Under Secretary (Backward Classes) and Under Secretary (Backward Classes and Media).
- Joint Secretary (Social Defence) is assisted by Deputy Secretary (Drug Abuse Prevention) and Director (Ageing)
- Joint Secretary (Disability Development and Chief Vigilance Officer) is assisted by Director (Disability Development), and Director (Disability Development and National Institutes) and Director (Disability Development).

- Economic Adviser (Planning, Monitoring and Coordination) is assisted by Director (Parliament), Deputy Secretary (Coordination), Director (Planning) and Joint Director (Research, Evaluation and Vigilance).

Besides this, Ministry of Social Justice and Empowerment has Standing Committee consisting of twenty one members from Lok Sabha and ten from Rajya Sabha.

The Ministry has Advisory Committee headed by Minister of the Ministry, nine members from Parliament, one from Rajya Sabha and two ex-officio members, i.e. two State Ministers of Parliamentary Affairs.

DIVISIONS OF MINISTRY OF SOCIAL JUSTICE AND EMPOWERMENT

There are divisions through which this Ministry functions. These are as follows:

(A) Scheduled Caste Welfare Division

1. This division monitors the efforts made by State Governments and Central Ministries for protecting and promoting the interests of Scheduled Castes.
2. This Ministry as the nodal Ministry to oversee the interests of the SCs, so this division has an important role to play.
3. Scheduled Caste Sub-Plan is being implemented by the Ministry through Scheduled Castes Development Bureau.
4. Special central assistance to Special Component Plan, in which cent per cent assistance is provided as additive to Scheduled Caste Sub-Plan of the States/UTs on the basis of certain criteria, i.e. SC population of States/UTs, relative backwardness of the area, percentage of SC families covered by composite economic development programmes in the State Plan to enable them to cross the poverty line etc.
5. The National Scheduled Castes Finance and Development Corporation has been set up under the Ministry to provide credit facilities to persons belonging to SCs living below double to poverty line limits (Rs. 40,000.00 p.a. for rural areas and Rs. 55,000.00 p.a. for urban areas) for income generating activities.
6. National Safai Karmacharis Finance and Development Corporation provides credit facilities to beneficiaries i.e. Safai Karmacharis, Scavengers and their dependents for income generating activities for socio-economic development through State channelising agencies.
7. The following two Acts are being implemented by the Ministry for the protection of SCs:
   (a) Protection of Civil Rights Act, 1955.

(b) The Scheduled Castes and Scheduled Tribes (Prevention of Atrocities) Act, 1989.

8. The Ministry also deals with the (a) monitoring of 11(a) point of 20 point programme, i.e. justice to Scheduled Castes, and (b) affirmative action including reservation in private sector for SCs/STs.
9. The associated organisations under this division are:
   (a) Babu Jagjivan Ram National Foundation
   (b) Dr. Ambedkar Foundation
   (c) National Commission for Safai Karmacharis
   (d) National Safai Karmachari Finance and Development Corporation
   (e) National Scheduled Castes Finance and Development Corporation
10. This Division implements varied kinds of schemes for educational and social development of SCs. These are as follows:
    (a) *Scholarships and Fellowships*: Various kinds of scholarships are being provided to SCs for their educational developments. These are: Pre-matric scholarships to SC students, post-matric scholarship to SC students, pre-matric scholarship to children of those engaged in unclean occupations, Rajiv Gandhi National Fellowship to SC students for pursuing Higher Education such as M.Phil. and Ph.D., Central Sector Scheme for Rajiv Gandhi National Fellowship, Central Sector Scholarship Scheme of Top Class Education for SC students, National Overseas Scholarship for SCs etc.
    (b) *Special Educational Development of SCs*: Certain special programmes are being run by this Division. These are: special educational development programme of scheduled castes girls belonging to low literacy levels, upgradation of merit of SC students and scheme of free coaching of SC and OBC students.
    (c) *Ideal Village Scheme*: Pradhan Mantri Adarsh Gram Yojana has been started on pilot basis to develop ideal villages having proper sanitation, housing, education etc.
    (d) *Hostel Scheme*: The Ministry has also started Baboo Jagjivan Ram Chattrawas Yojana for SC students who can live in these hostels.
    (e) *Rehabilitation Through Self-Employment and Credit Facilities*: The schemes of rehabilitation for SCs have also started through which these categories of persons are being given credit facilities through corporations known as National Scheduled Castes Finance and Development Corporation and National Safai Karmacharis Finance and Development Corporation.

    There is self-employment scheme for rehabilitation of manual scavengers also. Assistance is also provided to scheduled Castes

Development Corporations of States/UTs also.

(f) *Special Central Assistance to SC Sub-Plan*: The SC sub-plan, the Ministry provides assistance based on certain criteria.

(g) *Assistance to Voluntary Organisation*: There is scheme to assist Voluntary Organisations which are working for SCs.

(B) Welfare of Backward Classes Division

The main features are as follows:

1. The mandate of Ministry is to look after the welfare of Backward Classes through policy formulation, planning and implementation of programmes related to social and economic empowerment of OBCs.
2. This Division also deals with two institutions namely, National Backward Classes Finance and Development Corporation and National Commission for Backward Classes.
3. The following schemes are in operation for OBCs:
   (a) *Scholarship*. There are two schemes for OBCs i.e. Pre-matric and Post-matric scholarships.
   (b) *Construction of Hostel*. Under this scheme, the hostel is constructed for OBCs boys and girls.
   (c) *Assistance to Voluntary Organisations*. The voluntary organisations working for OBCs are given assistance for the programmes of OBCs.
   (d) *Credit Facility for Self-Employment*. National Backward Classes Finance and Development Corporation gives credit to OBCs for self-employment.

(C) Empowerment of Persons with Disabilities Division

The main features of this division are as follows:

1. The division facilitates empowerment of the persons with visual, hearing, speech, locomotors and mental disabilities.

2. The Government of India has enacted the Act namely "The Persons with Disabilities (Equal Opportunities, Protection of Rights and Full Participation) Act, 1995 for ensuring equal opportunities for persons with disabilities and full participation in nation building.

For this, a multi-pronged approach involving all the appropriate stakeholders is being followed in implementation of various provisions of the Act.

3. The following schemes are in operation:

(a) *Assistance to Disabled Persons for Purchase/Filing of Aids and Appliances*: The objective of this scheme to assist the needy disabled persons in procuring durable, sophisticated and scientifically manufactured, modern, standard aids and appliances that can promote their physical, social and psychological rehabilitation by reducing the effects of disabilities and enhance their economic potential.

(b) *Deendayal Disabled Rehabilitation Scheme to Promote Voluntary Action for Persons with Disabilities*: In order to facilitate delivery of various services to persons with disabilities by voluntary organisation, the Ministry is administering this scheme and providing grants-in-aid to NGOs for following projects:

(i) Vocational Training Centres,
(ii) Shelter and Workshops,
(iii) Special Schools for the Persons with Disabilities,
(iv) Project for Cerebral Palsied Children,
(v) Project for Pre-school and Early Intervention and Training,
(vi) Home-based Rehabilitation Programme/Home Management Programme
(vii) Project for Rehabilitation of Leprosy Cured Persons,
(viii) Project Relating to Survey, Identification Awareness and Sensitisation,
(ix) Project for Community Based Rehabilitation,
(x) Project for Human Resource Development,
(xi) Seminars/Workshops/Rural Camps,
(xii) Project for Legal Literacy Including Legal Counselling, Legal Aid, Analysis and Evaluation of Existing Laws,
(xiii) Environment Friendly and Eco-Primitive Projects for Handicapped,
(xiv) Grant for Purchase of Vehicle,
(xv) Construction of Building,
(xvi) Grant for Computer,
(xvii) Project for Low Vision Centres,
(xviii) Half-way Home for Psycho-Social Rehabilitation of Treated and Controlled Mentally Ill Persons,
(xix) District Disability Rehabilitation Centres

The Ministry supports up to 90 per cent of expenditure.

(c) *Scheme of National Awards for Empowerment of Persons with Disability*: Under this scheme, varied kinds of awards are given. The provision of separate awards have been made for:

(a) most efficient/outstanding employees with disabilities;
(b) best employer;
(c) best placement agency/officer;
(d) outstanding individual;
(e) outstanding institution;
(f) role model;

(g) outstanding creative disabled individuals;
(h) outstanding technological innovation and adaptation of innovation to provide cost-effective technology.

Awards are also given to Government sector, Public Sector Undertakings and Private Enterprises for creating barrier free environment for persons with disabilities.

(d) *Scheme of National Scholarships for Persons with Disabilities*: Every year 500 new scholarships are provided for pursuing post-matric professional and technical courses of duration more than one year.

In respect of students with cerebral palsy, mental retardation, multiple disabilities and profound or severe hearing impairment, scholarships are awarded for pursuing studies from IXth standard onwards.

(e) Schemes Arising Out of the Implementation of the Persons with Disabilities (Equal Opportunities, Protection of Rights and Full Participation) Act, 1995

These are as follows:

(a) Incentives to employers in the private sector for providing regular employment to persons with disabilities.
(b) Models to promote awareness about accessibility features in public building.
(c) Setting up of composite regional centres for persons with disabilities.
(d) Establishment of disability rehabilitation centres.
(e) Organisation of awareness generation programme.
(f) Technology development projects in mission mode.
(f) Trust Fund for Empowerment of Persons with Disabilities

The Supreme Court in its order dated April 16, 2004 had directed that the banks, who had collected an estimated excess amount of Rs. 723.79 crores annually from the borrowers through rounding of in collection of interest tax, should transfer it to a trust which would be used for welfare of persons with disabilities.

(D) Social Defence Division

This division caters the requirements of (a) neglected and marginalised people; (b) abandoned destitute; (c) neglected and delinquent juveniles who need care and protection for want of support or are in conflict with the society of the law; (d) the drug addicts and offenders; and (e) the aged and host of others who need special care, protection and support.

The aim is to equip these groups to sustain a life of respect and honour and to become useful citizens.

The division plays a role of catalyst and has promoted voluntary action.

National Institute of Social Defence functions under this division.

Schemes

This division implements following schemes:

1. *Scheme for Older Persons*: There is an integrated programme for older persons which provides assistance to voluntary organisations for various activities related to older people.

2. *Construction of Old Age/Multi-Service Centres*: In this scheme, assistance is provided to Panchayati Raj Institutions/Voluntary Organisations/ Self-Help Groups for the construction of old age homes/multi-service centres for older persons.

3. *Assistance for Prevention of Alcoholism and Substance Abuse and Social Defence Services*: Financial assistance is made available to voluntary organisations for the prevention of alcoholism and substance abuse.

Assistance is also provided for social defence services.

(E) Planning, Research, Evaluation and Monitoring (PREM) Division

I. Research and Evaluation

This division tries to know the impact of the schemes and programmes sanctioned to voluntary organisations, state governments and union territory administrations. It is also pertinent to identify emerging issues those require policy interventions. Consequently, the Ministry sponsors research and evaluation studies.

The types of schemes are in operation:

(a) Scheme of grant-in-aid for research and publication under which grants are provided for research/evaluation studies, seminars/ workshops/conferences and publications covering the areas of disabled development, social defence, other backward classes and general social welfare.

(b) Scheme for supporting projects of All India or Inter-state Nature for Scheduled Castes Development (Research and Training) under which grants are provided for research for evaluation studies, seminars/ workshops/conferences in the field of Scheduled Castes development.

II. Plan Coordination

Here coordination work is done for progress and planning activities such as preparation of annual reports, annual plans, five year plans and mid-term appraisal, review of plan expenditure in Ministry and by the Planning Commission, preparation of material for Reference Manual of I&B Ministry, Economic Survey, Parliamentary Standing Committee for approval of Budget, Finance Commission matters, advisory committee meetings of Indian Council of Social Science Research, Tata Institute of Social Sciences, University Grants Commission and Centre for Social Development.

III. Research/Statistical Publications

Here, reports of studies, statistical data and other matters related to Ministry are published.

SOCIAL WELFARE ADMINISTRATION AT STATE LEVEL

The State Governments and Union Territory Administrators implement the centrally sponsored social welfare and development schemes on the one hand and on the other hand they formulate their own welfare and development programmes (services for socially and economically weaker sections of society such as children, women, scheduled castes/tribes, backward classes, disabled, aged, unemployed, destitute, needy etc.). These programmes may be institutional such as education, health, homes, hostels, vocational training centres, etc. and non-institutional i.e. giving financial assistance in forms of unemployment allowance, children allowance, pensions, etc.

A large number of States/UT Administrations has established Department of Social Welfare for rendering these welfare services. The other states have given some different nomenclature of this Department such as Child Development and Social Welfare; Odisha; Sikkim – Social Justice, Empowerment and Welfare, etc.

Thus, it is clear that different states/union territory administrations have been providing these services through above mentioned departments as well as through other departments also, for example, Women and Child Welfare, Education, Health, Rural and Panchayati Raj Departments, etc.

Operational Structure

The main features are as follows:

1. Social welfare department is normally headed by a Cabinet or State Minister of the State.
2. Secretary to the State Government is the administrative head of Department.
3. The Secretariat helps, guides and advises the Minister in formulation of the policies of the Department and framing of legislation as well as supervising the execution of the policies, schemes, projects and programmes.
4. The Directorate is headed by Director who is assisted by Additional Director, Joint Director, Deputy Directors, Assistant Directors, Administrative Officers and other supporting staff.
5. The Directorate has Divisional Offices and representative at District Level. Normally, at district level, this representative of official functions under the Collector.

6. The Social Welfare Directorate has institutions also in the State such as Beggar Home, Observation Homes etc. which are normally headed by a Superintendent assisted by other supporting staff.

NATIONAL COMMISSION FOR SCHEDULED CASTES AND SCHEDULED TRIBES

The Indian Constitution has made special provisions for certain communities of the country who were suffering from extreme social, educational and economic backwardness arising out of age-old practice of untouchability and some others on account of the primitive agricultural practices, lack of infrastructure facilities and geographical as well as cultural isolation.

Historical Background

1. Under Article 338 of Indian Constitution, there is provision of appoint of Special Officer for looking after the effective implementation of various safeguards provided in the Constitution for the SCs/STs and other legislations providing varied kinds of protection. This Special Officer was designated as Commissioner for SCs/STs was assigned the duty to investigate all matters relating to safeguards for SCs and STs in various States and to report to the President upon the working of these safeguards.
2. The First Commissioner was appointed on November 18, 1950 for facilitating effective functioning of the Office of Commissioner for SCs and STS in accordance with the needs of time, 17 Regional Offices of Commissioner were set up in different parts of the country which were headed by Assistant Commissioners for SCs and STs who were, in July 1965, re-designated as Deputy Commissioners.
3. In June, 1967, the 17 Regional Offices were reorganised in five zonal offices and placed under the control of newly created Directorate General of Backward Classes Welfare in the Department of Social Welfare. Each Zonal Office was headed by Zonal Director, Backward Classes Welfare and the Post of Deputy Commissioner SCs/STs was re-designated as Deputy Director, Backward Classes Welfare and place under the control of Zonal Directors.
4. Only July 24, 1978, the Government decided to convert one member commission to multi-member commission and first Commission for SCs and STs was set up in August, 1978 with Chairman and other four members. The office of the Commissioner for SCs/STs and Commission for SCs/STs charged with the same functions continued to co-exist till September, 1987.

5. On September 1, 1987, the Commissioner for SCs/STs was renamed as National Commission for SCs/STs consisting of a chairperson and not more than 11 members. This resolution of formation of National Commission also demarcated the functions of Commissioner for SCs/STs and National Commission for SCs/STs.

   It was decided that only the Commissioner for SCs and STS would be submitting the report to the President. The National Commission of SCs/STs would conduct studies and function as a National Level Advisory Body to advise the Government on broad policy issues and levels of development of SCs and STs and would submit its report to Central Government.
6. The first Statutory Commission under the Constitution (Sixty Fifth Amendment) Act was constituted on 12.3.1992 and from the same date the Office of the Commissioner of SCs/STs was abolished. This Statutory Commission consisted of one Chairman, one Vice Chairman and five other members appointed by President of India.
7. After that, at different points of time following National Commissions were constituted:
   - Second National Commission for SCs/STs (constituted in October, 1995)
   - Third National Commission for SCs/STs (constituted in December, 1998)
   - Fourth National Commission for SCs/STs (constituted in march, 2002)
8. With the Constitution (Eighty-Ninth Amendment Act, 2003) coming into force on 19.2.2004, the erstwhile National Commission for SCs/STs has been replaced by:
   (a) National Commission for Scheduled Castes
   (b) *National Commission for Scheduled Tribes*: The National Commission for Scheduled Tribes has been created by inserting a new Article 338A in the Indian Constitution.
9. The First National Commission for Scheduled Tribes was constituted in March 2004 with one Chairman, one Vice Chairman and three other members.
10. The Second Commission for STs was constituted in June, 2007.

NATIONAL COMMISSION FOR SCHEDULED CASTES

Consequent upon the Constitution (Eighty Ninth Amendment) Act, 2003 coming into force on 19.2.2004, the erstwhile National Commission for

Scheduled Castes and Scheduled Tribes has been replaced by (a) National Commission for Scheduled Castes and (b) National Commission for Scheduled Tribes. The rules of this Commission were notified on February 20, 2004 by Ministry of Social Justice and Empowerment.

The Second National Commission for Scheduled Castes was constituted on 25.05.2007.

The Third National Commission for Scheduled Castes has been constituted on 18.11.2010, having one Chairperson, one Vice-Chairperson and three Members, which is still in operation.

ORGANISATIONAL STRUCTURE OF THE COMMISSION

See Chart 12.1.

NATIONAL COMMISSION FOR SCHEDULED TRIBES

This Commission has been constituted with one Chairman, one Vice Chairman and three members. The headquarters of Commission is located at New Delhi. This Commission has been constituted under Article 338A of the Indian Constitution.

Functions and Responsibilities of Commission

These are as follows:

1. To investigate and monitor all matters relating to the safeguards provided for Scheduled Tribes under the Constitution or under any other law for the time being in force or under any order of the Government and to evaluate the working of such safeguards.
2. To inquire into specific complaints with respect to the deprivation of rights and safeguards of Scheduled Tribes.
3. To participate and advise on planning process of socio-economic development of the Scheduled Tribes and to evaluate the progress of their development under the Union and State.
4. To present to the President, annually and at such other times as the Commission may deem fit, reports upon the working of those safeguards.
5. To make in such report recommendations as to the measures that should be taken by the Union or any State for the effective implementation of those safeguards and other measures for the protection, welfare and socio-economic development of the Scheduled Tribes.

Chart 12.1: Organisational Structure of the National Commission for Scheduled Castes

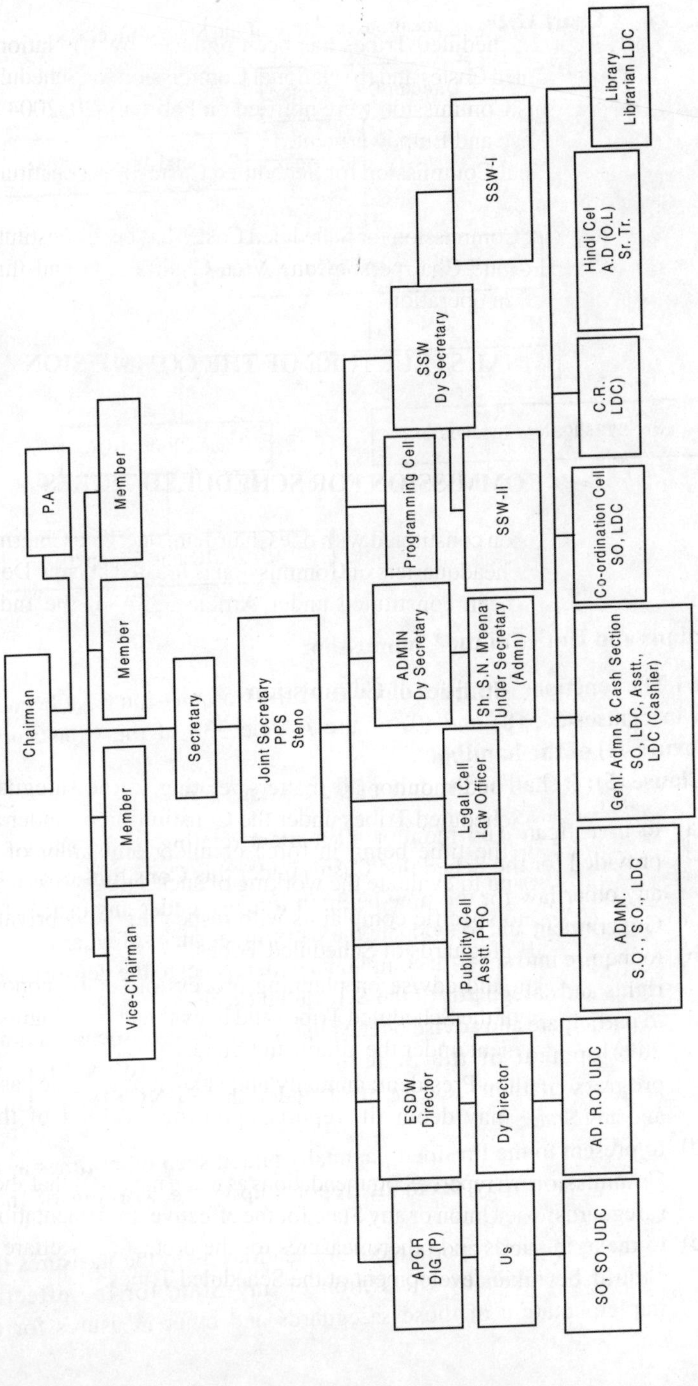

Chart 12.2: Organisation Structure of the State Offices

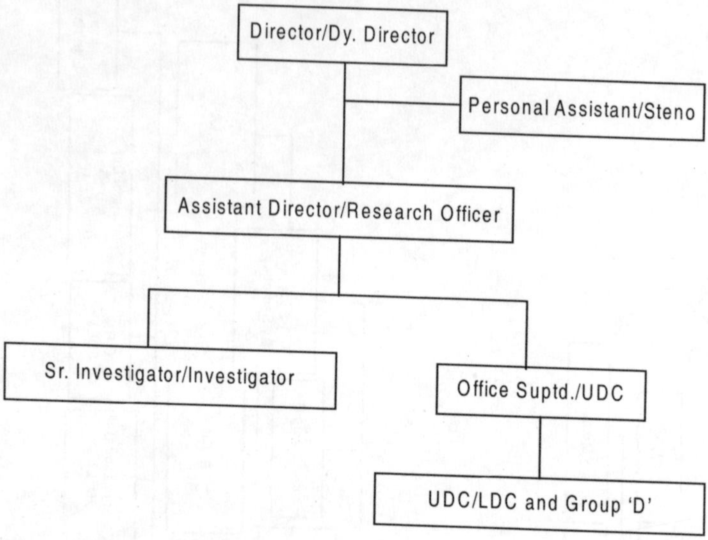

Functions and Duties of the Commission

1.1 The functions, duties and power of the Commission have been laid down in clauses(5), (8) and (9) of the Article 338 of the Constitution. **(Annexure-II) of the handbook**

Clause (5): It shall be the duty of the Commission:

(a) to investigate and monitor all matters relating to the safeguards provided for the Scheduled Castes under this Constitution or under any other law for the time being in force or under any order of the Government and to evaluate the working of such safeguards;

(b) to inquire into specific complaints with respect to the deprivation of rights and safeguards of the Scheduled Castes;

(c) to participate and advise on the planning process of socio-economic development of the Scheduled Castes and to evaluate the progress of their development under the **FUNCTIONS** Union and any State;

(d) to present to the President, annually and at such other times as the Commission may deem fit, reports upon the working of those safeguards;

(e) to make in such reports recommendations as to the measures that should be taken by the Union or any State for the effective implementation of those safeguards and other measures for the protection, welfare and socio-economic development of the Scheduled Castes; and

(f) to discharge such other functions in relation to the protection, welfare and development and advancement of the Scheduled Castes as the President may, subject to the provisions of any law made by Parliament, by rule specify.

Clause (8): The Commission shall, while investigating any matter referred to in sub-clause (a) or inquiring into any complaint referred to in sub-clause (b) of clause (5), have all the powers of a civil court trying a suit and in particular in respect of the following matters, namely:

(a) Summoning and enforcing the attendance of any person from any part of India and examining him on oath;
(b) Requiring the discovery and production of any documents;
(c) Receiving evidence on affidavits;
(d) Requisitioning any public record or copy thereof from any court or office;
(e) Issuing commissions for the examination of witnesses and documents;
(f) Any other matter which the President may by rule, determine;

Clause (9): The Union and every State Government shall consult the Commission on all major policy matters affecting Scheduled Castes.

Constitutional Safeguards

The important Constitutional Safeguards for Scheduled Castes is mentioned below:

(A) Development and Protective Safeguards

These safeguards are contained in the Directive Principles of State Policy of the Constitution and a specific provision in Article 46 which is a comprehensive provision comprising both the developmental and regulatory aspects. It reads as follows:-

Article 46—"The State shall promote with special care the educational and economic interests of the weaker sections of the people, and in particular, of the Scheduled Castes and the Scheduled Tribes, and shall protect them from social injustice and all forms of exploitation".

(B) Social Safeguards

Article 17—"Untouchability" is abolished and its practice in any form is forbidden. The enforcement of any disability arising out of "Untouchability" shall be an offence punishable in accordance with law.

To give effect to this Article, Parliament made an enactment viz., **Untouchability (Offences) Act, 1955.** To make the provisions of this Act more stringent, the Act was amended in 1976 and was also renamed as the **Protection of Civil Rights Act, 1955.** As provided under the Act, the Government of India also notified the Rules, viz, the PCR Rules, 1977, to carry out the provisions of this Act. As cases of atrocities on SCs/STs were not covered under the provisions of PCR Act, 1955, Parliament passed another important Act in 1989 for taking specific measures to prevent the atrocities. This Act known as the **Scheduled Castes and Scheduled Tribes (Prevention of Atrocities) Act, 1989,** became effective from 30-1-1990. For carrying out the provisions of this Act the Govt. of India have notified the SCs and STs (Prevention of Atrocities) Rules, 1995 on 31-3-1995. Copies of PCR Act, 1955, PCR Rules 1977, the SCs and the STs (POA) Act, 1989 and the SCs and STs (POA) Rules 1995 are placed at **Annexures-V, VI, VII and VIII of the handbook respectively.**

Article 23—prohibits traffic in human beings and beggar and other similar forms of forced labour and provides that any contravention of this provision shall be an offence punishable in accordance with law. It does not specifically mention SCs but since majority of bounded labour belong to SCs this Article has a special significance for these communities. In pursuance of this Article, Parliament has enacted the Bonded Labour System (Abolition) Act, 1976. For effective implementation of this Act, the Ministry of Labour is running a Centrally Sponsored Scheme for identification, liberation and rehabilitation of bonded labour.

Article 24—provides that no child below the age of 14 years shall be employed to work in any factory or mine or engaged in any other hazardous employment. There are Central and State laws to prevent child labour. This Article is also significant for SCs as a substantial portion of child labour engaged in hazardous jobs belong to these groups.

Article 25(2) (b)—provides that Hindu religious institutions of a public character shall be thrown open to all classes and sections of Hindus. This provision is relevant as some sects of Hindus used to claim that only members of the concerned sects had a right to enter their temples. This was only a subterfuge to prevent entry of SC persons in such temples. For the purpose of this provision the term Hindu includes Sikh, Jain and Buddhist.

(C) Economic Safeguards

The provisions of Articles 23, 24 and 46 mentioned above also form part of the economic safeguards for Scheduled Castes.

(D) Educational and Cultural Safeguards

Article 15(4)—empowers the State to make any special provision for the advancement of any socially and educationally backward classes of citizens or for SCs and STs. This provision w as added to the Constitution through the Constitution (First Amendment) Act, 1951, which amended several Articles. This provision has enabled the State to reserve seats for SCs and STs in educational institutions including technical, engineering and medical colleges and in Scientific & Specialized Courses. In this Article as well as in Article 16(4) the term 'backward classes' is used as a generic term and comprises various categories of backward classes, viz., Scheduled Castes, Scheduled Tribes, Other Backward Classes, De-notified Communities (Vimukta Jatiyan) and Nomadic/Semi nomadic communities.

(E) Political Safeguards

Article 164(1)—provides that in the States of Bihar, Madhya Pradesh and Orissa there shall be a Minister in charge of tribal welfare who may in addition be in charge of the welfare of the Scheduled Castes and backward classes or any other work.

Article 330—provides for reservation of seats for SCs and STs in the Lok Sabha.

Article 332—provides for reservation of seats for SCs/STs in the State Vidhan Sabhas (Legislative Assemblies).

Article 334—originally laid down that the provisions relating to the reservation of seats for SCs/STs in the Lok Sabha and State Vidhan Sabhas (and the representation of the Anglo-Indian community in the Lok Sabha and the State Vidhan Sabhas by nomination) would cease to have effect on the expiration of a period of ten years from the commencement of the Constitution, This Article has been amended five times, extending the said period by ten years on each occasion. This provision will now expire in January, 2010.

Article 371A—contains special provisions with respect to Nagaland.

Article 371B—contains special provisions with respect to Assam.

Article 371C—contains special provisions with respect to Manipur.

Article 371F—contains special provisions with respect to Sikkim.

(F) Service Safeguards

Article 16(4)—empowers the State to make "any provision for the reservation in appointments or posts in favour of any backward class of citizens which, in the opinion of the State, is not adequately represented in the services under the State".

Article 16(4A)—specific that nothing in this Article shall prevent the State from making any provision for reservation in matters of promotion, "with consequent seniority" to any class or classes of posts in the services under the State in favour of the Scheduled Castes and the Scheduled Tribes which, in the opinion of the State, are not adequately represented in the services under the State".

Article 16(4B)—"Specific that nothing in this article shall prevent the State from considering any unfilled vacancies of a year which are reserved for being filled up in that year in accordance with any provision for reservation made under clause (4) or clause (4A) as a separate class of vacancies to be filled up in any succeeding year or years and such class of vacancies shall not be considered together with the vacancies of the year in which they are being filled up for determining the ceiling of fifty percent reservation on total number of vacancies of that year".

Article 320 (4) provides that nothing in clause (3) shall require a Public Service Commission to be consulted as respects the manner in which any provision under Article 16(4A) may be made or the manner in which effect may be given to the provisions of Article 335.

Article 335 mentions that the claims of the members of the Scheduled Castes and the Scheduled Tribes shall be taken into consideration, consistently with the maintenance of efficiency of administration, in the making to appointments to services and posts in connection with the affairs of the Union or of a State"

"Provided that nothing in this Article shall prevent in making of any provision in favor of Member of SCs & STs for relaxation in qualifying marks in any examination or lowering the standards of evaluation, for reservation in matters of promotion to any class or classes of services or posts in connection with affairs of Union or of a State" **(Constitutional 82nd Amendment,-Act, 2000).**

Statutes and Legislations

There are a number of laws, both Central and State, which provide for safeguards to SCs. Some of these emanate from the various Constitutional provisions. An illustrative list of such laws is given below:

- The Protection ofCivil Rights Act- I955(in respect of Scheduled Castes)
- The Scheduled Castes and the Scheduled Tribes (Prevention of Atrocities) Act, 1989
- The Bonded Labour System (Abolition) Act, 1976 (in respect of Scheduled Castes)
- The Child Labour (Prohibition and Regulation) Act, 1986 (in respect of Scheduled Castes)
- The Minimum Wages Act 1948 (in respect of Scheduled Castes)
- Acts and regulations in force in different States to prevent alienation

of land belonging to SCs. In some States such provision exists in the Land Revenue Code,

Socio-economic Development

4.1 Section (9) of the Article 338 of the Constitution reads as follows:

"The Union and every State Government shall consult the Commission on all major policy matters affecting Scheduled Castes."

The Constitution has made it mandatory for the Union and every State Government to consult the Commission on all major Policy matters affecting SCs. This is very important function of the Commission, which has to keep track of all the major policy decisions, Legislative of Executive action taken by the Government of India or any State Government.

4.2 As per the provisions of Clause 5 (c) of Article 338, the Commission is required to participate and advise on the planning process of socio-economic development of SCs and evaluate the progress of their development under Union and any State. The role of the Commission in these areas involve interaction at various levels, i.e., with the Planning Commission, with the Central Ministries and with the State Governments. The Commission and its officers both at Headquarters and the State offices participate in formulation of policies and the developmental programmes for SCs including Special Component Plan for Scheduled Castes.

Procedure for Inquiry

5.1 Inquiry into specific complaints—The Commission is required to inquire into specific complaints with respect to the deprivation of rights and safeguards of Scheduled Castes. In order to enable the Commission to perform this function effectively and efficiently, the Commission would like the members of Scheduled Castes to know that it will be helpful to inquire into their grievances if they substantiate their complaints with supporting documents and quote the relevant provisions of the Act or Rules directions which have been violated.

5.2 The following aspect may be kept in mind while filing complaints before the Commission.

(a) The complaint should be directly addressed to the Chairman/Vice-Chairman/Secretary, National Commission for Scheduled Castes, New Delhi or the heads of its State Offices.

(b) The complaints should disclose his full identity and give his full address and should sign the representation.

(c) Complaints should be legibly written or typed and, where necessary, supported by authenticated documents.

(d) No action will be taken on matters which are sub-judice. Hence sub-judice matter need not be referred to the Commission as complaint(s).

(e) Cases pending in courts or cases in which a court has already given its final verdict may not be taken up afresh with the Commission.

5.3 Inquiry into cases of atrocities—

5.3.1 Whenever information is received in the Commission about any incident of atrocity against a person belonging to Scheduled Castes, the Commission would immediately get in touch with the law enforcing and administrative machinery of the State and the district to ascertain the details of incident and the action taken by the district administration.

5.3.2. The Commission ensures the following while by monitoring and issuing instructions to the concerned authorities.

(i) Whether the scene of occurrence of the crime has been visited immediately by Collector and Supdt. of Police of the district on receipt of information.

(ii) Whether proper FIR is registered in local Police Station.

(iii) Whether names of all the persons involved/cited by the complainant has been included in the FIR.

(iv) Whether investigation has been taken up by a Senior Police Officer as per provisions of SCS & STS (POA) Act-1989.

(v) Whether culprits has been apprehended and booked without loss of time.

(vi) Whether proper charge sheet is filed mentioning the relevant sections of IPC together with the PCR Act-1955 and SCS & STS (POA) Act-1989 in Court.

(vii) Whether the cases are tried by the Special Courts.

(viii) Whether special Public Prosecutors are appointed to handle these cases.

(ix) Whether Police assists the courts in bringing forward witnesses and see that the culprits are suitably punished by the courts.

5.3.3 The Commission will also monitor that—

(i) The victims are provided with suitable medical assistance and on time;

(ii) Adequate protection is arranged for the victims of such incidents by providing police protection by stationing a police party, by patrolling, etc;

(iii) To see that proper compensation is paid to the victims as per provisions of law.

5.3.4 The Commission will, wherever possible depending upon the gravity and circumstances of the case, visit the place of incident to oversee the arrangements and to console and infuse confidence among the victims.

5.3.5 The Commission has laid down detailed procedure for conducting such inquiries and monitoring at all levels. Such inquiries can be conduced by the Members of the Commission or Teams of Investigators from Headquarters or State office of the Commission.

5.4 Powers of the Commission to act as a Civil Court—While investigating any matter referred to in sub-clause (a) or inquiring into specific complaints under sub-clause (b) of the clause (5) of Article 338 of the Constitution, the Commission shall have the powers of a Civil Court trying a suit and in particular in respect of the following matters:

(a) Summoning and enforcing the attendance of any person from any part of India and examining him on oath;
(b) Requiring the discovery and production of any document;
(c) Receiving evidence on affidavits;
(d) Requisitioning of any public record or copy thereof from any court of office;
(e) Issuing commissions for the examination of witnesses the documents;
(f) Any other matter which the President may, by rule, determine.

5.5 Power to regulate its own procedure

(e) Clause 4 of the amended Article 338 of the Constitution empowers the Commission to regulate its own procedure for a meaningful performance. The Commission has framed the Rules of Procedure. A copy of the Rules of Procedure of the National Commission for Scheduled Castes as notified on 1st September, 2004 at given (Annexure x) of the Handbook.

Approach and Methodology Adopted by the Commission

6.1 Keeping in view its Constitutional obligations and the issues that are now critical, after almost half a century of independence, for the overall development and mainstreaming of the Scheduled Castes, the present Commission, constituted in February, 2004 has adopted a more vigorous approach in its functioning. The meetings of the Commission are held regularly and the implementation of decisions taken is monitored keenly.

6.2 In order to monitor and evaluate the impact of development schemes, the Commission has decided to interact with the State/UT Governments more actively by holding State level review meetings with the Chief Secretaries and other senior officers and conducting field level visits. The Commission feels that as a result of these visits and meetings, the State/UT Governments will become more conscious of the genuine problems of the Scheduled Castes and would take the necessary initiative in working out remedial measures and adopting appropriate strategies.

6.3 The Commission, through its Headquarters and State Offices has also conducted field level inquiries and studies. This process has been given a renewed vigour with a view to ensure prompt relief, specially in matters, relating to crimes and atrocities on Scheduled Castes and the grant of development benefits.

6.4 The procedure for investigating into complaints, especially with reference to violation of service safeguards, has also been streamlined to ensure prompt and speedy disposal of cases and relief in genuine cases. By calling officers and concerned Liaison Officers to the Commission with all relevant records, many long pending cases are being decided in one or two sittings. The Commission has also used its powers of Civil Court to summon documents and enforcing attendance in conducting the inquiries.

6.5 The Commission is of the view that it is only through proper planning and effective implementation of appropriate schemes for development that the Scheduled Castes can hope to catch up with the rest of the population and realize their full potential. The Commission has, thus, made a beginning by actively associating itself and participating in the planning process at the National and State levels. Regular communication is being maintained with the Planning Commission, Ministry of Social Justice & Empowerment and the State/UT Governments. The Annual Plans of the Central Ministries, States and UT Governments are being analysed in the Commission to this end with the support of its State Offices.

Consultation with Commission

Under the amended Article 338 (9), it has been provided that the Union and State Governments shall consult the Commission on all major policy matters affecting the Scheduled Castes. The Commission has impressed upon all concerned that this provision should be strictly enforced, as a result of which many Bills and other Policy matters affecting Scheduled Castes is now being received in the Commission for its views. The Commission would like to reiterate the obligatory nature of this provision and solicit the support of all concerned to bring to its notice new policies and change in existing policies, which have a bearing on the interests of SCs.

Commission's Report

8.1 Clause 5(d) of Article 338 provides "to present to the President, annually and at such other times as the Commission may deem fit, reports upon the working of those safeguards" and Clause 5(e) provides "to make in such reports, recommendations as to the measures that should be taken by the Union or any State for the effective implementation of those safeguards and other measures for the protection, welfare and socio-economic development

8.2 As per provision of these Clauses it is the duty of the Commission to present annually a report upon the working of Constitutional safeguards and measures taken by the Union and the States for the protection and welfare of the Scheduled Castes. In this series the erstwhile National Commission for Scheduled Castes and Scheduled Tribes has presented seven Annual Reports and four Special Reports during the period from 12th March, 1992 to 19th February, 2004 containing a number of recommendations.

8.3 Clause 6 of Article 338 provides, "The President shall cause all such reports to be laid before each House of Parliament along with a Memorandum explaining the action taken or proposed to be taken on the recommendations relating to the Union and the reasons for the non-acceptance, if any, of such recommendations.

8.4 Clause 7 of Article 338 provides, "Where any such report or any part thereof relates to any matter with which any State Government is concerned, a copy of such report shall be forwarded to the Governor of the State who shall cause it to be laid before the Legislature of the State along with a Memorandum explaining the action taken or proposed to be taken on the recommendations relating to the State and the reasons for non-acceptance, if any, of any of such recommendations.

Organisational set up of the Secretariat of the Commission

The National Commission for Scheduled Castes functions from the Headquarters located at New Delhi and from 12 State Offices of the Commission located in various States/UTs. The location and jurisdiction of these Offices and designation of office heads is given at Annexure-XI of the handbook.

9.1 There are four Wings at Hqrs.—

1. Administration & Coordination Wing
2. Service Safeguards Wing
3. Atrocities and Protection of Civil Rights Wing
4. Economic & Social Development Wing

9.2 Administration and Co-ordination Wing—

This Wing looks after personnel management of officers and staff of the Secretariat of the Commission and provide administrative support in the functioning of the Commission. The Co-ordination Wing co-ordinates the various activities being performed in the Commission, including making arrangements for holding internal meetings of the Commission as well as with State/UT Administrations for reviewing the implementation of constitutional safeguards.

9.3 Service Safeguards Wing—This Wing is dealing with the implementation of service safeguards provided to Scheduled Castes in the Central/State Government services as well as Central and State Government Public Sector Undertakings. All representations/complaints relating to Scheduled Castes persons about their service matters are dealt within this Wing. In addition, policy matters relating to enactment/Government orders and instructions pertaining to representation of Scheduled Castes in service, evaluation studies/surveys relating to implementation of the various Constitutional safeguards in respect of service matters are dealt in this Wing. Cases relating to false caste certificate and inclusion or exclusion of caste(s) in Scheduled Castes list are also dealt in this Wing.

9.4 Atrocities and Protection of Civil Rights Wing—This Wing is dealing with matters pertaining to atrocities caused on Scheduled Castes and cases relating to protection of Civil Rights Act, the Bonded Labour System (Abolition) Act, the Minimum Wages Act, etc. either on receipt of complaint from individuals or from newspapers report. Evaluation studies/surveys on these subjects are also conducted by this Wing.

9.5 Economic and Social Development Wing—This Wing is dealing with matters relating to development of Scheduled Castes particularly implementation and monitoring of plan schemes of the Central/State Governments. Some of the specific items of work handled by this Wing are:

(i) Special Component Plan for Scheduled Castes
(ii) National Scheduled Castes Finance and Development Corporation.
(iii) Representations/complaints made by Scheduled Castes persons regarding their grievances on matters other than atrocities, untouchability practices and service matters;
(iv) Social Research Institute and other research bodies;
(v) Land Reforms Acts and their implementation; (vi) Education Schemes for Scheduled Castes etc.

Functions of State Offices of the Commission

10.1 The State Offices of the Commission work as 'eyes and ears' of the Commission. They keep a watch on the formulation of policy and issue of guidelines relating to the welfare of Scheduled Castes in the respective States/UTs under their jurisdiction and keep the Commission Headquarters informed about the developments periodically. Policy decisions taken by any State Government/UT Administration affecting the interest of the Scheduled Castes are brought to the notice of the concerned authorities for necessary modifications. The State officers are requested to liaise with the State/UT Administration for taking up evaluation and other studies to assess the working of various development programmes implemented for the welfare of the Scheduled Castes and their impact on ameliorating the socio-economic conditions of the target groups. The findings of the studies are brought to the notice of the concerned State Government for taking remedial measures. The main observations are highlighted in the Commission's Report.

10.2 The State Offices of the Commission are required to interact with the State Administrations and guide them with a view to see that the interests of the Scheduled Castes is protected and promoted while in formulating plans and policies. The State Offices also monitor the utilization of funds earmarked for plans pertaining to Scheduled Castes including keeping a watch on diversion of funds from Special Component Plan.

10.3 Each of the State Offices sends Quarterly Report to the Commission Hqrs. on the activities undertaken by them highlighting major issues relating to welfare of Scheduled Castes in each States/UT under their jurisdiction. These reports contain useful information about the developments in a State and enable the Commission to have an overall view in respect of various States as well as national situation for taking appropriate action.

NATIONAL COMMISSION FOR SCHEDULED TRIBES

This Commission has been constituted with one Chairman, one Vice Chairman and three members. The headquarters of Commission is located at New Delhi.

This Commission has been constituted under Article 338A of the Indian Constitution.

FUNCTIONS AND RESPONSIBILITIES OF COMMISSION

These are as follows:

1. To investigate and monitor all matters relating to the safeguards provided for Scheduled Tribes under the Constitution or under any other law for the time being in force or under any order of the Government and to evaluate the working of such safeguards.
2. To inquire into specific complaints with respect to the deprivation of rights and safeguards of Scheduled Tribes.
3. To participate and advise on planning process of socio-economic development of the Scheduled Tribes and to evaluate the progress of their development under the Union and State.
4. To present to the President, annually and at such other times as the Commission may deem fit, reports upon the working of those safeguards.

5. To make in such report recommendations as to the measures that should be taken by the Union or any State for the effective implementation of those safeguards and other measures for the protection, welfare and socio-economic development of the Scheduled Tribes.
6. To discharge such other functions in relation to the protection, welfare and development and advancement of Scheduled Tribes as the President may, subject to the provisions of any law made by Parliament, by rule specify.

The Commission has been assigned the following additional functions vide the Ministry of Tribal Affairs' Notification dated 23 August, 2005 in relation to the protection welfare and development and advancement of the Scheduled Tribes:

(1) Measures that need to be taken over conferring ownership rights in respect of minor forest produce to STs living in forest areas.
(2) Measures to be taken to safeguard rights of the tribal communities over mineral resources, water resources etc. as laid down by law.
(3) Measures to be taken for the development of tribal to plug loopholes and to work more viable livelihood strategies.
(4) Measures to be taken to improve me efficacy of relief and rehabilitation measures for tribal groups displaced by development projects.
(5) Measures to be taken to prevent alienation of tribal people from land and to effectively rehabilitate such people in whose case alienation has already been taken place.
(6) Measures to be taken to elicit maximum cooperation and involvement of tribal communities for protecting forests and undertaking social afforestation.
(7) Measures to be taken to ensure full implementation of the provision of Panchayat (Extension to Scheduled Areas) Act, 1996
(8) Measures to be taken to reduce and ultimately eliminate the practice of shifting cultivation by tribal that lead to their continuous disempowerment and degradation of land and the environment.

DUTIES AND RESPONSIBILITIES OF OFFICIALS AND MEMBERS OF COMMISSION

Chairperson

1. The Chairperson shall have the residuary powers to decide on all questions and matters arising in the Commission.

2. He/she shall allocate subjects and responsibilities among the Members.
3. The Chairperson shall be the authority to sanction leave and approve tours of the Members.
4. The Chairperson shall preside over the meetings of the Commission.
5. All important decisions in the Commission pertaining to the subjects allotted to the Members shall be taken with the approval of the Chairperson.
6. The Chairperson may call for any records on any matter, which he/she considers s important and may take a decision on it himself/herself or, if necessary, place it at the meeting of the Commission.

Vice-Chairperson

1. The Vice-Chairperson shall preside over the meetings in the absence of the Chairperson.
2. The Vice-Chairperson shall perform such functions as are entrusted to him/her by the Chairperson.

Members

1. The Members shall have collective responsibility and shall function by participating in the 'meetings' and 'sittings' of the Commission and looking after the subjects allocated to them. Important actions and decisions of a Member may be brought at a meeting of the Commission which may review the same.
2. Any Member may suggest items for inclusion in the agenda and the same shall be so included after obtaining the consent of the Chairperson.
3. Each Member shall have overall responsibility of subjects and/or regions or State(s) as may be allocated to him.
4. The Members shall play the role of advising the State Governments under their jurisdiction on matters of planning and development relating to the welfare of Scheduled Tribes. The Commission's Secretariat at Headquarters and the Regional Offices shall assist the Members in keeping them fully informed of the problems and activities of the States and subjects under their respective charge.
5. One or more Members may, in accordance with the procedure specified in the rules elsewhere, hold sittings of the Commission to give hearing to the cases or to collect evidence or information on any matter, issue or case under investigation or inquiry of the Commission.

6. The Members shall communicate their tour programme well in advance to the Regional Offices indicating in detail the purpose of the visit and to the State Govt. Department and other concerned for discussions/inquiry, etc. The Members will observe the norms laid down during such tours.

Secretary

1. He shall be the administrative head and shall assist the Commission in the discharge of its functions with the assistance of the officers of the Commission.
2. All important administrative matters shall be placed before the Secretary who may pass general or specific orders on such matters.
3. The Secretary shall be responsible for having the agenda prepared for the meetings of the Commission and for circulating the minutes.
4. The Secretary shall assist the Commission in finalising the Reports.
5. The Secretary may, in his discretion, delegate any of his functions or authority to a subordinate officer of the Secretariat.

Investigation and Inquiry by the Commission

Methods of Investigation and Inquiry

The Commission may adopt any one or more of the following methods for investigating or inquiring into the matters falling within its authority:

(a) by the Commission directly;
(b) by an Investigating Team constituted at the Headquarters of the Commission; and
(c) through its Regional Offices

Investigation and Inquiry by the Commission Directly

The Commission may hold sittings for investigation into matters relating to safeguards, protection, welfare and development of the Scheduled Tribes for inquiry into specific complaints for which the Commission decided to take up investigation or inquiry directly. Such sittings may be held either at the Headquarters of the Commission or at any other place within the country.

The sitting(s) of the Commission would be held after giving due notice to the parties intended to be heard and also due publicity notice to the general public. Care will be taken to see that the members of the Scheduled Tribes who are affected in the mater under investigation or inquiry are given due information through notice or publicity.

When a decision for direct investigation is taken, an officer not below the rank of Assistant Director/ Research Officer/ Section Officer concerned with the subject matter of investigation, along with necessary staff may be attached to the Member(s) entrusted with such investigation or enquiry and they shall take all steps to arrange such sittings.

In accordance with clause 8 of Article 338A of the Constitution, while investigating in a matter referred to in sub-clause (a) or in inquiring into any complaint referred to in sub-clause (b) of clause (5) of Article 338A, the Commission shall have all the powers of civil court trying a suit and in particular in respect of the following matters, namely:

(a) summoning and enforcing the attendance of any person from any part of India and examining him on oath;
(b) requiring the discovery and production of any document;
(c) receiving evidence on affidavits;
(d) requisitioning any public record or copy thereof from any court or office;
(e) issuing commissions for the examination of witnesses and documents;
(f) any other matter which the President may, by rule, determine.

The Commission for the purpose of taking evidence in the investigation or inquiry may require the presence of any person and when considered necessary may issue summons to him/her. The summons for enforcing attendance of any person from any part of India and examining him/her during the course of investigation and inquiry by the Commission shall provide at least 15 days' notice to the person directed to be present before the Commission from the date of receipt of the summons.

Where the property, service/employment of Scheduled Tribes and other related matters are under immediate threat and prompt attention of the Commission is required, the matter shall be taken cognizance by issue of telex/fax to the concerned authority for making it known to them that the Commission is seized of the issue. Urgent reply by telegram or fax shall be called from the concerned authority. In case no reply is received within ten working days, the authority concerned may be required to appear before the Commission at a shorter notice for enquiry.

The Commission may issue commission/under clause 8 (e) of Article 338A of the Constitution to take evidence in any matter under investigation or inquiry and for this purpose appoint any person by an order in writing. The Commission may make further rules for payment of fee and travelling and other allowances to persons appointed to take evidence on commission.

After holding the required sittings, the Member(s) who conducted the investigation shall make a report which shall be sent to the Secretary or any other officer authorised to receive the report. After examination, action may be initiated on the report with the approval of the Chairperson.

Investigation or Inquiry by an Investigation Team Constituted at the Headquarters of the Commission

The Commission may decide about the matter that is to be investigated or enquired into by an Investigating Team of officials of the Commission, provided that in case the matter is urgent, the decision for such investigation or inquiry may be taken by the Chairperson.

The Investigating Team shall hold the investigation or inquiry, as the case may be, promptly and for this purpose, may initiate necessary correspondence including issuance of notices for production of documents in Form I, appended to these rules.

The Investigating Team may visit the area concerned after observing due formalities for obtaining approval of tours and other administrative requirements and after giving information to the concerned local authorities regarding the matter, purpose, scope and procedure of the investigation or inquiry. The Investigating Team may enlist the help of the officers and staff of the concerned Regional Office but the responsibility of preparing and presenting the report shall rest with the head of the Investigating Team.

The Investigating Team shall submit the report of the investigation or inquiry, as the case may be, to the Secretary or a subordinate officer of the Commission as may be directed by general or specific orders within the stipulated time, if any. If the time limit stipulated is likely to be exceeded, the head of the Investigating Team shall obtain the orders of the Secretary through the Officer-in-charge of the matter. The report shall be examined and put up to the competent authority for a decision regarding the action to be taken on the report.

The report shall be placed before the Chairperson of the Commission who will take appropriate action in the matter.

Investigation and Inquiry Through the Regional Offices

The Chairperson, the Vice-chairperson, the Members having jurisdiction over the subject or the Secretary of the Commission may decide about an investigation or inquiry that may be carried out through the Regional Offices of the Commission. The decision will be conveyed to the officer-in-charge of the concerned Regional Office who will be asked to get the matter investigated or inquired into within a stipulated time and send the report. The Regional Office shall conduct the investigation or inquiry through interrogation, on the spot visit, discussions and correspondence and examination of documents as may be necessary in the case and shall follow any special or general instructions issued in the matter by the Secretariat of the Commission from time to time.

If the investigation or inquiry cannot be completed within the stipulated time, the officer-in-charge of the Regional Office may send a communication to the Secretariat of the Commission before the expiry of the stipulated time and explain the circumstances and reasons for non-completion of the investigation or inquiry, as the case may be, within the stipulated time. The Secretary to the Commission or an officer acting under delegated functions may consider the request and communicate a revised date for the completion of the investigation or inquiry.

If during the course of investigation or inquiry, the Head of the Regional Office feels that it is necessary to invoke the powers of the Commission to require the production of any document or compelling the attendance of a person, he may make a special report with full facts to the Secretariat of the Commission. On receipt of such special report, the matter shall be placed before the Secretary/Member in-charge of the subject/State/UT who may make an order that necessary legal processes to compel attendance or to require production of any document may be issued. The summons and warrants issued for the purpose may be served on the person concerned either directly or through the officer-in-charge of the Regional Office as may be directed by the Secretary/Member authorising issue of such legal process.

After completion of the investigation or inquiry, as the case may be, the head of the Regional Office shall submit the report to the Secretary of the Commission suggesting the course of action that could be followed in the matter. The gist or findings of the report may be placed before the Secretary who may decide about further action in the matter.

Advisory Role of the Commission

Interaction of the Commission with the State Governments

The Commission shall interact with the State Governments through its Members, Secretariat and the Regional Offices.

The Members in-charge of the State/UT would interact with the State Government/UT Administration through meetings, personal contacts, visits and correspondence. The information in this regard may be sent to the concerned Deptt./Organisations well in advance and the Regional Offices should also be informed about the same. For this purpose, detailed guidelines may be formulated by the Commission. The Secretariat of the Commission through its concerned Wing(s) would provide necessary assistance and information to the Member for enabling him to discharge his functions effectively. The State Governments should provide facilities for transport, security, accommodation etc. to the Member as per his entitlement.

Interaction with the Planning Commission

The Commission shall interact with the Planning Commission at appropriate levels through representation in the various Committees, Working Groups or other such bodies set up by the Planning Commission. The Commission shall indicate this requirement through general or specific communication to the Planning Commission.

Interaction of the Regional Offices with the State Governments

The Regional Offices of the Commission shall work in a manner so as to provide a regular and effective link between the State Governments concerned and the Commission. For this purpose, the Commission may send communications to the State Governments suggesting that the officers-in-charge of the Regional Offices of the Commission may be taken on important Planning, Evaluation and Advisory bodies including Corporations concerned with the welfare, protection and development of the Scheduled Tribes.

Duties of the Regional Offices of the Commission

It shall be the duty of the Regional Offices of the Commission:

(i) To act as the "eyes and ears" of the Commission in the State(s) under their jurisdiction.

(ii) To maintain effective interaction and liaison with State Government/UT Administration on behalf of the Commission.

(iii) To serve on State Level Advisory Councils/Committees/Corporations, etc. on behalf of the Commission.

(iv) To provide information and documentation about the policies and programmes of the Union Government for the welfare and advancement of Scheduled Tribes to the States, NGOs, Media in their respective jurisdiction, and obtain similar information and documentation from such organisations and provide to the Headquarters of the Commission information/documentation about important developments, social movements, policy changes etc. in the State(s) affecting the interest of Scheduled Tribes.

(v) To monitor and inspect the working of voluntary and other non-governmental organisations receiving grant-in-aid from the Ministry of Tribal Affairs as also other Ministries/Departments of the Central Government, the concerned State Governments and Foreign Aid Agencies etc., engaged in Research Studies on Scheduled Tribes or welfare and development work relating to Scheduled Tribes and send reports to the Headquarters.

(vi) To conduct Research Studies, Seminars, Conferences, Surveys etc. either on their own or as entrusted to them by Headquarters from time to time and to organise Awareness Camps on the role of the Commission in ensuring the proper implementation of the safeguards available to members of STs including the schemes and programmes for their development in different districts in collaboration with the States/UTs.

(vii) To conduct on-the-spot inquiries into cases of atrocities on Scheduled Tribes either on their own or as entrusted to them by Headquarters and interact with the concerned Administrative/Police authorities having jurisdiction and submit report to the Headquarters.

(viii) To deal with complaints/representations from individuals, Scheduled Tribes Welfare Associations, etc., on various matters as also to deal with, suo-moto grievances of Scheduled Tribes published in print media.

(ix) To participate and advise in the planning process for socio-economic development of Scheduled Tribes as envisaged under Clause (5) of Article 338A of the Constitution of India.

(x) To collect, compile, analyse and monitor issues pertaining to development of Scheduled Tribes in the states especially with reference to Tribal Sub Plan (TSP) and Special Central Assistance (SCA) and prepare drafts of Reports pertaining to the State(s)/UT(s) under their jurisdiction.

(xi) To prepare and maintain a comprehensive and up-to-date database of Scheduled Tribes population, education, development etc. in the State(s)/UT(s).

(xii) To perform any other duty specifically assigned/entrusted to the Regional Office(s) by the Commission or the Secretary or any other officer empowered in this regard.

Monitoring Functions of the Commission

The Commission to Determine Subjects for Monitoring

The Commission may determine from time to time the subjects or matters and areas that it would monitor relating to safeguards and other socio-economic development measures provided for the Scheduled Tribes under the Constitution or under any other law for the time being in force or under any order of the Govt.

Prescribing Returns and Reports

The Commission may prescribe periodical returns or reports to be furnished by any authority responsible for or having control of the subject matter of which monitoring is being done by the Commission.

Follow-up Action

In order to ensure that monitoring is done effectively, the Commission, after getting the information as prescribed in the above rules and after reaching conclusions, may as early as possible send out communications to the concerned authority describing the shortcomings that have been noticed in the implementation of the safeguards and suggesting corrective steps.

The Commission may ask for the comments of the concerned authority on the action taken in pursuance of the communication sent under the Rule 76.

Working Structure

The National Commission for Scheduled Tribes functions from the Headquarters of New Delhi and from Regional Offices located in six States.

The Commission has six units namely (a) administration, (b) Coordination, (c) Research Unit – I, (d) Research Unit – II, (e) Research Unit – III, and (f) Research Unit – IV. These research units (I, II, III and IV) deal with all matters pertaining to socio-economic and educational development, service safeguards and atrocities in relation to STs as per allocation of work among these units.

The Regional Centres act as 'eyes and ears' of Commission regarding formulation of policy and issue of guidelines relating to the welfare of scheduled Tribes in the States/UTs periodically.

NATIONAL INSTITUTE OF SOCIAL DEFENCE

In order to implement the recommendations of Jail Manual Committee (1957-59), Central Bureau of Correctional Services was established in 1961 under the Ministry of Home Affairs, Government of India for the purpose of coordinating, developing and standardising the services in the field of social defence.

In 1964, this bureau was transferred to the then Ministry of Social Security, now Ministry of Social Justice and Empowerment.

In January 1975, the Central Bureau of Correctional Services was reorganised into National Institute of Social Defence.

Objectives

The objectives have been:

1. Reviewing policies and programmes in the field of social defence.
2. Anticipating and diagnosing defence problems.
3. Developing curative rehabilitative and curative policies in the field of social defence.
4. Identifying and developing the instrument for realising the objectives of social defence policies.
5. Reviewing and evaluating the implementation of social defence policies and programmes.
6. Developing and promoting voluntary effort in social defence.

Functions

These are as follows:

1. To undertake research in social defence.
2. To compile, process and analyse statistics on social defence.
3. To develop, promote, sponsor and undertake training/orientation in the field of social defence.
4. To draft model legislation and rules in the field of social defence.
5. To advise the Central/State Governments/Union Territory administrations on social defence problems.
6. To provide technical services/facilities for preparation of schemes, formulation of projects, drafting of legislation, etc.
7. To provide a forum for the exchange of information on social defence among State/Union Territories and voluntary organisations and thus to serve as a clearing house for information in the field of social defence.
8. To create public awareness on social problems specially in regard to preventive and rehabilitative role of the community.
9. To assist the Government of India for exchange of information on social defence with other countries and with the United Nations or other specialised agencies.
10. To establish liaison with universities, research institutes and voluntary organisations for appropriate attention to social defence.
11. To bring out publications in the field of social defence, both popular and scientific (Sachdeva, D.R. 1992-93).

Administrative Structure

This institute acts as an autonomous organisation under the administrative control of the Ministry of Social Justice and Empowerment. This is a nodal agency for training and research in field of social defence inventions.

The Institute functions under the overall executive control of a Director. Three divisions function under the Director.

(I) *Research, Evaluation and Statistics Division*: This Division functions under Deputy Director who is supposed to be Head of this Division. The Deputy Director has been assisted by Research Officers, Statistician and other concerned class three and class four employees.

(II) *Training Division*: This Division is also controlled by another Deputy Director and assisted by lecturers/trainers and other staff.

(III) *Common Service Facilities Division*: This Division has three wings:

(a) *Documentation, Clearing House, Library and Publication*: This wing is headed by Documentation Officer and consisted of other staff related to documentation, library maintenance and publication.

(b) *Publicity*: This is headed by a Research Officer. The other staff members are junior technical assistant etc.

(c) *Administration*: This is headed by an Administrative Officer and assisted by office staff. Hindi translator is also part of this.

Activities of Institute

These are as follows:

1. The institute has been concerned with wide range of preventive, correctional and rehabilitative services in the areas of social defence including welfare of prisoners, prison reform and administration, juvenile vagrancy and delinquency crime, probation, beggary, social and moral health, alcoholism, gambling, suicide, drug addiction, etc.
2. The Institute has been collecting data and factual information about above mentioned subjects.
3. It monitors and evaluates problems related to social defence.
4. It conducts/arranges training for various categories personnel engaged in the field of social defence in collaboration with State Governments, Union Territory Administrations, University Departments, Institutes of Research and Voluntary Organisations.
5. Conferences/Seminars/Discussions related to social defence issues are organised.
6. It networks with international and national organisations on the issues of social defence particularly neglected and marginalised people, abandoned destitute, neglected and delinquent juveniles who need care and protection for want of support or are in conflict with society or law, the drug addicts and offenders and the aged and host of others who need special care, protection and support.
7. It provides re-paragraphing, library and documentation services.
8. It assists to the Ministry in preparation of Model Rules and Regulations and in organising international meets on the issues of social defence.

Present Scenario

Presently the Institute is mainly concerned with following:

1. Care of senior citizens.
2. Care of drug addicts and offenders.
3. Training on these subjects.
4. Organisation of discussions/workshops/seminars/conferences on social defence problems.
5. Development of programmes for the care and treatment of persons suffering from problems related to social defence.

NATIONAL INSTITUTE OF PUBLIC COOPERATION AND CHILD DEVELOPMENT (NIPCCD)

This is a premier institute devoted to the promotion of voluntary action research, training and documentation regarding women and child development.

This institute was established in 1966 under the Societies Registration Act, 1860 as an autonomous institute. It has its headquarters in New Delhi and functions under the aegis of Ministry of Women and Child Development, Government of India. It has four regional centres at Guwahati (1978), Bangalore (1980), Lucknow (1982) and Indore (2001). The objective of these regional centres is to cater to region specific requirements.

Apex Institution and Nodal Agency

- The institute acts as an apex institution for training ICDS functionaries.
- The institute has been designated as nodal agency/organisation for training and capacity building of functionaries at national and regional level under the new scheme of Integrated Child Protection Scheme as well as for imparting training on two important issues of child rights and prevention of trafficking of women and children for SAARC countries.

Vision of Institute

The vision of the Institute is to become a Centre of Excellence in the field of women and child development in the South East Region by engaging in partnership with National and International Agencies and making its training and research activities relevant to the need of the clients.

Mission of Institute

To act as a think tank, catalyst and inventor of child rights, child protection and child development programmes by pursuing capacity building of child development functionaries, research and evaluation, networking, consultancy and advisory services as well as provision of specialised services through inter-disciplinary teams.

Objectives

1. Develop and promote voluntary action in social development, promote and develop relevant need-based programmes in pursuance of the National Policy for Children.
2. Evolve measures for coordination between government and voluntary action in social development.

3. Develop framework and perspective for organising children's programmes through government and voluntary efforts.
4. Establish liaison with international and regional agencies, research institutions, universities and technical bodies engaged in activities similar to those of institute.
5. Develop and promote voluntary action in social development through training and capacity building of government and non-governmental functionaries.
6. Taking of comprehensive view of child development through research and develop tools/design for supporting implementation of government schemes and programmes.
7. Coordinate meeting of Ministry of Women and Child Development with stakeholders under different schemes/programmes and policies for furthering the objectives and provide feedback.

Functions

1. Acts as apex institution for the training of functionaries of Integrated Child Development Services (ICDS) and functionaries of Integrated Child Protection Scheme(ICPS).
2. Building the training capabilities of institutions engaged in the training of ICDS/ICPS functionaries and trainings.
3. Providing training to the functionaries engaged in implementation of Rajiv Gandhi Scheme for Empowerment of Adolescent Girls – SABLA.
4. Imparting training to the functionaries engaged in implementation of Conditional Maternity Benefit Scheme – Indira Gandhi Matritya Sahyog Yojana (IGMSY).
5. Preparing and procuring training materials for ICDS/ICPS.
6. Monitoring and supervision of ICDS.
7. Functioning as a technical support arm of the Government in matters pertaining to development/welfare of both mother and child.
8. Completing national policies and programmes for women's development through training, research and documentation at the policy and macro level.
9. Conducting research and training programme sponsored by various Central Ministries and State Governments.
10. Providing demonstration services for capacity building of trainees through child care centre, Child Guidance Clinic and Adolescent Guidance Services Centre.
11. Advocacy and capacity building of officers of Central and State Government departments on gender issues.

12. Awareness generation, sensitisation and training to NGOs for prevention of trafficking of women and children.
13. Finding gaps in legislative framework through evaluating different schemes of various departments of central and state government.
14. Providing support of Childline India Foundation for organising training programme.
15. Coordinating meetings of Ministry of Women and child Development with stakeholders and providing feedback.

Areas of Interest of Institute

These are as follows:

1. Early childhood care and development.
2. Health and nutrition of the young child and mothers.
3. Infant and young child feeding.
4. Prevention of micronutrient malnutrition.
5. Adolescent health, reproductive health and HIV/AIDS.
6. Growth monitoring.
7. Nutrition and health education.
8. Child guidance and counselling.
9. Early detection and prevention of childhood disabilities.
10. Learning and behavioural problems of children and parent education.
11. Child rights and child protection.
12. Juvenile justice.
13. Women's empowerment and gender mainstreaming.
14. Holistic development of adolescent girls and family life education.
15. Prevention of child marriage, female foeticide and female infanticide.
16. Counselling and support services for women in distress.
17. Formation and management of self-help groups.
18. Prevention of trafficking of women and children.
19. Prevention of gender based violence.
20. Gender budgeting.
21. Gender sensitisation of law enforcement agencies.
22. Partnership initiatives of governmental/social organisations in the area of child development.
23. Manpower development in social development sector.
24. Capacity building of civil society organisations.

Constitutional Bodies/Committees

The institute has two constitutional bodies:

(a) *General Body*. Constituted by the representative of government and voluntary organisations. It is responsible for formulating overall policies of the institute.

(b) *Executive Council.* It is also constituted by the representatives of government and voluntary organisations. The council is responsible for management and administration of the institute.

The Minister of State for Women and Child Development is the President of General Body and Chairperson of Executive Council (*see* Fig. A).

Working Structure

The Director of Institute is the administrative head.

There are two departments, namely (a) Department of Mother Care and Child Development, and (b) Department of Training.

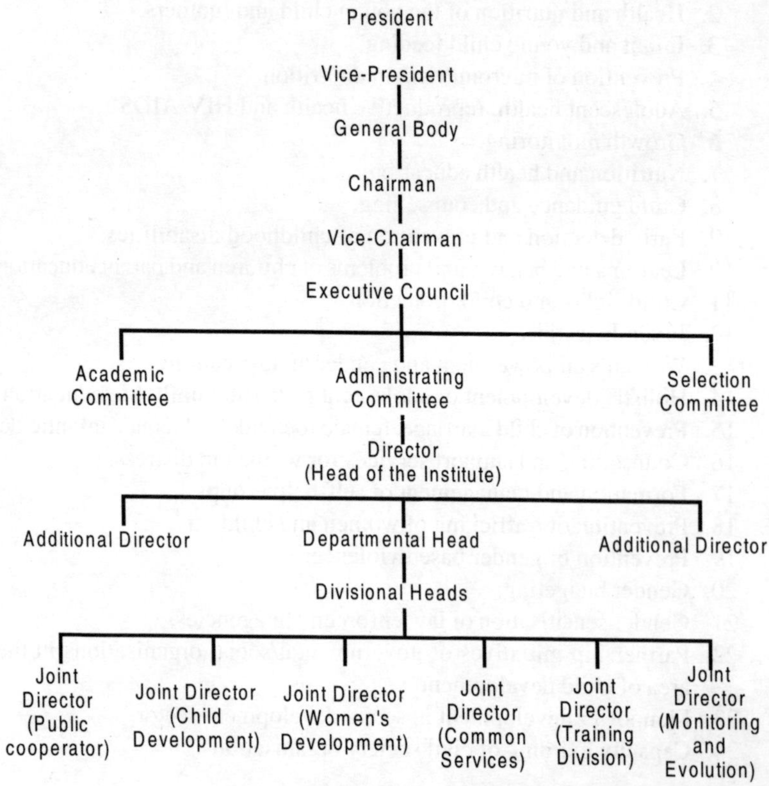

Fig. A: Organisational Structrue

Each department is headed by an Additional Director and there are six divisions working under these two departments. The details are as follows:

(a) Department of Mother Care and Development

1. *Public Cooperation Division*: This division undertakes the following activities:

(a) Promotion of voluntary action.
(b) Organisation of communities.
(c) Management of community resources.
(d) Rehabilitation of children victim of difficult situations.
(e) Capacity building of voluntary organisations and constitution of project for that.

There is proposal to constitute Child Protection Division under Integrated Child Protection Scheme. Presently the work of child protection is seen by this department.

2. *Child Development Division*: This division acts as policy associate related to mother and child development issues. The main subjects of this division are: (a) mother and child health, (b) early childhood care, (c) education and (d) taking of nutrients.

3. *Common Services Division*: This division performs the activities related to administrative, financial and internal maintenance as well as provides support services to headquarters and other divisions of regional centres.

(b) Department of Training

1. *Training Division*: This division is related to following activities:

(a) Planning for training of functionaries of Integrated Child Development Schemes.
(b) Coordination of training programme.
(c) Monitoring and operation of training programme.
(d) Capacity building of and preparation of infrastructure for institutions involved in training of ICDS functionaries.
(e) Preparation of and modifications in training modules.
(f) Preparation of training material.
(g) Procurement of training material.

2. *Monitoring and Evaluation Division*: This division provides technical inputs for monitoring social units related to ICDS and other programmes. This division also monitors and supervises ICDS projects through its Central Monitoring Unit.

3. *Women's Development Division*: This division organises different activities for the fulfilment of women development and empowerment policies and programmes in a big way through training research, documentation, clearing house and management services.

This division develops and implements programmes related to gender issues, violence against women, immoral trafficking of women and children, sexual harassment of women at work place, women empowerment etc.

The each division is headed by a Joint Director.

The Regional Centres fulfil the training, research and consultancy needs of Institute. Each regional centre is headed by a Regional Director.

Mother and Child Documentation Centre. The Institute has this centre which contains a rich collected literature regarding women and children. This centre presents a review of research studies and books related to women and children.

It publishes literature and propaganda material for the publicity of issues related to women and children. It has also developed a computer data base containing published and unpublished material and data.

Programmes and Activities

The Institute conducts training and research as core activities along with field demonstration services and varied kinds of publications at its headquarters and regional centres. The programmes are as follows:

(A) Training Programmes

The categories of these programmes are as follows:

1. Regular Training Programme

Under this, Institute organises following programmes:

(a) Orientation/training courses for representatives of voluntary organisations and officials of government.
(b) Workshops/seminars for categories of persons mentioned in point (a)
(c) Programmes on subjects of topical interest.
(d) Strengthening service delivery system.

2. Training under ICDS Programme

The Institute is an apex institution for training of functionaries of ICDS programme. So following programmes are being organised:

(a) Job training courses.
(b) Refresher courses for CDPOs/ACDPOs and trainers.
(c) Workshops/Consultation Meets/Training under ICDS.
(d) Orientation, refresher and skill training of trainers.
(e) Conducting research/evaluation/documentation/compilations.
(f) Strengthening of monitoring and supervision system in ICDS programme through Central Monitoring Unit. The monitoring set up has three-tier set up i.e. monitoring at community, state and national level.
(g) Publication of research studies.

(h) Organisation of demonstration services.
(i) Maintaining data base.
(j) Conducting full time Advanced Diploma in Child Guidance and Counselling.

ADMINISTRATION OF CENTRAL SOCIAL WELFARE BOARD (CSWB)

The Board was set up on August 12, 1953 by a Resolution of the Government of India (Ministry of Education's Resolution No. F.2-6/53, D.2). It functioned as an autonomous body which was part of administrative set up of the Government.

To foster healthy growth of social service organisations through well-planned and directed financial aid was the major objective.

Functions of Board

1. To cause a survey to be made of the needs and requirements of social welfare organisations.
2. To evaluate the programmes and projects of the aided agencies.
3. To coordinate the assistance extended to social welfare activities by various ministries in Central and State Governments.
4. To promote the setting up of social welfare organisations on voluntary basis in places where no such organisations exist.
5. To render financial aid, when necessary to deserving organisations or institutions on terms to be prescribed by the Board.

Formation of Panels and Experts Committees

In order to survey the needs and requirements of the existing social welfare organisations, the following panels were constituted:

(a) Panel on child welfare.
(b) Panel on women welfare.
(c) Panel on welfare of juvenile delinquents and physically handicapped.

Following committees were framed:

(a) Committee on after care services and social and moral hygiene.
(b) Committee on after care services for the handicapped.
(c) Committee on social and moral hygiene.

State Social Welfare Advisory Boards

These boards (now known of State Boards) were constituted in 1954. With the result, 26 State Boards came into existence. Presently there are 33.

These boards have been in operation as counterpart to Central Social Welfare Board. These boards are acting as liaison bodies between CSWB, State Government and voluntary welfare institutions. These Boards also receive, scrutinise and examine the applications received for grants-in-aid before inspecting and recommending these institutions to CSWB for grant.

Organisational Structure of CSWB

The main features of this structure are as follows:

1. The Board is headed by a chairperson.
2. It has General Body consisting of 58 members.
3. It has Executive Committee also which consists of 16 members.
4. The composition of General Body of CSWB is as follows:
   - Chairperson, CSWB.
   - All chairpersons of State Social Welfare Boards (33).
   - Representatives for the Parliament (Two from Lok Sabha and one from Raya Sabha).
   - Five professionals (one each from law, medicine, social work, education and social development/nutrition).
   - Three eminent persons with extensive experience of social work.
   - Representative from Ministries/Departments (rank of Joint Secretary) of Government of India.

     (a) Ministry of Women and Child Development
     (b) Ministry of Rural Development
     (c) Ministry of Health and Family Welfare
     (d) Ministry of HRD
     (e) Department of Secondary and Higher Education
     (f) Ministry of Social Justice and Empowerment
     (g) Ministry of Labour and Employment
     (h) Ministry of Finance
     (i) Department of Expenditure
     (j) Planning Commission
     (k) Financial Adviser
     (l) Ministry of Women and Child Development.
   - Executive Director, Central Social Welfare Board
5. The composition of Executive Committee is as follows:
   - Chairman, CSWB
   - Chairperson of State/Union Territories – Maharashtra, Karnataka, Assam, Rajasthan, Andaman and Nicobar Islands
   - Representatives of Ministries/Department of Government of India (Level of Joint Secretary) Ministry of Rural Development,

Ministry of Finance, Ministry of HRD, Director of Secondary and Higher Education, Ministry of Social Justice and Empowerment, Financial Advisor, Ministry of Women and Child Development

- Professionals (Two)
- Executive Director, CSWB

The General Body governs the Central Social Welfare Board and Executive Committee supervises the administrative functions of Board.

The organisational set up of CSWB is as follows:

General Body
↓
Executive Committee
↓
Chairperson
↓
Executive Director
↓
Joint Director (Four in Number)
↓
Deputy Directors (Twelve in number)
↓
Two Editors, one SRO and one IFA-Cum-CAO
↓
Assistant Director (26 in number)
↓
One RO, one P and AO
↓
One Account Officer

Mission of CSWB

As a National Organisation, strive to be recognised as the most progressive entity for providing services of unequivocal excellence to women and children for their protection, capacity building and total empowerment. To raise awareness about the legal and human rights of women and girl child and to run campaigns against social evils affect them.

Vision Statement of CSWB

The Board must:

- Act as change maker with a humanitarian approach reinforcing the spirit of voluntarism.
- Create an enabling mechanism to facilitate networking of committed social workers for the empowerment of women and children.
- Develop a cadre of sensitive professionals with a gender centric vision committee to equity, justice and social change.
- Recommend gender specific policy initiatives to meet the new challenges for women and children in emerging areas.
- Strengthen voluntary organisations and expand coverage of 'engendered' schemes in areas where they have not yet reached.
- Initiative and strengthen its monitoring role to act as social audit and guide for the voluntary sector so as to access government funds as resource.
- Generate awareness about the challenges of society in transition where negative use of technologies and practices are impacting on the wellbeing of women and children.

Programmes of Central Social Welfare Board

Since its inception, the Board has launched several programmes for women, children, families and upliftment of weaker sections, socially and economically.

Discontinued Programmes

The following programmes were stared successfully and with the passage of time, these programmes were discontinued and other programmes were launched in their place.

1. General grant-in-aid programme.
2. Welfare extension projects.
3. Family and child welfare projects.
4. Border area projects.
5. Balwadis (Demonstration projects)
6. Mahila mandal programme
7. Working women hostels
8. Socio-economic programme.
9. Holiday camps for children

Programmes of CSWB during the Period of Eleventh Plan

These are as follows:

1. Awareness Generation Camp for Rural and Poor Women

This programme was introduced in the ear 1986-87.

The main aim of the programme was disseminating information amongst women and community and their rights, status and problems of women and other concerns.

Objectives:

(a) To identify the needs of rural and poor women.
(b) To increase actual participation of women in development and other allied programme.
(c) To train organisers of this camping activities.

2. Condensed Course of Education for Women

This programme was initiated in 1958 with the aim 'to provide educational opportunities to girls/women above the age of 15 years along with additional inputs of skill development and vocational training.

3. The courses are organised through voluntary organisations engaged in the field of women welfare and education which are identified and recommended by State Boards. Here, more than 60 per cent courses have been sanctioned for middle and high school levels and about 40 per cent for primary levels as per need of the area.

3. Rajiv Gandhi National Crèche Scheme

This is the scheme of the Ministry of Women and Child Development under which assistance is made available to NGOs for running crèches for children of 0-6 years. This provides sleeping facilities, health care, supplementary nutrition, immunisation etc. for running a crèche for 25 infants for eight hours i.e. from 9 a.m. to 5 p.m.

4. Family Counselling Centres

This scheme was launched in March 1983. This is described as flagship programme. The objectives are as follows:

(a) To provide preventive, counselling and rehabilitation services to women in distress due to atrocities, family maladjustment and social ostracism etc.
(b) To provide crisis intervention as well as counselling services for victims.
(c) To provide trauma counselling services to women and children in case of disaster of crisis.

These centres work in close collaboration with the local administration, police, courts, legal aid cell, etc. They also create awareness and mobilise public opinion on issues affecting status of women.

5. Short Stay Homes

This scheme was launched in 1969. The objective of this scheme is to rehabilitate women and girls who are facing social, economic, and emotional distress due to family problems, social ostracism, exploitation, violence, being forced into prostitution or are in moral danger.

These homes provide temporary accommodation, maintenance and rehabilitative services to women and girls rendered homeless due to family discard or crime.

Temporary shelter is made available through voluntary organisations to those women and girls with facilities of case work, counselling services, medical care, psychiatric treatment, skill development training, education, vocational and rehabilitative services.

The scheme has an inbuilt component of 10 per cent increase for rent every year and 15 per cent under maintenance of inmates every three years.

6. Integrated Scheme for Women's Empowerment for North Eastern Region

This scheme has been developed to address the socio-economic needs of the women and children of selected eight most backward districts in the region.

This scheme is being implemented on pilot basis from 2008 and has the objectives of (a) meeting the felt needs of the area by mobilising community action; (b) converging available services and resources of the area; (c) income generation through feasible and sustainable activities for women; and (d) providing service for health awareness, career counselling, vocational training, preventing child trafficking and other social evils.

7. Disaster Relief

This programme has been envisaged to provide relief during disaster period through voluntary organisations.

8. Dr. Durgabai Deshmukh Award for Women's Development

This award has been implemented and an amount of Rs. 5.00 lakhs is awarded every year for recognised work in the field of women development.

9. Publications

The CSWB publishes 'Social Welfare' magazine in English and 'Samaj Kalyan' in Hindi.

10. Innovative Scheme

The CSWB has provision to introduce innovative schemes in the area of women and child development, implemented through voluntary organisations recommended by State Boards.

Bibliography

Ali, Shum Shun Nisa (1947): *Eminent Administrative Thinkers*: Associated Publishing House: New Delhi.

Appleby, Paul H. (1961): *Public Administration for Welfare State*: Asia Publishing House, Bombay.

Atwater, Liece (1940): *Problem of Administration in Social Work*: University of Minnesota Press: Minneapolis.

Bhattacharya, Sanjay: *Social Administration and Development*: Rawat Publication: Jaipur.

Bigger Staff, Marilyn A. (1978): "Preparation of Administration in Social Welfare: A Follow-up Study of Administration Concentration Graduates": Administration in Social Work 2.

Birrell, W.D., P.A.R. Hillyard, S. Murie and D.J.D. Roche (ed.) (1973): *Social Administration*: Penguin Books Ltd., England.

Bose, A.B. (1990): "Social Welfare: Some Issues" in H.Y. Siddique (ed.). *Social Welfare in India*: Harnam Publications, New Delhi.

Bulsara, J.F. and Verma, R.M. (ed.) (1985): *Perspective Social Welfare in India*: S. Chand and Co., New Delhi.

Carlisle, H.M. (1979): *Management Essentials: Concepts and Applications*: Science Research Associates Inc. Chicago.

Carrier, Johan and Ian Kendall (1977): "Social Administration as Social Science" in Helmuth Neisler (ed.): *Foundations of Social Administration*: London.

Chaturvedi, T.N. and Kohli Shanta Chandra (eds.) (1980): *Social Administration: Development and Change*: Indian Institute of Public Administration: New Delhi.

Chowdhry, D.P. (1962): *Social Welfare Administration*: Atma Ram and Sons: Delhi.

Compton, B.R. (1980): *Introduction to Social Welfare and Social Work – Structure, Function and Process*: The Dorsey Press: Homewoods: Illinios.

Donnison, D.V. (1968): "*Teaching of Social Administration*", Vol. XII.

Donnison, D.V. and Valerie Chapman (1965): *Social Policy and Administration*: George Allen and Unwin Ltd., London.

Department of Publications (1972): *Special Number of the Administration of Social Welfare Services*: Tata Institute of Social Sciences, Bombay.

Dubey, S.N. (1973): *Administration of Social Welfare Programmes in India*: Somiya: Bombay.

Durham, Arthur (1962): *Community Welfare Organisation: Principles and Practice*: Thomas Y. Crowell Company: New York.

Elwood Street (1933): "Social Work Administration", *Social Work Year Book*: Russell Sage Foundation: New York.

Fayol, Henri: "*General Principles of Management*" reprinted in Harry A. Schatz (ed.) (1970): Social Work Administration: A Resource Book: Council on Social Work Education: New York.

Flippo, E.B. and Garry M. Munsinger (1978): *Management* (Fourth Edition): Allyn and Bacon Inc.: Basin.

Forder, Anthony (1974): *The Concept of Social Administration: A Framework for Analysis*: Routledge and Kegan Paul, London.

Friedlander, W.A. (1955): *Introduction to Social Welfare*: Prentice International Inc., London.

Fulmer, Robert M. (1978): *The New Management* (2nd edition): Macmillan Publishing Company, Inc.: New York.

Gangrade, K.D. (1978): *Social Legislation in India,* Vol. I and II: Concept, Delhi.

Garden, R.K. and H.O. Judd (1959): *The Development of Social Administration*: Oxford University Press: London.

Gilbert, Neil, Armin Rosenkranz and Harry Specht (1973): "Dialects of Social Planning", *Social Work*: 18.

Goel, S.L. and Jain, R.K. (1988): *Social Welfare Administration* Vol. I and Vol. II: Deep and Deep Publications: New Delhi.

Gokhale, S.D. (ed.) (1974): *Social Welfare: Legend and Legacy*: Popular Prakashan, Bombay.

Gummer, Burton (1975): "Social Planning and Social Administration: Implication for Curriculum Development", *Journal of Education for Social Work* 11.

Hagenbuch, W. (1958): *Social Economics*: Nisbet, Welwyn.

Hamilton, Gorden (1949): "Education for Social Work – The Interaction of School and Agency": *Social Work Journal* 30.

Hasan, Saiyed Zafar (1965): "Teaching of Social Administration in India", Paper submitted to the Seminar on Social Administration of the Association of Schools of Social Work in India, held in 1965 at Udaipur School of Social Work, Rajasthan, India, quoted in Rajeshwar Prasad (1982): Social Administration: Shree Publishing House, Delhi.

Herman, Resnick and Rino J. Patti (1986): *Change From Within, Humanising Social Welfare Organisations*: Temple University Press: Philadelphia.

Herzberg, F. (1966): *Work and Nature of Man*: Thomas Y. Crowell Company: New York.

Herzberg, F. (1976): *The Managerial Choice: To Be Efficient and To Be Human*: DOW Jones-Irwin: Homewood: Illinois.

Herzberg, G., Bernard Mausner, and Barbara Snyderman (1959): *The Motivation to Work*: John Wiley and Sons: New York.

Jagannadham, V. (1967): *Social Welfare Organisations*: Indian Institute of Public Administration: New Delhi.

Jagannadham, V. (1978): *Administration and Social Change*: Uppal Publishing House: New Delhi.

Janssen, B.S. and Samuel H. Taylor (1978): "The Planning Contradiction in Social Agencies: Great Expectations vs. Satisfaction with Limited Performance," *Administration in Social Work* 2.

Johnson, Arlien (1947): "The Administration Process in Social Work": Proceedings of the National Conference of Social Work: Columbia University Press: New York.

Kenneth J. Kazmerski and David Macarov (1976): *Administration in Social Work Curriculum*: Council on Social Work Education: New York.

Khinduka S.K. (1962): Social Work in India: Sarvodaya Sahitya Samaj, Jaipur.

Kidneigh, John C. (1950): "Social Work Administration – An Area of Social Work Practice 3": *Social Work Journal* 31, April.

Kulkarni, P.D. (1965): *Social Policy in India: Tata Institute of Social Sciences*: Bombay.

Kulkarni, P.D. (1979): *Social Policy and Social Development*: Association of Schools of Social Work in India: Madras.

Kulkarni, V.M. (1972): *Essays in Social Administration*: Research: Delhi.

Lochhead, A.V.S. (ed.) (1968): *A Reader in Social Administration*: Constable: London.

Likert, Rensis (1967): *The Human Organisation: Its Management and Value*: McGraw-Hill Book Co.: New York.

Madison, Berice (1980): *The Meaning of Social Policy: The Comparative Dimensions of Social Welfare*: Groom Helso Ltd.: London.

Marsh, David (ed.) (1965): *Introduction to the Study of Social Administration*: Routledge and Kegan Paul.

Marshall, T.H. (1975): *Social Policy in Twentieth Century*: Hutchinson: London.

McGregor, Douglas (1960): *The Human Side of Enterprise*: McGraw Hill Book Company: New York.

Metcalf, H.C. and Urwick (eds.) (1942): *Dynamics of Administration*: The Collected Papers of Marry Parker Follet: Harper and Brothers: London.

Misra, Ramesh (1984): *The Welfare State in Crisis: Social Thought and Social Change*: The Harvester Press Publishing Group (Wheatsheaf Books Ltd.): Great Britain.

National Association of Social Workers (1968): *Social Work Administration*: New York.

Nigro, Felix. (1970): *Modern Public Administration*: Harper and Row, London.

Odiorone, George S. (1965): *Management by Objectives: A System of Managerial Leadership*: Pitman Publishing Corporation, California.

Patty, Rino J. (1983): *Social Welfare Administration: Managing Social Welfare Programmes in a Development Context*: Prentice Hall Inc., Englewood Cliffs: New Jersey.

Patti, Rino (1975): "The New Scientific Management: Systems Management for Social Welfare", *Public Welfare*, 33.

Parker, Julia M. (1966): "Pinning Down a Subject" *Review*: New Society, May 19.

Pathak, Shankar (2012): *Social Work and Social Welfare: A Historical-Cultural Perspective*: Nirula Publications, Bangalore.

Pfiffner, John M. and F.P. Sherwood (1968): *Administrative Organisation*: Prentice Hall of India (Pvt.) Limited.

Prasad, Rajeshwar (1982): *Social Administration*: Shree Publishing House: Delhi.

Proceedings of the Seminar on Social Administration in Developing Countries (1960): India International Centre, New Delhi.

Proceedings of the Seminar on Social Administration in Developing Countries (1964): India International Centre, New Delhi.

Pugh, D.S., D.J. Hickson and C.R. Hinigs (ed.) (1964): *Writers on Organisations*: Penguin Books: New York.

Radin, Norma (1976): "A Follow-up Study of Social Work Graduates", *Journal of Education for Social Work*, 12.

Raymond Monsour Scurfield (1980): "Social Work Administrators: Their Educational Preparation, Value Orientation, Role Transition and Satisfaction": *Administration in Social Work*: 4.

Reid, E.W.: *Social Welfare Administration*, Columbia University Press.

Romanyshyn, John M. (1971): *Social Welfare – Charity to Justice*: Random House: New York.

Ruesch, Jurgen and Weldon Rees (1956): *Non-verbal Communication*: University California Press: Berkeley.

Schwartz, Edward E. (1970): "Some Views of the Study of Social Welfare Administration", in Harry A. Schatz (ed.): *Social Work Administration – A Resource Book*: Council of Social Work Education: New York.

Sharma, G.B. (1970): *Social Administration in India*, Ellora Printers, Jaipur.

Siddique, H.Y. (ed.) (1990): *Social Welfare in India*: Harnam Publications: New Delhi.
Simon, Herbert A. (1970): "New Techniques for Programmed Decision Making" in Harry A. Schatz (ed.): *Social Work Administration: A Resource Book*: Council on Social Work Education: New York.
Simon, Herbert A. (1970): "Traditional Decision Making" in Harry A. Schatz (ed.): *Social Work Administration: A Resource Book*: Council on Social Work Education: New York.
Simon, Herbert, A. (1954): *Administrative Behaviour: A Study of Decision Making Processes in Administrative Organisation*: Macmillan Company: New York.
Singh, Atul and Arun Kumar Singh (2010): *Social and Human Development*: New Royal Book Company, Lucknow.
Singh, Surendra and K.S. Soodan (ed.) (1986): *Horizons of Social Work*; Jyotsna Publications, Lucknow.
Skidmore, Rex A. (1983): *Social Work Administration: Dynamic Management and Human Relations*: Prentice Hall Inc.: New Jersey.
Slack, K.M. (1966): *Social Administration and Citizen*: Michael Joseph, London.
Specht, Harry (1978): "The Gross Roots and Environment in Social Planning and Community Organisation", *Administration in Social Work*: 2".
Spencer, Sue (1959): *The Administration Method in Social Work*, Council on Social Work Education, America.
Spencer, Sue W. (1961): "The Administration Process in Social Welfare Agency", in Ela W. Reed (ed.): *Social Welfare Administration*, Columbia University Press: New York.
Spicker, Paul (1988): *Principles of Social Welfare*: Routledge, London.
Stein, Herman (1970): "Social Work Administration" in Harry A. Schatz (ed.): *Social Work Administration – A Resource Book*: Council on Social Work Education: New York.
Street, Elwood (1947): *A Handbook for Social Agency Administration*, Harper and Brothel: New York.
Stretch, John J. (1979): "Seven Key Managerial Functions of Sound Fiscal Budgeting: An Internal Management and External Accountability Perspective", *Administration in Social Work*: 3.
Szilagyi, A.D. Jr. and Marc J. Wallace Jr. (1980): *Organisational Behaviour and Performance* (Second Education), Goodyear Publishing Company Inc.: Santa Monica.
Titmuss, R.M. (1951): "Social Administration in a Changing Society", *British Journal Sociology*, Vol. II, No. 30, September.
Titmuss, R.M. (1958): *Essays on the Welfare State*: George Allen and Unwin Ltd.: Great Britain.
Titmuss, R.M. (1968): *Commitment to Welfare*: George Allen and Unwin Ltd.: Great Britain.
Titmuss, R.M. (1974) (edited by Brian Abel-Smith and Kay Titmuss): *Social Policy: An Introduction*: George Allen and Unwin Ltd., London.
Trecker, H.B. (1946): *Group Process in Administration*: The Woman's Press: New York.
Trecker, Harleigh (1971): *Social Work Administration: Principles and Practices*: Association Press: New York.
U.S. Department of Health, Education and Welfare (1966): *Social Development–Key to Great Society*: Government Printing Office: Washington, D.C.
Verma, R.B.S. (1982): *Supervisory Management*: Deep and Deep Publications: New Delhi.
Verma, R.B.S. (2009): *Case Studies: Teaching Material in Social Work*: New Royal Book Company: Lucknow.
Verma, R.B.S. (2012): "Empowerment: A Conceptual Analysis", in M.M. Verma (ed.)

Empowerment of Weaker Sections in India, Serial Publications, New Delhi".

Verma, R.B.S. (ed.) (2012): *Field Work Practicum: Challenges and Opportunities*: Rapid Book Company: Lucknow.

Verma, R.B.S. (ed.) (2012): *Social Work: The Ethical and Spiritual Paradigm*, Rapid Book Service, Lucknow.

Verma, R.B.S. and Atul Pratap Singh (2001): *Inclusive Development in India*: New Royal Book Company: Lucknow.

Verma, R.B.S. and Atul Pratap Singh (2011): *Handbook of Field Work Practice Learning in Social Work Texts and Cases*: New Royal Book Company: Lucknow.

Verma, R.B.S. and Atul Pratap Singh (2013): *Standard Manual For Field Work Practicum in Social Work*: New Royal Book Company, Lucknow.

Verma, R.B.S. and Rajkumar Singh (eds.) (2007): *Facets of Empowerment*: New Royal Book Company: Lucknow.

Verma, R.B.S., H.S. Verma and Nadeem Hasnain (eds.) (2007): *Study of Women's Problematic in India: Assessing Contemporary State of Art*: Serial Publications: New Delhi.

Verma, R.B.S., H.S. Verma and Nadeem Hasnain (eds.) (2007): *The Indian State and Women's Problematic: Running with the Hare and Hunting with The Hounds*: Serial Publications: New Delhi.

Verma, R.B.S., H.S. Verma and Nadeem Hasnain (eds.) (2007): *Towards Empowering Indian Women: Mapping Specifics of Tasks in Crucial Sectors*: Serial Publications: New Delhi.

Verma, R.B.S., Manoj Agarwal and Raj Kumar Singh (eds.) (2007): *Socio-Economic Development and Population Dynamics in India*: New Royal Book Company: Lucknow.

Verma, R.B.S., Raj Kumar Singh and Pooja Verma (eds.) (2012): *Shades of Inclusion and Exclusion in India*: New Royal Book Company: Lucknow.

Verma, R.B.S.; H.S. Verma and Raj Kumar Singh (eds.) (2006): *Empowerment of Weaker Sections in India*: Serial Publications: New Delhi.

Waldo (1955): *The Study of Administration*: Double Day and Company: Garden City.

Walters H. Ehlers, Michael J. Austin and John C. Protheso (1976): *Administration for the Human Services*: Harper and Row Brothers: New York.

Walters, J.E. (1959): *Basic Administration*: Adams and Coy.

Warham, Joyce (1967): *An Introduction to Administration for Social Workers*, Routledge and Kegan Paul, London.

Weinberger, Paul E. (1969): *Perspectives on Social Welfare*: The Macmillan Company Limited, London.

Weinshall, T.D. (1979): *Managerial Communication: Concepts, Approaches and Techniques*: Academic Press: London.

Wickendon, Elizabeth (1965): *Social Welfare in a Changing World*: U.S. Department of Health, Education and Welfare: Government Printing Office: Washington D.C.

Wilensky, H.L. and C.N. Lebeaux (1958): *Industrial Society and Social Welfare*: Russell Sage Foundation: New York.

Williams, J.D. (1980): *Public Administration: The People's Business*: Little Brown and Company: Boston.

Zelko, H.P. (1968): *Art of Communicating Your Ideas*: Reading Rack Service Inc.: New York.

Zey-Ferrell, Mary (1979): *Dimensions of Organising: Environment, Context, Structure, Process and Performance*: Goodyear Publishing Company: Santa Monica.

Index